The Economist

POCKET USA

The
Economist

=== POCKET ===

USA

THE ECONOMIST IN ASSOCIATION WITH
HAMISH HAMILTON LTD

Published by the Penguin Group
Penguin Books Ltd, 27 Wrights Lane, London W8 5TZ, England
Penguin Books USA Inc., 375 Hudson Street, New York,
New York 10014, USA
Penguin Books Australia Ltd, Ringwood, Victoria, Australia
Penguin Books Canada Ltd, 10 Alcorn Avenue, Toronto,
Ontario, Canada M4V 3B2
Penguin Books (NZ) Ltd, 182–190 Wairau Road, Auckland 10,
New Zealand

Penguin Books Ltd, Registered Offices: Harmondsworth,
Middlesex, England

First published by The Economist Books Ltd 1993
This edition published by Hamish Hamilton Ltd in association
with The Economist 1994

1 3 5 7 9 10 8 6 4 2

Contributors
Alastair Burnet, John Grimond, Elizabeth Jelliffe,
Paul Maidment, Jesse Malkin, John Micklethwait,
Carrie Robinson, Dominic Ziegler

Printed in Great Britain by William Clowes Limited,
Beccles and London

A CIP catalogue record for this book is available
from the British Library

ISBN 0-241-00282-6

Contents

INTRODUCTION

The United States is perhaps the most open society in the world; it is widely visited by tourists and businessmen alike; it is familiar through newspapers, magazines, movies and, above all, television; and it produces information about itself in almost bewildering quantities. Yet it is still misunderstood.

The reason for this paradox is that America is very much more strange than it seems. In three ways in particular it is quite unlike most other countries.

Democracy at work

The first of these is its system of government. The president of the United States, often cast as the most powerful man in the world, may be utterly incapable of getting some seemingly modest piece of legislation passed into law. He is the commander-in-chief, but does not have the right to declare war. He is head of state and head of government, but has no power to call elections. Most American presidents look with envy on the ability of prime ministers in parliamentary systems who can have laws enacted at the crack of a whip and hold general elections at will.

The American Congress is of far greater importance than legislatures in most other countries. Its powers, especially over matters like taxation, are formidable; they are exercised with independence and, sometimes, unpredictability. Within Congress committees wield enormous influence, shaping legislation and conducting far-reaching investigations. A committee chairman may well be more powerful than a cabinet member.

Adding to the mix is the Supreme Court, the third, unelected branch of government. Through its interpretation of the law, it plays a much bigger part in the life of the country than high courts generally do. Policies that are elsewhere usually left to legislatures – on abortion, racial segregation in schools or the application of capital punishment, for instance – are in America often, in effect, made by the nine justices of the Supreme Court.

Any outsider, then, who goes to the United States and expects to find a single government speaking with one voice, and able to see its words promptly translated into actions, is in for a shock. Further shocks are in store when it becomes clear that the federal government is replicated on a smaller scale in each of the 50 states. Yet even when the significance of the USA's multi-dimensional government has been appreciated, there are further surprises for anyone seeking to understand America.

Big differences

The next of these, and the second discovery necessary to an understanding of America, is that nothing much of consequence has ever started in Washington. To get the measure of what is going on, and why, it is necessary to travel. Exactly where to go is harder to say. The writer A.J. Liebling used to complain that his fellow-writers in New York were forever working on novels about the places they had grown up in – Nebraska, or Arkansas, or Ohio, or wherever. That, by implication, was the real America, whereas New York, where Liebling had spent his childhood, was not. In truth, as Liebling proudly argued, New York was, and is, as American as anywhere else. Yet it is certainly not typical, any more than Miami is, or Los Angeles or Minneapolis or Chicago.

It is a mistake to believe that any one city is representative of a country as large and varied and effervescent as America. To get an understanding of the place it is necessary to see a fair bit of it, something that few Americans – let alone visitors – do. Only when the different regions, states and cities have been experienced at first hand do some of its peculiarities make sense: why cars are seen as basic necessities, for instance, and petrol taxes so disliked; why hunting is a working-man's sport in Pennsylvania; why southerners still feel misjudged by Yankees; why Alaskans both loathe government and depend upon it; why weathermen get paid more than anchormen on television stations.

Framework for the Dream

The third way in which America is so strangely singular lies in the very essence of its nationhood. Whereas other peoples are defined by language or history or culture, even by literature or cuisine, Americans are defined by ideas. The country's origins lie not in an accident of conquest, but in an idealistic venture whose principles were set out in the Declaration of Independence. Next came the constitution, the Bill of Rights and then, less formally, the American Dream, the belief that a better life awaits every American who is prepared to work hard and make the most of the opportunities that his country affords him.

Americans differ about almost everything, but not about this fundamental set of ideas. They are the cement that holds the country together, and their enduring popularity helps to explain as much about modern America as about its revolutionary predecessor. They explain the reverence for law, the constant appeals to the constitution, the ubiquitousness of lawyers and the propensity to litigate. They explain some of the importance attached to morality in public affairs: the perennial need for a morally based foreign policy, for instance. And they explain the absence, unique among modern industrial democracies, of a socialist party of any size.

In a country where everyone, whether Boston Brahmin or Vietnamese immigrant, southern redneck or Jewish refugee, holds to the same ideals, there is simply no need for socialism. Rebels and Republicans may disagree about many things, but they have always shared a belief in the importance of the individual, and they have always shared a suspicion of government, and especially of government control of the means of production, distribution and exchange. The ideology of America is not socialism; it is Americanism.

Opportunities for influence

These three quirks of government, geography and history that have set America apart have also helped to make it preeminently successful, both as a standard-bearer of liberal democratic values and as a generator of prosperity. Today this pre-eminence is in doubt as never before. The United States' roll as chief promoter of western values seems, in a world no longer challenged by communism, suddenly less important. In fact, the opportunities for influencing events may be greater than at any time since the end of the second world war. The collapse of the Soviet Union has left the United States as the world's only superpower, just at a time when a variety of countries, from Albania to Zambia, are turning against the old certainties of autocracy and central planning and looking instead to plural politics and market economics.

America, however, has lost its missionary zeal. That does not mean it is incapable of taking action in any circumstances. In 1990 President George Bush showed that it was possible to overcome the misgivings of many Americans, including many congressmen, and to mobilise a huge force to expel Saddam Hussein from Kuwait. It was by no means clear at the outset of the ensuing war, in 1991, that the United States would suffer so few casualties. In the end the Gulf war proved a triumph for the Americans, not least for their president, and with that success behind him Mr Bush chose to embark on another intervention, in December 1992 in Somalia, little more than a month before he was due to leave office. At the time, this expedition to an insignificant country in the Horn of Africa seemed a much less risky venture than the Gulf war had done.

By then, however, it had become clear that Americans were less interested in foreign affairs than in domestic ones: that had been a main reason for Mr Bush's defeat by Bill Clinton in the 1992 election. Moreover, it was soon also to become clear that Somalia was not another magnificent Desert Storm, but rather a painful and often ignominious Shambles in the Horn. In 1994, a few months after 18 American rangers had been killed in a single incident in the Somali capital, Mogadishu, all American troops were pulled out of Somalia, and the prevailing mood at home returned to the familiar post-Vietnam one of intense suspicion of foreign intervention. A few months later, when it became clear something akin to genocide was taking place in Rwanda, there was no question of American peacekeepers getting involved. And though the war in Bosnia aroused feelings of outrage among some Americans, even the most interventionist among them (paradoxically many Bosnian hawks had been Vietnam doves) were agreed that America should not send ground troops until a peace was in place.

In his first 18 months of office at least, President Clinton seemed to have judged the mood of the people well; like him they were more interested in the economy than in foreign policy. Accordingly, when the president did take the initiative in foreign affairs, it was generally to promote economic policy: in turning the United States towards its trading partners in Asia and the countries of the Pacific, for instance, and to win congressional approval for the North American Free-Trade Agreement with Canada and Mexico. This, the securing of NAFTA, probably represented the greatest – some would say only – foreign-policy success of Mr Clinton's first year in the White House.

America has continued to give support, more with words than with money, to the efforts of reformers in Eastern Europe and Russia. As the leading member of NATO, it helped in 1994 to launch the Partnerships for Peace that are designed to build security among the new democracies emerging from the rubble of communism. And NATO itself has, for the first time in its history, taken aggressive action (using air power against Bosnian Serbs) rather than merely responding defensively to an attack. But nothing is now heard of Mr Bush's "new world order". President Clinton has shown himself to have no new ideas for the United Nations, whether in Haiti or in Rwanda. He has been in no hurry to enunciate a "Clinton doctrine", even one that elaborated just how little America was prepared under his presidency to do abroad. Indeed, in his first 500 days he offered no new lead to the peoples of the West who were wondering what, after the collapse of communism, it meant to be a member of a liberal western democracy. Thus for the first time for at least 50 years, the United States seemed utterly unclear about what it stood for in world affairs.

Richly indebted

Some of this bewilderment is born of economic uncertainty, especially of doubts about America's ability to compete abroad and balance its books at home. With a persistent budget deficit, born of a refusal to meet public spending by taxation, the world's richest country has been turned into the world's biggest debtor. At the same time the United States has watched its dominance of the world economy being eroded by countries like Japan and Germany. After the second world war, when America's power was at its zenith, its share of gross world product was 40%; today it is less than 10%. Some shrinkage was inevitable, if other countries were to grow richer. Less inevitable was the decline, an absolute decline, in wages. Real average earnings rose steadily from 1947 to 1972, in all by more than half. Since 1972 they have been falling.

That does not mean that living standards have fallen in the same way. What it does mean is that Americans are having to work harder if they are not to feel poorer. The middle classes – and the vast majority of Americans consider themselves to be middle-class – complain that two people must now go out to work to maintain a family's standard of living, whereas in the past one breadwinner was enough. The baby-boomers, the group born after the second world war, worry that their generation will be the first to be less well-off than its parents. And their children, they fear, thanks to the indestructible federal debt, will be born not with silver spoons but with IOUs in their mouths. That single-storey ranch-style home in the suburbs, which was the aspiration of many a young couple of yesterday, is unthinkable for most newlyweds today. In short, it is becoming harder and harder to turn the American Dream into reality.

Downside extremes

For some, life is even more bleak. More than 30m Americans live in poverty, fully a third of them children. And whereas the America of old always offered the prospect of getting on, nowadays, it seems, an underclass has emerged that is stuck at the bottom. A cycle of poverty, involving single mothers, truancy, drugs, unemployment, crime and often violence, stubbornly prevents them from becoming useful members of society. A disproportionate number are black.

It is in the cities that the problems of the underclass are felt. It is there, too, that most of America's new arrivals and its minorities congregate. The cities are changing fast. Already by the mid-1980s racial minorities accounted for more than half the populations of Baltimore, Chicago, Cleveland, Detroit, New York and Philadelphia. Blacks are the biggest minority, but Hispanics and others are growing fast, both in absolute and in proportionate terms. Whereas blacks were 12.5% of the population in 1991, and other races just 3.5%, the Bureau of the Census expects other races to increase to 8.8% by 2025, while blacks go up to just 14.5%. Hispanics – who may be of any race – are expected to become 16.2%.

This change will be especially noticeable in some parts of the country. Two-thirds of all Hispanics live in just four states: California, Florida, New York and Texas. By 2010 the majority of the population in California and Texas may be Hispanic.

Melting-pot consequences

The political consequences of these changes will be enormous. It is not unimaginable that some Californians will be campaigning in the next century for the secession of their state and its return to Mexico. The use of Spanish, both for official and unofficial purposes, is already common in some parts of the country. At universities, the old curriculums are coming under attack for their emphasis on European history, thought and values. New demands for "multiculturalism", with its implication that ethnic minorities should not subordinate their values to the prevailing one (often cast as white, male, Judeo-Christian), are seen by some as a growing threat to the established ideology of Americanism.

Farewell old order

Other forces are tearing at the old order. The family, long the central unit of American society, is in decline. In 1950, 70% of the labour force consisted of married men at work with a wife and two children at home; by the late 1980s, that figure had dropped to 15%. An increase in divorce means that, among women in their 30s, a quarter have been divorced in their 20s. One child in four is born out of wedlock; among blacks the proportion is nearly two out of three.

In politics, too, disintegration is at work. The two old political parties that have dominated the scene this century have been losing cohesion and authority for more than 20 years. Congressmen have been acting more independently since the 1970s, when they started to raise more of their campaign money from their own sources and less from the parties. Single-issue interest groups have come to play an increasingly important role. More recently, the voters, especially in the west, have been taking more and more decisions directly, by use of the referendum. And since the collapse of communism, the distrust of politicians that is ever-present in America has been manifesting itself with even more bravura than before.

Voters seem to believe that the old constraints, the need in the end to behave responsibly, no longer apply, especially in presidential elections. Why should they? In the past, after all, Americans knew that the main task of their president was to safeguard the republic from attack, which has, for 50 years, meant from communists. Now attack is almost unthinkable, so the man in the White House no longer has to perform that role. Choosing a president has thus become an opportunity in which the voters can register their protests with a licence they have not had for decades. In 1992 many chose to do that by voting for the anti-politician, Ross Perot.

Juggling crystal balls

Enduring peculiarities; rapidly changing economic, demographic, social and political features. Not much can be said with certainty about what the mix will bring in the coming years except that it is bound to be interesting. America will continue to absorb the attention of the outside world, and those who think they understand it but don't will be those most wrong-footed by events.

=Part I=
Background

A BRIEF HISTORY

When Christopher Columbus stepped ashore in 1492, after a 33-day voyage westwards from the Canaries, everything was new. Each human being, animal and plant the Europeans met was unexpected, strange and different. Columbus, expecting either Japan or China, was disappointed. To the tens of millions of Europeans who followed him westwards in the succeeding centuries it was America's newness, its opportunities, its difference from the past which mattered, and which endowed them and America with a hope and a destiny.

Early colonies

In what was to be the United States the English were the first with a permanent settlement at Jamestown, in Virginia, in 1607. The first black slaves were sold there by Dutch traders in 1610. A year later the Puritans in the *Mayflower*, escaping from religious intolerance, landed on Plymouth Rock. To the north, the French explorer Champlain founded Quebec in 1608. At the mouth of the Hudson river Dutch fur traders took over the island of Manhattan in 1624. The English were the most committed to colonial life because private enterprise was encouraged and, reinforced by successive waves of the persecuted and poor, they were also the most numerous and enterprising.

Scotch-Irish and German settlers helped to push the frontier of European life westwards through the Appalachian mountains. British sea power and alliances with native Indian tribes ensured military superiority, and by 1763 the whole of the continent east of the Mississippi had been ceded to Britain. The total population was put at 1.5m, ranging from trappers and traders in the west and the tobacco and rice plantations of the south to the small, prosperous towns and ports of the east, proud of their universities and even theatres. Distance from London had made the colonies essentially self-governing. Their people were used to a form of democracy and to free speech; above all, they had a sense of being American.

Revolution

The colonies had an educated class of practising politicians, lawyers and merchants as able as and more experienced in representative government than George III and his ministers. When the London government tried to impose taxation to run the colonial federation and regulations to control trade, the result was rebellion and the Declaration of Independence in 1776. The military determination of George

Washington and the vast distances which confronted the British forces might not have been decisive without the help of the French fleet which trapped Cornwallis's army at Yorktown in 1781. The royal government was discredited, and though the British still held New York and much of the south, peace was agreed in 1783.

The ingenious new constitution, which defined how the republic was to work, was based on the principle of the balance of powers. The legislative, executive and judicial bodies had independent duties but were interlocked by methods meant to achieve harmony without any one interest – congress, president or supreme court – being dominant. It was a classic of 18th-century thought and experience, suiting a new and isolated country and the individuality of its people. With amendment and manipulation, it has served American needs through succeeding generations of society.

Growth and civil war

The United States wished to turn its back on the wars of the old world, but it first had to survive an undeclared war against revolutionary France before the third president, Thomas Jefferson, bought the immense stretch of land, called Louisiana, west of the Mississippi from Napoleon for $15m in 1803. Then, irritated by the British seizure of American ships trading with Napoleon's empire and searches for deserters, it declared war on Britain in 1812. The British burned the White House but the fighting was inconclusive and was ended in 1815. The young country needed peace and it made the best use of it. A high tariff protected its new industry in the east. Emigrants pushed west to conquered Indian lands. Between 1810 and 1820 the population beyond the Appalachians doubled. It was not just the covered wagons rolling westwards. Steamboats appeared on the Ohio river; New York began to dig the Erie canal.

It was the west that made Andrew Jackson president, and he personified the demanding wishes of the small farmer, the mechanic and the frontiersman. He committed himself to removing Indians from their lands in a series of bloody campaigns. Texas, in the south-west, after declaring itself independent from Mexico, succeeded (after defeat at the Alamo) in defeating Santa Anna and gaining international recognition. Texas joined the union in 1845. But a new president, Polk, had to go to war to get Mexican agreement, and with it took California as well. The western empire had been established.

But the occupation of the land west of the Mississippi

and, especially, the creation of states where slavery was allowed, had begun to divide Americans. The anti-slavery movement had made steady progress in the north through its publicists, William Lloyd Garrison and Harriet Beecher Stowe (author of *Uncle Tom's Cabin*), but the southern states retained effective control of Congress and the presidency. The election of a moderate opponent of slavery, Abraham Lincoln, in 1860 prompted the secession of the slave-holding states, the formation of their confederacy, the taking of Fort Sumter and four years of bitter and destructive war. The north was slow to make its numbers, industry and wealth take effect and the south fought gallantly until it was exhausted. Lincoln abolished slavery in 1863; he did not abolish the problems of the ex-slaves.

Developing the west

Paying for the civil war and the capital cost of developing the west made the United States an international debtor, chiefly to the City of London. The rate of progress accelerated. Railroads spread across the country; the first transcontinental line was completed at Promontory Point, Utah, in 1869. The prairie wheatfields, using the McCormick reaper, fed the industrial cities in the United States and Europe. America's own factories and mines grew and flourished.

But there were discontents. For instance, the administration of Ulysses S. Grant, who had been the north's most successful general, proved to be corrupt. Labour unions appeared. Farmers faced international competition and resented both industrial protection and the gold standard. Later in the century, in what turned out to be three presidential elections, the Democrat William Jennings Bryan tried and failed to dislodge the sound money men. Whenever credit contracted, an inefficient banking system set off panics. But the solidity of dollar capitalism was not jolted.

World stage

It was Grant who settled Anglo-American differences when arbitration made Britain pay modest compensation for the depredations of the Confederate commerce raider *Alabama*, built at Liverpool. He hankered after annexing the island of Santo Domingo (now the Dominican Republic) but the Senate refused. The French were warned to abandon their venture in Mexico. The American strategic interest in the Caribbean grew with each proposal to dig a canal joining the Atlantic and Pacific oceans. Hawaii was acquired in 1898, the origin of the naval base at Pearl Harbor. The war with Spain to liberate Cuba brought the conquest of the Philippines too. Imperial America believed it had a responsibility to keep an open door to trade with the decaying Chinese empire; it also faced the early ambitions of a resurgent Japan.

The turn of the century saw American economic power ahead of Britain's and Germany's, with its big corporations like Standard Oil and Andrew Carnegie's steel works. Henry Ford developed the cheap automobile. Invention was prolific: Alexander Graham Bell's telephone, Thomas Edison in electricity and the Wright brothers' airplane. But there was a cost. The United States was resented in continental Europe and the strength of its trusts, the giant industrial combinations, was feared at home. There was corruption in city and state government and in industry's relations with the courts. The railroad, oil and steel corporations faced, and usually survived, legal battles to trim their power.

The American consumer was dissatisfied, and a split developed in the Republican party after years of domination since the Civil War which let in the liberal, free-trade President Woodrow Wilson. He believed in moral influence and the sanctity of treaties. Although intellectually he was firmly aligned with the Anglo-French cause against the Kaiser's Germany, he kept the United States out of the first world war until 1917, when he believed Germany's unrestricted submarine warfare left him no option.

Boom and bust

America's intervention in the war was conclusive and Wilson used his prestige to influence the peace settlement at Versailles, but enough of the Senate refused to endorse his concept of a League of Nations and American opinion reverted to isolation from Europe's troubles. War production for the allies had turned the United States from a debtor to a creditor country and although Europe was reluctant to pay its debts, America felt itself rich.

The 1920s were a decade of optimism, high employment, car ownership, radio, the cinema and jazz. Women got the vote. Prohibition was put in the constitution and enforced. It was supposed to stop the production and sale of alcohol, but chiefly it encouraged illegality and gangsterism. Not all the prosperity was confined to a narrow class, but when worries about markets and the over-expansion of credit prompted the Wall Street crash of 1929, industrial labour, the farmers and the blacks were almost wholly unprotected. Bankruptcies, unemployment and destitution gripped the country. Up to 15m were unemployed and as many as 40m of a population of 120m were reduced to poverty.

The New Deal introduced by Franklin D. Roosevelt from 1933 onwards took several forms and its results were frequently disappointing; some of its measures were thrown out by the Supreme Court. However, Roosevelt inspired popular confidence, he brought in overdue social reforms, and he persevered with his economic experiments. He asked America questions about itself and he upheld democratic solutions when countries like Germany, the Soviet Union, Japan, Italy and Spain followed totalitarian ones. After the outbreak of war in Europe in 1939 he managed to persuade Congress to start dismantling the neutrality laws which prevented the sale of arms to Britain and France. Lend-lease was his way of supplying Britain and the Soviet Union against the Nazis but it was not until Japan attacked Pearl Harbor in 1941 that the United States entered the war.

Victory and the cold peace

The American industrial machine, producing ships, tanks and aircraft in unprecedented numbers, ensured allied success in the battle of the Atlantic and in the campaigns which liberated North Africa, Italy and western Europe. The United States was much the predominant power in the defeat of Japan, before and after the first atomic bombs were dropped on Hiroshima and Nagasaki. It emerged from the war the strongest and richest country in the world, but its preoccupations were such that it could not withdraw into itself again. The secretive and hostile behaviour of the Soviet Union aroused mistrust among the western countries, and the destruction of Europe in the war left it dispirited and vulnerable to a communist takeover.

In 1947 Harry S. Truman organised help for Greece and Turkey and set out his doctrine to support free peoples who were resisting attempted subjugation. The Marshall Plan was launched to initiate European recovery. In 1948 the Berlin airlift countered the Soviet blockade of the western sectors of the city. In 1949 Nato was set up to organise military security against aggression. In 1950 the United States and allies intervened to throw back the North Korean invasion of South Korea. The cold war gave Americans the unwanted and unpopular role of confronting communist power and its encroachment and subversion around the world. This meant difficulty at home when security tipped over into witch-hunting, and commotion abroad when the American presence was resented.

World role

This world role was possible only because of the continued success of the American economy, its financial power, its technological innovation and the strength of its market. It became a triple strain. In 1962 the Soviet Union exacerbated the cold war; it shipped missiles to Cuba to upset Americans' sense of security. President John F. Kennedy insisted on their removal. The black community at home insisted on reforms, especially in voting, education and the ending of segregation in the unregenerate south. Their leaders, like the Rev. Martin Luther King, were persuasive and successful; federal investment was devoted to social reform. And when Kennedy was assassinated in 1963 his successor, Lyndon Johnson, tried to promote simultaneously his idea of a great society and the defence of South Vietnam against pro-communist attacks from the north. The outcome was inflation and liberal animosity.

Johnson was forced to abandon the idea of re-election in 1968, and after him Richard Nixon, swiftly unpopular for continuing the war, was found obstructing justice to defend agents hired by his subordinates who were caught breaking into the Democratic party's offices in the Watergate building in Washington in 1972. He was driven from office. Nixon and his secretary of state, Henry Kissinger, had reopened relations with both the Soviet Union and China, but he was succeeded by two weak and ineffectual presidents.

It was not until Ronald Reagan entered the White House in 1980 that a policy of rearmament and sustained pressure on the precarious Soviet economy helped to bring down the Soviet system and its empire during the Bush presidency from 1988 onwards. Reagan's fiscal policies left a crushing budget deficit which he was reluctant to alleviate and could not force Congress to do for him. Nor could Bush, whose record in the country's estimation deteriorated steadily after his success in evicting the Iraqi Saddam Hussein from Kuwait in 1991. Bush himself was duly evicted from the White House by the Democrat Bill Clinton in 1992.

The United States found itself the victor of the cold war, but confronted with pressing problems of its own. Economic superiority had given way to vigorous competition from Japanese and European producers. The financial consequences of the 1980s meant a struggle to reorganise the federal budget and its social demands. The problems of the urban underclass were publicised by crime and rioting, as in Los Angeles in 1992. American self-confidence had found the problems of peace more disconcerting than the remaining superpower had supposed.

GOVERNMENT

The United States has the oldest written constitution in the world, drawn up in 1787 and operated continuously ever since. It was framed for another age but has been accepted (with amendments) in a constantly changing society and is still the fundamental Act of the world's most powerful state. The national preference in facing its anomalies had been to make them work.

The constitution was ratified by a majority of the 13 original states by June 1788; the system went into effect in March 1789; and George Washington was inaugurated as the first president in April 1789.

Balance of powers

The aims of the constitution were to secure "a more perfect union", justice, domestic tranquillity, common defence, general welfare and liberty. It divided power and responsibility between the legislators, executive and judiciary. The legislators themselves were divided into a house of representatives directly elected every two years, and a senate, a third of which was indirectly elected every two years. (The senate was opened to popular election by a constitutional amendment in 1913.) Each element in government was given its own duty and function, but each has depended on adaptation to the interests of the whole to achieve its aims.

Within the triangular balance of power much of American political and legal history has been determined by the outcome of differences between the three sources of authority. Each has had its periods of predominance. Equally, all the federal authorities have had to compromise with the powers of the individual states, who have remained suspicious of attempts to override their rights.

It is the president, Congress and Supreme Court who daily suffer the attentions of the media and the publicity they confer. Many of the modern issues -- black rights, women's rights, abortion, homosexuality, economic initiatives, welfare policies -- would have taken the authors of the constitution by surprise, but the system they devised is still able to accommodate them, and no better one has been endorsed by the indispensable source of political power -- the people.

The president and executive

The president is at the centre of the system, and, politically, at its heart; when he is incapacitated, or is deemed to have incapacitated himself, he must be replaced. He is the head of state, the chief executive, the commander-in-chief of the armed forces, the chief diplomat and (as the head of a political party) the chief initiator, or regulator, of legislation.

The influence of mass communications has added a new dimension to the job and its ascendancy. For the same reason it has increased its vulnerability. When the country has felt comfortable with its president and itself he has been awarded re-election; when uncomfortable, it has been remorseless in ensuring only a single term in the White House.

Electing the president

The president is elected for a four-year term and can serve (since the 1951 amendment) for only two terms. He (there have been no women presidents) and the vice-president dependent on him are the only members of the government elected from a nationwide constituency; this direct link with the public is an essential part of the office's significance.

Manoeuvring by potential candidates begins two years or more before voting day, but the campaign by hopefuls becomes important in the early weeks of election year. The outcome of the first presidential primary election (New Hampshire) and party caucuses (usually Iowa) can have a disproportionate influence on public opinion, and so on the contenders' prospects of raising enough funds to remain in the race. Jimmy Carter's success in taking four of the first five primaries in 1976 began an almost inexorable advance to the nomination and set the modern pattern of campaigning. Now that most delegates at national conventions are committed to their candidates and the strengths are known, the prospect of a compromise one emerging from what used to be called a "smoke-filled room" has virtually disappeared.

More attention is paid than in the past to the choice of vice-presidential candidates, who used to be picked as an afterthought. The aim is to appeal to a particular constituency in the party or country (as Reagan took the more liberal Bush in 1980 and Walter Mondale the first woman, Geraldine Ferraro, in 1984), but neither Democrats nor Republicans have repeated the gesture of Adlai Stevenson in 1956 when the choice of his running-mate was thrown open to the whole convention.

Campaigning

The campaign proper is dominated by television and the other media and by the opinion polls. The party managers and publicists put particular emphasis on spectacle and brief "sound-bites" for repetition on the network evening news. Debates between the candidates, usually to a stylised formula, seldom produce outright winners. Third candidates of substance run on occasion but have influenced the result only rarely. The migration of population to the south and west has increased the electoral importance of states like California, Texas and Florida (usually to the Republicans' advantage), but New York, Pennsylvania, Illinois, Ohio and Michigan remain highly important.

The state of the national economy and its regional subdivisions (such as the farm belt and the Rustbelt of old heavy industry) is invariably the decisive issue, although ethnic votes (sometimes disguising conservative blue-collar workers), the black and Hispanic votes, and the votes of women's rights, evangelical and single-issue campaigners are all sought after. Voting day is the Tuesday of the first full week in November. Up to 105m vote but turnout, at just over 55%, is low by European standards; voters in some western states argue that no results should be given in the east until after all polls close.

The administration

The voters do not just elect a president and legislators but an entire administration. The president-elect has two months to decide his chief cabinet and other appointments (sometimes meeting the men and women concerned for the first time), and after taking office in January the new man will sweep out the occupants of over 2,000 of the higher posts in the bureaucracy in Washington and ambassadors abroad. Even if the incomer succeeds a president of his own party, he will have his own clients and favourites to instal to ensure that the administration is plainly his own.

Executive departments

There are 14 executive departments with separate responsibilities, from the most senior, the State Department (foreign policy), the treasury and defence, to agriculture, energy and transportation. In disputacious times the attorney-general's appointment will be important. All the departments are represented in the cabinet, whose members implement the president's policies through the civil service and hold office at his pleasure. Also in the public eye are the chairmen and administrators of such agencies as the Federal Reserve System (with great influence over the economy), the Environmental Protection Agency, the Federal Trade Commission and the Securities and Exchange Commission.

The executive office

In the White House and in neighbouring buildings like the Old State Department are the offices of the president's inner team, with particular clout, relatively small (about 5,000 employees) and devoted to his policies and political interests. The president relies on it for information, analysis and policy proposals and, through his press spokesman, to enlighten and influence the media and public opinion. Certain of its specialists, especially the National Security Council and the Office of Management and Budget (preparing the federal budget) are central to the president's decisions, enabling him to consider and accept alternatives to the regular recommendations by departments and agencies.

Congress

The congress is the legislative body with powers of most consequence in the world. Its two separate houses, the Senate and the House of Representatives, sit at opposite ends of the Capitol Building. There are 100 senators (2 from each state), each with six-year terms, and 435 members of the house of representatives, or congressmen, elected every two years. The allocation of congressmen from each state is adjusted every ten years according to population.

Congress possesses all legislative powers, both initiating bills (all bills for raising revenue having to originate in the House, but with the Senate allowed to propose amendments) and voting them into law. Forceful presidents have normally managed to impose their particular legislative ideas on their own parties, or coalitions of supporters, in Congress. So, occasionally, have external pressure groups. Presidents have the right to veto bills to which they object, but Congress can override vetoes by majorities of two-thirds in each house. The Senate alone is empowered to advise on and consent to (or reject) the appointment of cabinet secretaries, ambassadors and justices of the supreme court, duties which it takes seriously.

Presidents in the past were able to rely on having one or both of the Senate and House controlled by their own party. But habitual Democratic domination of the House has meant that Eisenhower in 1952 was the last Republican to carry both the Senate and House in with him. The Senate has been more closely fought and both Nixon and Reagan were able to assemble majorities there on first being elected. But Bush in 1988 managed to win the White House with the Democrats controlling both sides of Capitol Hill. Until the 1992 results, indeed, it seemed as if the Republicans had, by design or default, concentrated on becoming the presidential party and the Democrats the congressional one. Nor have recent Republicans been able to rely on conservative feelings among senior southern Democrats to organise anti-liberal coalitions whenever they needed them. This division had become an unexpectedly major factor in politics, being partly responsible for both parties' failure to accept responsibility for the consequences of deficit financing.

The rise of committees

Congress's committees have grown in number and stature over the past 25 years. They had always been vehicles for the ambitious, especially of those capable of exploiting the press and radio. The power and scope of television have made them even more important. Joseph McCarthy's harassment of suspected communists, Estes Kefauver's campaign against corruption, the several denouements in the eclipse of Nixon, the cross-examinations of Oliver North and John Poindexter in the Iran-Contra affair, and the rejection of John Tower as defence secretary all turned the committee system into an uninhibited public stage.

Now nearly all proposed legislation is sent to the relevant standing committee, which then commissions a subcommittee to make a thorough investigation. After the subcommittee reports, the standing committee seeks approval to introduce the bill to the full house for debate, amends it or ditches it altogether.

Supreme Court

The court is composed of nine justices who are appointed by the president and hold their offices during good behaviour. It has appellate jurisdiction (except in diplomatic cases); it determines for itself which cases it will hear. Its vital power of judicial review was established early in the 19th century. A Supreme Court decision can be reversed only by an amendment to the constitution.

The court is highly respected but is not immune from political and economic controversy. As many justices are long-lived, the court has been accused of failing to keep up with altered priorities and needs, let alone political trends, so that new presidents use each opportunity provided by death or resignation to bring in justices sympathetic to their point of view.

Franklin D. Roosevelt conducted a campaign against the court he inherited, which rejected much early New Deal legislation as unconstitutional. Reagan and Bush were equally concerned to rectify the court the other way, but all such appointments need Senate approval, and Reagan had two successive selections thrown out until a more moderate one was accepted. Party men have normally put the court first. Earl Warren, a former Republican governor of California and vice-presidential candidate, turned out to be the most liberal chief justice the court has seen. The same sort of thing happened with Nixon's choice of Warren Burger. The court has been instrumental in bringing an end to racial segregation of black and white, in encouraging affirmative action to promote equality and in taking a balanced view of abortion and other issues.

Rival powers

Presidents and Congress have both contrived to increase their power and influence in a complicated and dangerous world. Their rivalry has been augmented by the political differences between a president from one party and a congress controlled by the other.

In 1973 what was called the imperial presidency (personified by Nixon) raised mounting opposition over its use of war-making powers, secrecy prosecutions and even illegal espionage and sabotage of its domestic opponents. Congressional feelings were so high that the idea of impeaching the president was revived. Impeachment had been attempted only once, against Andrew Johnson, and its failure in 1868 had seemed to discredit it for ever. The Watergate affair, a minor matter in many ways, had its importance in raising the important constitutional issue of presidential accountability after decades in which it had been largely ignored.

Presidential power

The president's power has increased in times of war and the threat of war. Active presidents relish the opportunity that the sense of urgency brings. They resort to executive action and glory in the name of commander-in-chief; they dominate the terms of the national debate; Congress, in turn, is reluctant to jeopardise the national interest.

Presidents have done more than use the authority the constitution gives them. Congress may control taxation but it is seldom going to stint funds for men and women defending the country. Even in 1907 when Theodore Roosevelt wanted the navy to show the flag round the world and had funds for only half the voyage, he calculated Congress could not leave the ships laid up in a foreign port.

Until the Japanese attack on Pearl Harbor in 1941 Franklin Roosevelt preferred to consult Congress, but his exchange of old destroyers for British bases in 1940 upset constitutional purists, as did Johnson's use of the Gulf of Tonkin resolution in 1964 to endorse the whole Vietnam war effort.

Head of state

The role of head of state carries respect. Eisenhower was the popular epitome of legitimacy, morality and continuity, even when his grasp of economic policy could be questioned. Reagan's patriotism and modesty, the popular reluctance to believe he would knowingly mislead, helped him through the Iran-Contra troubles. By contrast Ford and Carter, both honest and open, were seen to be weak and unrepresentative of an American ideal. Nor have active presidents given up the advantages accruing to them from new legislation, the modern growth of government services and the incessant demands of the media.

Growing responsibility

Government activity has grown impressively since 1945, even under presidents who sought to diminish it. Economic and budgetary policies are critical to the modern society and up to 1970 at least congress was mainly content to leave management to the executive branch, where practical expertise was supposed to lie. Social programmes and mandatory spending have become a crucial problem: entitlement cheques now make up half the federal budget. Throughout the cold war defence and space spending added to the executive's command and influence. The concentration of much attention on foreign policy gave the administration increased prestige. Congress did not have the resources to compete.

The power of initiative matters decisively in American politics. In foreign affairs secrecy and speed are invariably at the executive's disposal; so is having the virtual monopoly of producing the authoritative answers to the media's questioning. Congress's most effective methods of reply, through legislation and committee inquiries, can seem dramatic but have an air of retrospection. American governments' publicity techniques are unchallenged internationally.

Distrust

It has only been when the presidency has overreached itself

in using its unmatched advantages that it has been worsted. Both Democrats and Republicans in the White House have been apt to fear and quarrel with the national media even when their lieutenants have become expert in exploiting the opportunities they offer. They have not trusted the bureaucracy and have relied on their own inner circle of committed advisers, whose own remoteness from the daily political process has increased the sense of isolation that normally overtakes men at the top.

The White House itself is a court whose members compete for attention and leverage; those in the west wing, closest to the president, are still competing with each other for his notice, however superior they may feel to the outer functionaries. Secretaries of state are aware of the inherent rivalry with the national security advisers even when the national security council is not headed by a Henry Kissinger.

It is a shifting stage. In almost all presidencies the swings of public opinion are great and often sudden. Truman, Johnson, Nixon, Carter and Bush, in particular, have experienced giddy heights and depths in a job that is predictable chiefly in its insecurity. Tradition and the modern constitution envisage a standard presidency of eight years, but in the past 70 years (besides Franklin Roosevelt's four terms) only Eisenhower and Reagan have survived two full terms.

Congressional power

Congress took priority in the minds of the men who wrote the constitution because they thought of the president chiefly as a manager. Congress has contrived its periods of dominance, usually in reaction to presidential ones. From 1919 to 1939 it had the whip hand over foreign policy after Wilson, replacing his League of Nations with isolation. It nearly defeated Truman. It made Nixon pay the penalty for the Vietnam war and the presidency's part in it. Reagan's deficiency was exposed in the Iran-Contra hearings and his Nicaraguan policy was closed down. The perception of authority returned to Capitol Hill.

Both the Senate and the House have reinforced their political presence and challenged administrations by taking on sizeable staffs of experts, lawyers and researchers. Much subcommittee work has become sufficiently demanding to justify numerous and resourceful staff teams -- as do the demands of two-yearly re-election. Congress came later to harnessing television but now uses the courtroom procedure to advantage. A congressional Office of the Budget shadows the executive one and is an investment in a decisive issue of the 1990s.

Committee power

Congress's power lies in its many standing committees and subcommittees. There is particular competition for places on the more important ones. In the senate these include budget, finance, appropriations, armed services and foreign relations. In the house they are budget, ways and means, appropriations and rules. Chairmen are regarded as eminent; subcommittee chairmen can find themselves overseeing whole industries. The chairmen, who set the agendas, are nominated by the majority party and membership reflects the party proportions. When appointments simply reflected the seniority rule control was kept by the elderly holders of safe seats (mainly conservative southern Democrats) but this has been partially adjusted.

Rules Committee

This has particular power in the house because it regulates the flow of legislative business. The members consider the many bills reported out of other committees. They decide on whether or not to grant special consideration, so effectively determining success or failure by their political priorities.

Watchdog committees

Congress has routine powers to scrutinise the executive's actions, originating in its financial responsibility. The power of examining members of the administration is both prized and conducive to publicity. Special investigations into apparent scandals can achieve, in practised hands, the status of national political occasions, which can become popular indications of a change in the political initiative.

Lobbying

Lobbying in Washington, DC is an ever-expanding industry. Its practitioners range from those with exceptional skills and experience in legislation to others who specialise in entertainment. The rapid development of single-issue politics has added impressively to the industry's numbers and financial backing. All who seek to influence congress are required to register their trade. They are highly professional and fully aware of their importance.

Major pressure groups

The most influential of the pressure groups tend to be those representing business and commercial interests, such as the National Association of Manufacturers and the US Chamber of Commerce. Big corporations employ their own expert staff. Politicians rely on the help of financial support, with campaign contributions raised and distributed as the law requires through political action committees. The farmers, oil interests, tobacco and liquor corporations are generous whenever, as often, they feel themselves threatened. The defence industries seldom lack for friends. Foreign countries are hard-working in their own interests; the China (later Taiwan), Israel and Arab lobbies are often conspicuous.

Professional associations are active, led by the American Medical Association and the American Bar Association. So are the trade unions, the veterans and various enthusiasts for countless causes, such as pro- and anti-abortion, small business, education, car dealers and the gun clubs who uphold the constitutional right of American citizens to carry arms. Civil rights campaigners are prolific, as are environmentalists, consumerists and political activists like the Americans for Democratic Action, the American Civil Liberties Union and the League of Women Voters.

These are legitimate contributors to the democratic process, although there is regular criticism of politicians who show undue dependency on financial contacts and of experts who switch easily between the bureaucracy and the private sector.

State power

State and local government retain power and influence, encouraged by regional interests and Republican efforts to favour the states against federal authority. Within limits the states set their own taxes on top of federal ones and draft their own laws regulating commerce, education, social services and the criminal justice system. Some are pioneers in social reform; others are testbeds of fiscal innovation; most are protective of local interests. Sales tax rates vary. Kentucky is mindful of tobacco growers, Texas of oil producers.

State governors are potential White House candidates: Carter, Reagan and Clinton all came up that way. At election times states allow their voters the opportunity of referenda which occasionally acquire national significance. California is especially interested in taxation and environmental issues. Its efforts in rolling back property taxes have had imitators. Other states concern themselves with gambling and lotteries, and with worthy causes such as countering discrimination against handicapped people. There are always surprises engendered by the system.

Party politics

The two-party system has had many detractors and even challengers, but its resilience still seems to meet the wishes of a majority of Americans. The Democrats had their origin in Jefferson's days and the Republicans, formed in 1854, had Lincoln as their first president. No independent or third-party candidate has even come close to the presidency. Theodore Roosevelt, running as a Progressive, got 27% of the vote in 1912; Ross Perot, an independent, 19% in 1992 and Robert M. LaFollette (Progressive) 17% in 1924. Intrusions into Congress or state governorships are rare.

The Democrats

The party has been, by tradition, the one more inclined to deficit economics, high taxation, social welfare, free trade and internationalism. But tradition falters after repeated defeats, and Bill Clinton's campaign presented businesslike qualities, caution on tax and spend, and elements of protection and even of isolation. Many of his supporters expected to see Democratic policies in the tradition of Roosevelt's New Deal, Truman's Fair Deal and Johnson's Great Society.

The party's chief constituencies have been among unionised industrial workers, black voters and the urban poor, but with a liberal middle-class wing of particular influence. Although this wing has seldom hankered after European socialist ideals, the choice of what were seen as left-wing candidates in 1968, 1972, 1984 and 1988 played a substantial part in the failure to keep customary Democratic support. The radical changes in the industrial and social composition of the south, aided by migration to the booming sunbelt suburbs, meant that the party lost states and seats which it had once relied on.

Despite persistent Democratic strength in both houses of congress, the putting together of a modern national coalition to take the presidency was a prolonged and uncertain process. The 1992 success may have owed most to the accumulated economic failures of the Bush term in office.

The Republicans

The Republicans recovered from the experience of Nixon, Vietnam and Watergate with the comfortable popularity of Ronald Reagan, a firm policy to win the political confrontation of the cold war, and attractive ideas on supply side economics and tax cutting. The party ran strongly in the 1980s in the west and south, the farm states and among the right-of-centre ethnic blue-collar families, as well as in the upwardly mobile suburbs. It came to see itself as the natural American majority combining prosperity, patriotism and what were admired as small town virtues.

These electoral advantages did not persist, despite the success of the Reagan and Bush administrations in discrediting communism and breaking up the Soviet empire, plus the humiliation of Saddam Hussein of Iraq after his invasion of Kuwait. The obduracy of the recession, the shifting of American antagonism from Russia to the Japanese and their commercial success, and the apparent exhaustion of both Bush himself and Republican ideas all counted for more in 1992. The loss of the White House was a particular blow to a party without a strong congressional and governorship base.

Weakened parties

American voters are changing and with them are the parties. Voters have been losing a partisan identification for two generations now. Parties are no longer symbols for loyalties that can be taken for granted. New voters no longer follow their parents' example. People increasingly prefer to register as independents rather than Democrats and Republicans. So party organisations are weakening. For modern presidential campaigns the organisations are personal and are created anew every four years.

In return, voters are more interested in issues and personalities. This is encouraged by the media, especially the new media outlets. Whereas national TV news, news magazines and broadsheet papers adhered to traditional politics, the latest technology has been put to use by cable TV, supermarket tabloids, talk-shows and "infomercials" (developed by Ross Perot's 1992 campaign). Sceptics say this will lead to more emphasis on personalities and short-term interests. .

In Congress candidates have become more independent of party and party platforms. Incumbents had relied on their instant media access to beat off challengers. In the house 95% of congressmen running again had become used to reelection, but in 1992 public sentiment changed after a congressional banking scandal and a high pay rise. Region, class and religion still have an influence on voters' decisions but all are weaker factors than before. Adaptability is the watchword of the new politics.

USA: the basic facts

Area	9,372,614 sq km	Currency	US dollar ($)
Capital	Washington DC		

People

Population	255.4m	Life expectancy: men	73 yrs
Pop. per sq km	27	women	79 yrs
Av. ann. growth		Adult literacy	99%
in pop. 1985–90	0.8%	Fertility rate (per woman)	2.1
Pop. under 15	21.9%		
Pop. over 65	12.6%		*per 1,000 pop.*
No. of men per 100 women	95	Crude birth rate	15.9
Human Development Index	98	Crude death rate	8.3

The economy

GDP	$5,951bn	GDP per head	$23,120
		GDP per head in purchasing	
Av. ann. growth in real		power parity (USA=100)	100
GDP 1985-92	2.3%		

Origins of GDP		Components of GDP	
	% of total		*% of total*
Agriculture	2.3	Private consumption	68.6
Industry, of which:	24.4	Public consumption	18.8
manufacturing	18.3	Investment	13.0
Services	73.3	Exports	10.6
		Imports	-11.1

Structure of manufacturing

	% of total		*% of total*
Agric. & food processing	12	Other	52
Textiles & clothing	5	Av. ann. increase in industrial	
Machinery & transport	31	output 1985–92	2.0%

Energy

	quadrillion Btus		
Total output	67.5	% output exported	7.7
Total consumption	81.5	% consumption imported	22.6
Consumption per head,			
m Btu	326.2		

Inflation and finance

Consumer price		*av. ann. increase 1985–92*	
inflation 1993	3.0%	Narrow money (M1)	7.5%
Av. ann. inflation 1988–93	4.1%	Broad money (M3)	3.9%

Exchange rates

	end 1993		*end December 1993*
$ per SDR	1.37	Effective rates	*1985 = 100*
$ per Ecu	1.12	– nominal	67.0
		– real	65.3

Principal exports

	$bn fob		$bn fob
Machinery & transport equipment	224.0	Agric. products & foodstuffs	40.6
Other manufactures	180.2	Total incl. others	**448.2**

Main export destinations

	% of total		% of total
Canada	20.2	Germany	4.7
Japan	10.7	South Korea	3.3
Mexico	9.0	EU	22.9
United Kingdom	5.0		

Principal imports

	$bn fob		$bn fob
Other manufactures	273.3	Agric. products & foodstuffs	28.0
Machinery & transport equipment	231.4	Total incl. others	**532.7**

Main origins of imports

	% of total		% of total
Canada	18.5	Taiwan	4.6
Japan	18.2	United Kingdom	3.7
Mexico	6.6	EU	17.7
Germany	5.4		

Balance of payments, reserves and aid, $bn

Visible exports fob	440.1	Capital balance	36.6
Visible imports fob	-536.3	Overall balance	-42.0
Trade balance	-96.1	Change in reserves	-6.4
Invisibles inflows	290.4	Level of reserves	
Invisibles outflows	-227.6	end Dec.	71.3
Net transfers	-32.9	No. months import cover	1.6
Current account balance	-66.3	Aid given	11.7
– as % of GDP	-1.1	– as % of GDP	0.2

Family life

No. of households	95.6m	Marriages per 1,000 pop.	9.4
Av. no. per household	2.6	Divorces per 1,000 pop.	4.7

Note   See Notes on pages 206–207 for explanations of terms.

The presidential election

Electoral college votes		1992 Clinton, %	1988 Bush,%
Alabama	9	41	59
Alaska	3	32	60
Arizona	8	37	60
Arkansas	6	53	56
California	54	47	53
Colorado	8	41	53
Connecticut	8	42	52
Delaware	3	44	56
DC	3	87	14
Florida	25	39	61
Georgia	13	43	60
Hawaii	4	49	45
Idaho	4	29	62
Illinois	22	48	51
Indiana	12	37	60
Iowa	7	44	44
Kansas	6	34	56
Kentucky	8	44	56
Louisiana	9	46	54
Maine	4	39	55
Maryland	10	50	51
Massachusetts	12	48	47
Michigan	18	42	54
Minnesota	10	44	46
Mississippi	7	41	60
Missouri	11	44	52
Montana	3	44	52
Nebraska	5	30	60
Nevada	4	38	56
New Hampshire	4	39	63
New Jersey	15	43	56
New Mexico	5	46	52
New York	33	49	48
North Carolina	14	44	58
North Dakota	3	32	56
Ohio	21	40	55
Oklahoma	8	43	58
Oregon	7	42	47
Pennsylvania	23	46	51
Rhode Island	4	48	46
South Carolina	8	40	62
South Dakota	3	41	53
Tennessee	11	47	58
Texas	32	37	56
Utah	5	26	66
Vermont	3	46	51
Virginia	13	41	60
Washington	11	45	48
West Virginia	5	49	48
Wisconsin	11	41	47
Wyoming	3	34	61

1992
Overall % vote
Clinton 43
Bush 38
Perot 19

Electoral college votes
Clinton 370
Bush 168

1988
Overall % vote
Bush 54
Dukakis 46

Electoral college votes
Bush 426
Dukakis 111

=Part II=
Rankings

Area and population

Area	'000 sq miles	Population	millions
1 Alaska	656.4	1 California	30.9
2 Texas	268.6	2 New York	18.1
3 California	163.7	3 Texas	17.7
4 Montana	147.0	4 Florida	13.5
5 New Mexico	121.6	5 Pennsylvania	12.0
6 Arizona	114.0	6 Illinois	11.6
7 Nevada	110.6	7 Ohio	11.0
8 Colorado	104.1	8 Michigan	9.4
9 Oregon	98.4	9 New Jersey	7.8
10 Wyoming	97.8	10 Georgia	6.8
11 Michigan	96.7	North Carolina	6.8
12 Minnesota	86.9	12 Virginia	6.4
13 Utah	84.9	13 Massachusetts	6.0
14 Idaho	83.6	14 Indiana	5.7
15 Kansas	82.3	15 Missouri	5.2
16 Nebraska	77.6	16 Washington	5.1
17 South Dakota	77.1	17 Tennessee	5.0
18 Washington	71.3	Wisconsin	5.0
19 North Dakota	70.7	18 Maryland	4.9
20 Oklahoma	69.9	20 Minnesota	4.5
21 Missouri	69.7	21 Louisiana	4.3
22 Florida	65.8	22 Alabama	4.1
23 Wisconsin	65.5	23 Arizona	3.8
24 Georgia	59.4	Kentucky	3.8
25 Illinois	57.9	25 South Carolina	3.6
26 Iowa	56.3	26 Colorado	3.5
27 New York	54.6	27 Connecticut	3.3
28 North Carolina	53.8	28 Oklahoma	3.2
29 Arkansas	53.2	29 Oregon	3.0
30 Alabama	52.4	30 Iowa	2.8
31 Louisiana	51.8	31 Mississippi	2.6
32 Mississippi	48.4	32 Kansas	2.5
33 Pennsylvania	46.1	33 Arkansas	2.4
34 Ohio	44.8	34 West Virginia	1.8
35 Virginia	42.8	Utah	1.8
36 Tennessee	42.1	36 Nebraska	1.6
37 Kentucky	40.4	New Mexico	1.6
38 Indiana	36.4	38 Maine	1.3
39 Maine	35.4	Nevada	1.3
40 South Carolina	32.0	40 Hawaii	1.2
41 West Virginia	24.2	41 New Hampshire	1.1
42 Maryland	12.4	Idaho	1.1
43 Hawaii	10.9	42 Rhode Island	1.0
44 Massachusetts	10.6	44 Montana	0.8
45 Vermont	9.6	45 Delaware	0.7
46 New Hampshire	9.4	South Dakota	0.7
47 New Jersey	8.7	47 Alaska	0.6
48 Connecticut	5.5	District of Columbia	0.6
49 Delaware	2.5	North Dakota	0.6
50 Rhode Island	1.5	Vermont	0.6
51 District of Columbia	0.07	51 Wyoming	0.5

Population growth and density

Av. ann. growth 1980–92			Pop. per sq. mile of land	
1	Nevada	4.3	1	District of Columbia	9,649.5
2	Alaska	3.2	2	New Jersey	1,049.9
3	Arizona	2.9	3	Rhode Island	961.8
4	Florida	2.7	4	Massachusetts	765.3
5	California	2.2	5	Connecticut	677.2
6	Georgia	1.8	6	Maryland	502.1
	Texas	1.8	7	New York	383.7
	Utah	1.8	8	Delaware	352.3
	Washington	1.8	9	Ohio	269.0
10	New Hampshire	1.6	10	Pennsylvania	267.9
	New Mexico	1.6	11	Florida	249.8
12	Colorado	1.5	12	Illinois	209.2
	Hawaii	1.5	13	California	197.9
	Virginia	1.5	14	Hawaii	180.5
15	Maryland	1.3	15	Michigan	166.1
	North Carolina	1.3	16	Virginia	161.0
17	Delaware	1.2	17	Indiana	157.8
	South Carolina	1.2	18	North Carolina	140.5
19	Idaho	1.0	19	New Hampshire	123.8
	Oregon	1.0	20	Tennessee	121.9
21	Vermont	0.9	21	South Carolina	119.7
22	Maine	0.8	22	Georgia	116.6
	Minnesota	0.8	23	Louisiana	98.4
	Tennessee	0.8	24	Kentucky	94.5
25	Alabama	0.5	25	Wisconsin	92.2
	Arkansas	0.5	26	Alabama	81.5
	Connecticut	0.5	27	Washington	77.1
	Kansas	0.5	28	Missouri	75.4
	Missouri	0.5	29	West Virginia	75.2
	New Jersey	0.5	30	Texas	67.4
	Oklahoma	0.5	31	Vermont	61.6
	Rhode Island	0.5	32	Minnesota	56.3
	Wisconsin	0.5	33	Mississippi	55.7
34	Massachusetts	0.4	34	Iowa	50.3
	Montana	0.4	35	Oklahoma	46.8
36	Indiana	0.3	36	Arkansas	46.1
	Mississippi	0.3	37	Maine	40.0
	New York	0.3	38	Arizona	33.7
39	Kentucky	0.2	39	Colorado	33.5
	Lousiana	0.2	40	Oregon	31.0
	Michigan	0.2	41	Kansas	30.8
	Nebraska	0.2	42	Utah	22.1
	Ohio	0.2	43	Nebraska	20.9
	South Dakota	0.2	44	New Mexico	13.0
45	Illinois	0.1	45	Idaho	12.9
	Pennsylvania	0.1	46	Nevada	12.1
47	Wyoming	-0.1	47	South Dakota	9.4
48	North Dakota	-0.2	48	North Dakota	9.2
49	Iowa	-0.3	49	Montana	5.7
50	West Virginia	-0.6	50	Wyoming	4.8
51	District of Columbia	-0.7	51	Alaska	1.0

Society

Pop. living in urban areas	%	Pop. white	%
1 District of Columbia	100.0	**1** Vermont	98.6
2 California	92.6	**2** Maine	98.4
3 New Jersey	89.4	**3** New Hampshire	98.0
4 Hawaii	89.0	**4** Iowa	96.6
5 Nevada	88.3	**5** West Virginia	96.2
6 Arizona	87.5	**6** North Dakota	94.6
7 Utah	87.0	**7** Idaho	94.4
8 Rhode Island	86.0	Minnesota	94.4
9 Florida	84.8	**9** Wyoming	94.2
10 Illinois	84.6	**10** Nebraska	93.8
11 Massachusetts	84.3	Utah	93.8
New York	84.3	**12** Oregon	92.8
13 Colorado	82.4	**13** Montana	92.7
14 Maryland	81.3	**14** Wisconsin	92.2
15 Texas	80.3	**15** South Dakota	91.6
16 Connecticut	79.1	**16** Rhode Island	91.4
17 Washington	76.4	**17** Indiana	90.6
18 Ohio	74.1	**18** Kansas	90.1
19 Delaware	73.0	**19** Massachusetts	89.8
New Mexico	73.0	**20** Pennsylvania	88.5
21 Michigan	70.5	Washington	88.5
Oregon	70.5	**22** Colorado	88.2
23 Minnesota	69.9	**23** Ohio	87.8
24 Virginia	69.4	**24** Missouri	87.7
25 Kansas	69.1	**25** Connecticut	87.0
26 Pennsylvania	68.9	**26** Nevada	84.3
27 Missouri	68.7	**27** Michigan	83.4
28 Louisiana	68.1	**28** Florida	83.1
29 Oklahoma	67.7	**29** Tennessee	83.0
30 Alaska	67.5	**30** Arkansas	82.7
31 Nebraska	66.1	**31** Oklahoma	82.1
32 Wisconsin	65.7	**32** Kentucky	82.0
33 Wyoming	65.0	**33** Arizona	80.8
34 Indiana	64.9	**34** Delaware	80.3
35 Georgia	63.2	**35** New Jersey	79.3
36 Tennessee	60.9	**36** Illinois	78.3
37 Iowa	60.6	**37** Virginia	77.4
38 Alabama	60.4	**38** New Mexico	75.6
39 Idaho	57.4	North Carolina	75.6
40 South Carolina	54.6	**40** Alaska	75.5
41 Arkansas	53.5	**41** Texas	75.2
42 North Dakota	53.3	**42** New York	74.4
43 Montana	52.5	**43** Alabama	73.6
44 Kentucky	51.8	**44** Georgia	71.0
45 New Hampshire	51.0	Maryland	71.0
46 North Carolina	50.4	**46** California	69.9
47 South Dakota	50.0	**47** South Carolina	69.0
48 Mississippi	47.1	**48** Louisiana	67.3
49 Maine	44.6	**49** Mississippi	63.5
50 West Virginia	36.1	**50** Hawaii	33.4
51 Vermont	32.2	**51** District of Columbia	29.6

Highest birth rate
No. of live births per '000 population, 1991

1	Alaska	21.1	6	Arizona		18.3
2	Utah	20.1	7	New Mexico		18.0
3	California	19.8	8	Hawaii		17.5
4	Nevada	18.8		Maryland		17.5
	Texas	18.8	10	Louisiana		17.2

Highest death rate
No. of deaths per '000 population, 1991

1	District of Columbia	11.7		Florida	10.2
2	West Virgina	11.0	7	Mississippi	9.9
3	Missouri	10.4	8	Oklahoma	9.6
4	Pennsylvania	10.3	9	Kentucky	9.5
5	Arkansas	10.2	10	Alabama	9.3

Highest marriage rate
No. of marriages per '000 population (1991)

1	Nevada	106.3	6	Tennessee	13.7
2	Arkansas	15.7	7	Kentucky	12.7
3	Hawaii	15.4	8	Alaska	11.3
4	South Carolina	14.8	9	Virginia	11.0
5	Idaho	13.9	10	Georgia	10.6

Highest divorce rate
No. of divorces per '000 population (1991 or latest year)

1	Nevada	11.9	6	Tennessee	6.5
2	Arkansas	7.8		Alabama	6.5
3	Oklahoma	7.4	8	Idaho	6.3
4	Wyoming	7.0		Georgia	6.3
5	Arizona	6.7	10	Florida	6.2

Highest black population
%

1	District of Columbia	65.8	11	Delaware	16.9
2	Mississippi	35.6	12	Tennessee	16.0
3	Louisiana	30.8	13	Arkansas	15.9
4	South Carolina	29.8		New York	15.9
5	Georgia	27.0	15	Illinois	14.8
6	Alabama	25.3	16	Michigan	13.9
7	Maryland	24.9	17	Florida	13.6
8	North Carolina	22.0	18	New Jersey	13.4
9	New Mexico	20.0	19	Texas	11.9
10	Virginia	18.8	20	Missouri	10.7

Highest Hispanic population
%

1	New Mexico	38.2	6	New York	12.3
2	California	25.8	7	Florida	12.2
3	Texas	25.5	8	Nevada	10.4
4	Arizona	18.8	9	New Jersey	9.6
5	Colorado	12.9	10	Illinois	7.9

Age

Aged under 18		%
1	Utah	36.1
2	Alaska	31.5
3	Idaho	30.4
4	New Mexico	29.7
5	Wyoming	29.6
6	Louisana	28.9
7	South Dakota	28.7
	Texas	28.7
9	Mississippi	28.6
10	Arizona	27.4
	Montana	27.4
12	California	27.3
	Nebraska	27.3
14	North Dakota	27.0
15	Kansas	26.9
	Minnesota	26.9
17	Georgia	26.7
	Oklahoma	26.7
19	Michigan	26.6
	Wisconsin	26.6
21	Washington	26.4
22	Arkansas	26.2
	Colorado	26.2
	South Carolina	26.2
25	Iowa	26.1
26	Alabama	26.0
	Illinois	26.0
	Missouri	26.0
29	Indiana	25.8
30	Kentucky	25.7
	Oregon	25.7
32	Ohio	25.6
33	Nevada	25.5
34	Vermont	25.3
35	Hawaii	25.2
	New Hampshire	25.2
37	Delaware	25.0
	Maryland	25.0
39	Maine	24.8
	Tennessee	24.8
41	Virginia	24.5
42	New York	24.4
43	North Carolina	24.3
44	West Virginia	24.2
45	New Jersey	23.9
46	Pennsylvania	23.7
47	Connecticut	23.5
48	Rhode Island	23.2
49	Massachusetts	23.1
50	Florida	23.0
51	District of Columbia	19.9

Aged over 65		%
1	Florida	18.4
2	Pennsylvania	15.7
3	Iowa	15.4
4	Rhode Island	15.2
	West Virginia	15.2
6	Arkansas	14.9
7	South Dakota	14.7
8	North Dakota	14.6
9	Missouri	14.1
	Nebraska	14.1
11	Connecticut	13.9
	Kansas	13.9
13	Massachusetts	13.9
14	Oregon	13.8
15	Maine	13.6
	New Jersey	13.6
17	Oklahoma	13.5
18	Arizona	13.4
	Montana	13.4
20	Wisconsin	13.3
21	Ohio	13.2
22	District of Columbia	13.1
	New York	13.1
24	Alabama	13.0
25	Indiana	12.7
	Kenucky	12.7
	Tennessee	12.7
28	Illinois	12.6
29	Minnesota	12.5
	Mississippi	12.5
31	North Carolina	12.4
32	Delaware	12.3
33	Michigan	12.2
34	Vermont	12.0
35	Idaho	11.9
36	New Hampshire	11.8
37	Washington	11.7
38	South Carolina	11.6
39	Hawaii	11.4
40	Louisiana	11.2
41	Maryland	11.0
	Nevada	11.0
43	New Mexico	10.9
	Virginia	10.9
45	Wyoming	10.7
46	California	10.5
47	Texas	10.2
48	Georgia	10.1
49	Colorado	10.0
50	Utah	8.8
51	Alaska	4.3

Causes of death[a]

Cancer

1	District of Columbia	261.7	6	Rhode Island	241.9
2	Florida	254.9	7	New Jersey	232.0
3	Pennsylvania	251.2	8	Maine	227.4
4	West Virginia	245.8	9	Missouri	226.8
5	Arkansas	242.6	10	Massachusetts	223.5

Heart disease

1	West Virginia	395.8	6	New York	353.7
2	Michigan	367.3	7	Arkansas	346.7
3	Pennsylvania	366.1	8	Missouri	343.2
4	Mississippi	358.3	9	Rhode Island	342.4
5	Florida	354.3	10	Iowa	340.9

Motor accident

1	California	5,105	6	Illinois	1,748
2	Texas	3,395	7	Ohio	1,700
3	Florida	3,016	8	Michigan	1,633
4	New York	2,239	9	Georgia	1,632
5	Pennsylvania	1,877	10	North Carolina	1,464

Suicide

1	Nevada	23.1	6	Alaska	16.9
2	Montana	20.0	7	Oregon	16.7
3	New Mexico	19.5	8	Colorado	16.6
4	Arizona	18.9		Vermont	16.6
5	Wyoming	17.3	10	Florida	16.4

AIDS cases[b]

1	District of Columbia	117.7	6	Maryland	24.6
2	New York	46.4	7	Georgia	19.5
3	Florida	37.8	8	Illinois	17.6
4	California	27.2	9	Louisiana	16.5
5	New Jersey	26.2		Texas	16.5

Highest murder rate[c]

1	District of Columbia	80.6		Georgia	12.8
2	Louisiana	16.9	7	California	12.7
3	Texas	15.3	8	Nevada	11.8
4	New York	14.2	9	Maryland	11.7
5	Mississippi	12.8	10	Alabama	11.5

Lowest murder rate[c]

1	North Dakota	1.1	6	Iowa	2.0
2	New Hampshire	1.2	7	Vermont	2.1
	Maine	1.2	8	Utah	2.9
4	South Dakota	1.7	9	Minnesota	3.0
5	Idaho	1.8	10	Nebraska	3.3

a   Data refer to rates per 100,000 population, 1990.
b   1992.
c   1991.

The economy

	Gross st. prod. (GSP) $bn, 1989			Tot. personal income $bn, 1992	
1	California	697.4	1	California	656.8
2	New York	441.1	2	New York	426.4
3	Texas	340.1	3	Texas	315.9
4	Illinois	256.5	4	Florida	261.6
5	Pennsylvania	227.9	5	Illinois	251.3
6	Florida	227.0	6	Pennsylvania	243.2
7	Ohio	211.5	7	New Jersey	206.1
8	New Jersey	203.4	8	Ohio	205.2
9	Michigan	181.8	9	Michigan	184.1
10	Massachusetts	144.8	10	Massachusetts	144.3
11	Virginia	136.5	11	Virginia	131.6
12	North Carolina	130.1	12	Georgia	122.4
13	Georgia	129.8	13	North Carolina	120.9
14	Indiana	105.3	14	Maryland	112.8
15	Missouri	100.1	15	Washington	104.8
16	Maryland	99.1	16	Indiana	102.2
17	Washington	96.2	17	Missouri	97.8
18	Wisconsin	94.0	18	Wisconsin	93.8
19	Minnesota	93.6	19	Minnesota	89.8
20	Tennessee	92.3	20	Connecticut	88.5
21	Connecticut	88.9	21	Tennessee	87.1
22	Louisiana	79.1	22	Colorado	69.8
23	Alabama	67.9	23	Louisiana	67.4
24	Colorado	66.2	24	Alabama	67.1
25	Kentucky	65.9	25	Arizona	65.6
26	Arizona	65.3	26	Kentucky	62.1
27	South Carolina	60.2	27	South Carolina	57.6
28	Iowa	52.6	28	Oregon	54.2
29	Oklahoma	52.3	29	Oklahoma	52.0
30	Oregon	52.1	30	Iowa	51.4
31	Kansas	48.8	31	Kansas	48.9
32	District of Columbia	39.4	32	Arkansas	37.0
33	Mississippi	38.1	33	Mississippi	36.8
34	Arkansas	37.2	34	Nebraska	30.6
35	Nebraska	31.1	35	Utah	27.8
36	Utah	28.1	36	West Virginia	27.3
37	Nevada	28.0	37	Nevada	26.9
38	West Virginia	27.9	38	New Hampshire	25.5
39	Hawaii	25.8	39	Hawaii	24.6
40	New Mexico	25.4	40	New Mexico	24.3
41	New Hampshire	24.5	41	Maine	22.5
42	Maine	23.5	42	Rhode Island	20.4
43	Alaska	19.6	43	Idaho	17.1
44	Rhode Island	18.8	44	District of Columbia	15.5
45	Idaho	16.3	45	Delaware	14.8
46	Delaware	15.4	46	Montana	13.2
47	Montana	13.1	47	Alaska	12.7
48	Vermont	11.5	48	South Dakota	11.8
49	North Dakota	11.2	49	Vermont	10.7
50	South Dakota	11.1		North Dakota	10.7
	Wyoming	11.1	51	Wyoming	8.1

In receipt of most federal funds
$bn, 1992

1	California	139.7	6	Ohio	43.5
2	New York	83.9	7	Virginia	40.9
3	Texas	69.9	8	Michigan	34.7
4	Florida	62.7	9	New Jersey	34.3
5	Pennsylvania	55.7	10	Massachusetts	32.8

Biggest exporters
$bn, 1992

1	California	56.3	6	Ohio	16.3
2	Texas	43.5	7	Louisiana	16.2
3	Washington	28.0	8	Illinois	15.3
4	New York	22.6	9	Florida	14.4
5	Michigan	20.4	10	Massachusetts	10.4

Most innovative
No. of patents, 1991

1	California	9,002	6	Michigan	3,024
2	New York	4,965	7	Pennsylvania	2,935
3	Texas	3,474	8	Ohio	2,930
4	New Jersey	3,295	9	Massachusetts	2,211
5	Illinois	3,176	10	Florida	1,950

Highest business failure rate
1992

1	California	169	6	Rhode Island	133
	Georgia	169	7	Florida	130
3	Arizona	164	8	Oklahoma	124
4	New Hampshire	146	9	Tennessee	120
5	Massachusetts	135	10	New York	117

Lowest business failure rate[a]

1	Iowa	47	6	Wyoming	60
2	Alsaka	51	7	South Dakota	63
	Montana	51	8	Arkansas	65
4	South Carolina	52	9	Mississippi	70
5	North Dakota	55	10	Wisconsin	73

Most social security recipients
m, 1991

1	California	3.7	6	Ohio	1.8
2	New York	2.9		Illinois	1.8
3	Florida	2.7	8	Michigan	1.5
4	Pennsylvania	2.3	9	New Jersey	1.2
5	Texas	2.2	10	North Carolina	1.1

a Per 10,000 listed concerns. Failures consist of businesses involved in court proceedings or voluntary actions involving losses to creditors.

Leading companies and banks

Top 50 US companies
by sales, 1993

1 General Motors, Detroit, MI
2 Ford Motor, Dearborn, MI
3 Exxon, Irving, TX
4 Intl. Business Machines, Armonk, NY
5 General Electric, Fairfield, CT
6 Mobil, Fairfax, VA
7 Philip Morris, New York, NY
8 Chrysler, Highland Park, MI
9 Texaco, White Plains, NY
10 E.I. Du Pont De Nemours, Wilmington, DE
11 Chevron, San Francisco, CA
12 Procter & Gamble, Cincinnati, OH
13 Amoco, Chicago, IL
14 Boeing, Seattle, WA
15 Pepsico, Purchase, NY
16 Conagra, Omaha, NE
17 Shell Oil, Houston, TX
18 United Technologies, Hartford, CT
19 Hewlett-Packard, Palo Alto, CA
20 Eastman Kodak, Rochester, NY
21 Dow Chemical, Midland, MI
22 Atlantic Richfield, Los Angeles, CA
23 Motorola, Schaumberg, IL
24 USX, Pittsburgh, PA
25 RJR Nabisco Holdings, New York, NY
26 Xerox, Stamford, CT
27 Sara Lee, Chicago, IL
28 McDonnell Douglas, St Louis, MO
29 Digital Equipment, Maynard, MA
30 Johnson & Johnson, New Brunswick, NJ
31 Minnesota Mining & Mfg., St Paul, MN
32 Coca-Cola, Atlanta, GA
33 International Paper, Purchase, NY
34 Tenneco, Houston, TX
35 Lockheed, Calabasas, CA
36 Georgia-Pacific, Atlanta, GA
37 Phillips Petroleum, Bartlesville, OK
38 AlliedSignal, Morris Township, NJ
39 IBP, Dakota City, NE
40 Goodyear Tire, Akron, OH
41 Caterpillar, Peoria, IL
42 Westinghouse Electric, Pittsburgh, PA
43 Anheuser-Busch, St Louis, MO
44 Bristol-Myers Squibb, New York, NY
45 Rockwell International, Seal Beach, CA
46 Merck, Whitehouse Station, NJ
47 Coastal, Houston,TX
48 Archer Daniels Midland, Decatur, IL
49 Ashland Oil, Russell, KY
50 Weyerhaeuser, Federal Way, WA

Biggest banks
by capital, $m, 1992

#	Bank	Capital	#	Bank	Capital
1	BankAmerica Corp	8,580	11	Bank of New York	2,904
2	Citicorp	7,752	12	Wachovia Corporation	2,741
3	Chemical Banking Corp	7,400	13	Fleet Financial	2,729
4	NationsBank	7,174	14	NBD Bancorp	2,661
5	JP Morgan & Co.	6,820	15	Wells Fargo & Co	2,648
6	Chase Manhattan Corp	4,831	16	First Chicago Corporation	2,615
7	Banc One Corp	4,668	17	Norwest Corp	2,591
8	PNC Financial Corp	3,651	18	SunTrust Banks	2,540
9	Bankers Trust New York Corp	3,637	19	First Interstate Bancorp	2,414
10	First Union Corp	2,925	20	National City Corp	2,143

Living standards

Average income per head $		Pop. below pov. line %, 1989	
1 Connecticut	26,979	1 Mississippi	25.2
2 New Jersey	26,457	2 Louisiana	23.6
3 District of Columbia	26,360	3 New Mexico	20.6
4 Massachusetts	24,059	4 West Virginia	19.7
5 New York	23,534	5 Arkansas	19.1
6 Maryland	22,974	6 Kentucky	19.0
7 New Hampshire	22,934	7 Alabama	18.3
8 Illinois	21,608	8 Texas	18.1
9 Alaska	21,603	9 District of Columbia	16.9
10 Delaware	21,451	10 Arizona	16.7
11 California	21,278	Oklahoma	16.7
12 Hawaii	21,218	Tennessee	16.7
13 Virginia	20,629	13 South Carolina	16.4
14 Washington	20,398	14 Montana	16.1
15 Rhode Island	20,299	15 South Dakota	15.9
16 Nevada	20,266	16 Georgia	14.7
17 Pennsylvania	20,253	17 North Dakota	14.4
18 Colorado	20,124	18 Idaho	13.3
19 Minnesota	20,049	Missouri	13.3
20 Michigan	19,508	20 Michigan	13.1
21 Florida	19,397	21 New York	13.0
22 Kansas	19,376	North Carolina	13.0
23 Nebraska	19,084	23 Florida	12.7
24 Missouri	18,835	24 California	12.6
25 Vermont	18,834	25 Ohio	12.5
26 Wisconsin	18,727	26 Oregon	12.4
27 Ohio	18,624	27 Illinois	11.9
28 Iowa	18,287	Wyoming	11.9
29 Maine	18,226	29 Colorado	11.7
30 Oregon	18,202	30 Iowa	11.5
31 Georgia	18,130	Kansas	11.5
32 Indiana	18,043	32 Utah	11.4
33 Texas	17,892	33 Nebraska	11.1
34 North Carolina	17,667	Pennsylvania	11.1
35 Wyoming	17,423	35 Washington	10.9
36 Tennessee	17,341	36 Maine	10.8
37 Arizona	17,119	37 Indiana	10.7
38 North Dakota	16,854	Wisconsin	10.7
39 South Dakota	16,558	39 Minnesota	10.2
40 Kentucky	16,354	Nevada	10.2
41 Alabama	16,220	Virginia	10.2
42 Oklahoma	16,198	42 Vermont	9.9
43 Idaho	16,067	43 Rhode Island	9.6
44 Montana	16,062	44 Alaska	9.0
45 South Carolina	15,989	45 Massachusetts	8.9
46 Louisiana	15,712	46 Delaware	8.7
47 Arkansas	15,439	47 Hawaii	8.3
48 New Mexico	15,353	Maryland	8.3
49 Utah	15,325	49 New Jersey	7.6
50 West Virginia	15,065	50 Connecticut	6.8
51 Mississippi	14,088	51 New Hampshire	6.4

Cities and airports

Largest cities
Population '000, 1990

1	New York, NY	7,322.6	31	Kansas City, MO	435.1
2	Los Angeles, CA	3,485.4	32	Long Beach, CA	429.4
3	Chicago, IL	2,783.7	33	Tucson, AZ	405.4
4	Houston, TX	1,630.6	34	St Louis, MO	396.7
5	Philadelphia, PA	1,585.6	35	Charlotte, NC	395.9
6	San Diego, CA	1,110.6	36	Atlanta, GA	394.0
7	Detroit, MI	1,028.0	37	Virginia Beach, VA	393.1
8	Dallas, TX	1,006.9	38	Albuquerque, NM	384.7
9	Phoenix, AZ	983.4	39	Oakland, CA	372.2
10	San Antonio, TX	935.9	40	Pittsburgh, PA	369.9
11	San Jose, CA	782.2	41	Sacramento, CA	369.4
12	Indianapolis, IN	742.0	42	Minneapolis, MN	368.4
13	Baltimore, MD	736.0	43	Tulsa, OK	367.3
14	San Francisco, CA	724.0	44	Honolulu, CDP, HI	365.3
15	Jacksonville, FL	673.0	45	Cincinnati, OH	364.0
16	Columbus, OH	633.0	46	Miami, FL	358.6
17	Milwaukee, WI	628.1	47	Fresno, CA	354.2
18	Memphis, TN	610.3	48	Omaha, NE	335.8
19	Washington, DC	607.0	49	Toledo, OH	333.8
20	Boston, MA	574.3	50	Buffalo, NY	328.1
21	Seattle, WA	516.3	51	Wichita, KS	304.0
22	El Paso, TX	515.3	52	Santa Ana, CA	293.7
23	Nashville-Davidson, TN	510.8	53	Mesa, AZ	288.1
24	Cleveland, OH	505.6	54	Colorado Springs, CO	281.1
25	New Orleans, LA	497.0	55	Tampa, FL	280.0
26	Denver, CO	467.6	56	Newark, NJ	275.2
27	Austin, TX	465.6	57	St Paul, MN	272.2
28	Fort Worth, TX	447.6	58	Louisville, KY	269.1
29	Oklahoma City, OK	444.7	59	Anaheim, CA	266.4
30	Portland, OR	437.3	60	Birmingham, AL	266.0

Largest metro areas[a]
Population

1	New York–Northern New Jersey–Long Island New York, New Jersey, Connecticut	18,087,251
2	Los Angeles–Anaheim–Riverside, California	14,531,529
3	Chicago–Gary–Lake County, Illinois, Indiana, Wisconsin	8,065,633
4	San Francisco–Oakland–San Jose, California	6,253,311
5	Philadelphia–Wilmington–Trenton, Pennsylvania, New Jersey, Delaware, Maryland	5,899,345
6	Detroit–Ann Arbor, Michigan	4,665,236
7	Boston–Lawrence–Salem, Massachusetts, New Hampshire	4,171,643
8	Washington, District of Columbia, Maryland, Virginia	3,923,574
9	Dallas–Fort Worth, Texas	3,885,415
10	Houston–Galveston–Brazoria, Texas	3,711,043

a CMSA.

Fastest growing cities
% change in population, 1980–90

1	Moreno Valley, CA	319.6	16	Glendale, AZ	52.4
2	Mesa, AZ	89.0	17	Mesquite, TX	51.3
3	Rancho Cucamonga, CA	83.5	18	Ontario, CA	49.9
4	Plano, TX	77.9		Virginia Beach, VA	49.9
5	Irvine, CA	77.6	20	Scottsdale, AZ	46.5
6	Escondido, CA	68.8	21	Santa Ana, CA	44.0
7	Oceanside, CA	67.4	22	Stockton, CA	42.3
8	Santa Clarita, CA	65.8	23	Pomona, CA	42.0
9	Bakersfield, CA	65.5	24	Irving, TX	41.0
10	Arlington, TX	63.5	25	Aurora, CO	40.1
11	Fresno, CA	62.9	26	Raleigh, NC	38.4
12	Chula Vista, CA	61.0	27	San Bernardino, CA	38.2
13	Las Vegas, NV	56.9	28	Santa Rosa, CA	37.1
14	Modesto, CA	54.0	29	Overland Park, KA	36.7
15	Tallahassee, FL	53.0	30	Vallejo, CA	36.0

Fastest declining cities
% change in population, 1980–90

1	Gary, IN	-23.2	16	Birmingham, AL	-7.7
2	Newark, NJ	-16.4	17	Richmond, VA	-7.4
3	Detroit, MI	-14.6		Chicago, IL	-7.4
4	Pittsburgh, PA	-12.8	19	Atlanta, GA	-7.3
5	St Louis, MO	-12.4	20	Kansas City, KA	-7.1
6	Cleveland, OH	-11.9	21	Baltimore, MD	-6.4
7	Flint, MI	-11.8	22	Akron, OH	-6.1
8	New Orleans, LA	-10.9		Toledo, OH	-6.1
9	Warren, MI	-10.1		Philadelphia, PA	-6.1
	Chattanooga, TN	-10.1	25	Dayton, OH	-5.9
11	Louisville, KY	-9.9	26	Knoxville, TN	-5.7
12	Peoria, IL	-9.1	27	Memphis, TN	-5.5
13	Macon, GA	-8.8		Cincinnati, OH	-5.5
14	Erie, PA	-8.7	29	Denver, CO	-5.1
15	Buffalo, NY	-8.3	30	District of Columbia	-4.9

Busiest airports
Aircraft departures per year, '000, 1991

1	Chicago, IL (O'Hare)	329	6	St Louis	160
2	Dallas/Ft. Worth, TX	269	7	Denver, CO	151
3	Atlanta, GA	206	8	Phoenix	145
4	Los Angeles (International), CA	199	9	Detroit	132
5	San Francisco (International), CA	168	10	Newark	128

Jobs, education and health

Highest unemployment
% of civilian workforce, 1992

1	West Virginia	11.3	6	Massachusetts	8.5
2	Alaska	9.1		New York	8.5
	California	9.1	7	District of Columbia	8.4
4	Rhode Island	8.9		New Jersey	8.4
5	Michigan	8.8	10	Florida	8.2

Lowest unemployment
% of civilian workforce, 1992

1	Nebraska	3.0	6	North Dakota	4.9
2	South Dakota	3.1		Utah	4.9
3	Kansas	4.2	8	Minnesota	5.1
4	Hawaii	4.5		Wisconsin	5.1
5	Iowa	4.6	10	Wyoming	5.6

Highest spending per pupil
$, 1992

1	New Jersey	10,219	6	Vermont	6,992
2	Alaska	9,248	7	Pennsylvania	6,980
3	New York	8,658	8	Rhode Island	6,834
4	Connecticut	8,299	9	Massachusetts	6,323
5	District of Columbia	8,116	10	Maryland	6,273

Lowest spending per pupil
$, 1992

1	Utah	3,092	6	Arkansas	3,770
2	Mississippi	3,344	7	Oklahoma	3,939
3	Idaho	3,528	8	North Dakota	4,119
4	Alabama	3,675	9	South Dakota	4,255
5	Tennessee	3,736	10	Louisiana	4,378

Most doctors
per 100,000 population, 1990

1	Massachusetts	337	6	Vermont	253
2	Maryland	334	7	New Jersey	246
3	New York	315	8	California	244
4	Connecticut	275	9	Hawaii	236
5	Rhode Island	254	10	Pennsylvania	235

Least doctors
per 100,000 population, 1990

1	Idaho	125	6	Oklahoma	147
2	Mississippi	133	7	Arkansas	150
3	Wyoming	139	8	Iowa	151
4	South Dakota	140	9	Indiana	157
5	Alaska	146	10	Alabama	158
				Montana	158

=Part III=
State profiles

ALABAMA

The first evidence of taming of this raw land comes with prehistoric Indian culture whose mounds are visible to this day along the Black Warrior river in the west. And in its violent history no incident can have been bloodier than Hernando de Soto's attack in 1540 upon a collection of Creeks, Choctaws and Chickasaws led by Chief Tuscaloosa; several thousand Indians were slaughtered. In 1814 Andrew Jackson finished the job by crushing an uprising of the great Creek Confederacy at the battles of Talladega and Horseshoe Bend. The whole state then lay open for white American planters – and their black slaves.

From King Cotton to chemicals

Cotton then was truly king. Between 1800 and 1860, production doubled every ten years to satisfy apparently insatiable British and New England markets. The rich loam of Alabama's central Black Belt proved ideal soil. Deep rivers made booming towns out of Montgomery, the state capital on the Alabama river (where Jefferson Davis was inaugurated as president of the Confederacy), and Mobile on the Gulf coast. Cotton continued to dominate the state's economy long after the Civil War – until the arrival of the boll weevil, in fact, during the first world war. Today, in the town of Enterprise, stands a monument to the weevil put up by farmers grateful for being taught the benefits of diversification into the corn, soybeans and peanuts which are still grown in Alabama.

For most of this century Alabama's focus shifted northwards as the state industrialised. The start of the great hydroelectric projects of the Tennessee Valley Authority (TVA) in 1933 tamed rivers that flooded their banks so often that nearby farmers were guaranteed a life of poverty. Before long, the steel town of Birmingham overtook Montgomery to become the state's biggest. Today manufacturing – textiles, paper, chemicals – may not be as vibrant as it once was. Yet it accounts still for 23.2% of the state's product, compared with a national average of 19%. Meanwhile high-tech companies, many drawn by the Huntsville national space centre in northern Alabama, have thrived.

To many Americans, Alabama evokes images of a civilrights movement, led by Martin Luther King, which met the implacable hostility of governor George Wallace. The state's racial politics is a thing of the past. But it is to Alabama's enduring economic cost that its cities chose not to desegregate like nearby Atlanta, Georgia, where peace and prosperity, hand in hand, won Atlanta the right to become the south's main metropolis.

State facts

Date of statehood	14 December 1819	Total area	52,423 sq miles
Capital	Montgomery	Highest point ft	Cheaha Mountain
Other cities	Birmingham,		2,405
	Mobile, Huntsville	Main rivers	Alabama, Tombigbee, Tennessee

Climate   Long hot summers; mild winters; generally abundant rainfall.
Geography   Coastal plains including Prairie Black Belt give way to hills, broken terrain.
Time zone   Central

People

			%
Population m	4.14	Under 18	26.0
% av. ann. growth 1980–92	0.5	Over 65	13.0
Pop. per sq mile	81.5	Urban	60.9
Birth rate per 1,000 pop.	15.7	Male	47.9
Death rate per 1,000 pop.	9.3	White	73.6
Pop. below poverty line %	18.3	Hispanic	0.6
Doctors per 100,000 pop.	158	Black	25.2
Hospital beds per 100,000 pop.	565	School spending per head	$3,675

The economy

GSP $m	67,886	Av. income per head $	16,220
No. of new corporations '000	6.1	% of national average	82

Structure of GSP	%		%
Construction	3.1	Manufacturing	23.2
Transportation, public utilities	10.7	Wholesale/retail trade	14.6
Services	14.8	Finance, insurance, real estate	14.1
Government	15.1	Other	4.4

Principal industries   Pulp and paper, chemicals, electronics, apparel, textiles, primary metals, lumber and wood, food processing, fabricated metals, automotive tyres
Main crops   Peanuts, cotton, soybeans, hay, corn, wheat, potatoes, pecan

Politics

Senate   Howell Heflin (D; term expires 1997), Richard C. Shelby (D; term expires 1999)
House   Glen Browder, Tom Bevill, Bud Cramer, Earl Hilliard (all D); Sonny Callahan, Terry Everett, Spencer Bachus (all R)

State government
Governor   Guy Hunt (R; term expires 1995)
State Legislature   Senate 28D, 7R; House 82D, 23R.
Total expenditure (1992) $9,285m

ALASKA

The Aleuts native to Alaska named it simply "Great Land", but the 49th state commands a host of superlatives. Occupying the northwest extremity of the continent, it is the nation's largest state, stretching nearly 600,000 square miles over vast tundra, icy peaks and frozen islands. Mt McKinley, the highest point in North America, stands over 20,000 feet.

Closer to Tokyo than to cities in the "lower 48", Alaska was a wilderness largely ignored by America until 1967, when a rig hit oil on the 11 billion-barrel North Slope field which now provides a tenth of the country's domestic supply. At that moment, the state that had been dubbed "Uncle Sam's stepchild" discovered its raison d'être.

Boomerangs

Alaska's abundant natural resources have drawn newcomers over the centuries, but non-native residents have been speculators and prospectors quick to pull up stakes when boom went bust, rather than "settlers" *per se*. Russians sold the territory to America for 2 cents per acre in 1867 when they had exhausted the supply of fur seal and otter pelts which they had sought. The purchase was regarded as "Seward's folly" (after the Secretary of State who had urged it) until 1880 when Joseph Juneau discovered gold outside the rude frontier town that would become Alaska's capital.

Only green as in greenback

As oil goes, so goes Alaska. The oil business dominates Alaska's economy, accounting for most employment and about 90% of the state's revenue. People poured out of the state in the mid-1980s as oil prices slumped. They came back after the Iraqi invasion of Kuwait pushed prices back up, but oil prices have since fallen again.

The state's extreme dependence on oil and government makes for a peculiar politics. Despite regional partisanship, virtually all Alaskans are in favour of development. Every day nearly 80m gallons of oil are pumped through the Trans-Alaska pipeline from Prudhoe Bay to Valdez, where oil is loaded into tankers – and was spilt in 1989 when an Exxon supertanker hit rocks in Prince William Sound. Not even an environmental disaster of that calibre turns Alaskans into greens; the state's Congressmen are unabashed boomers whose pet priorities are to build an $11 billion natural gas pipeline and to open the Arctic National Wildlife Refuge to oil exploration.

State facts

Date of statehood	3 January 1959	Total area	656,424 sq miles
Capital	Juneau	Highest point ft	Mt McKinley 20,320
Other cities	Anchorage, Fairbanks, Sitka	Main rivers	Yukon

Climate South-east, south-west and central regions, moist and mild; far north extremely dry. Extended summer days, winter nights, throughout.
Geography Includes Pacific and Arctic mountain systems, central plateau and Arctic slope. 10 highest mountains in USA are in Alaska.
Time zone Pacific

People

			%
Population m	0.59	Under 18	31.5
% av. ann. growth 1980–92	3.2	Over 65	4.3
Pop. per sq mile	1.0	Urban	67.5
Birth rate per 1,000 pop.	21.6	Male	52.7
Death rate per 1,000 pop.	3.8	White	75.5
Pop. below poverty line %	9.0	Hispanic	3.3
Doctors per 100,000 pop.	146	Black	nil
Hospital beds per 100,000 pop.	320	School spending per head	$9,248

The economy

GSP $m	19,582	Av. income per head $	21,603
No. of new corporations '000	1.3	% of national average	109

Structure of GSP	%		%
Construction	6.9	Manufacturing	4.8
Transportation, public utilities	9.4	Wholesale/retail trade	8.0
Services	10.4	Finance, insurance, real estate	9.4
Government	17.9	Other	33.2

Principal industries Oil, gas, tourism, commercial fishing
Main crops Barley, hay, greenhouse nursery products, potatoes, lettuce, milk

Politics

Senate Ted Stevens (R; term expires 1997), Frank Murkowski (R; term expires 1999)
House Don Young (R)

State government
Governor Walter Hickel (Ind; term expires 1994)[a]
State Legislature Senate 10R, 9D, 1 Ind; House 20D, 18R, 2 Ind
Total expenditure (1992) $4,369m

a December.

ARIZONA

The desert state's hot, dry climate is ideal for precision manufacturing, and the dramatic scenery of the Grand Canyon gives the state America's most popular tourist attraction. Constructed out of sand by copper barons and wheeling-dealing developers at the turn of the century, Arizona has a reputation for innovation and entrepreneurial daring.

In the last generation its economy doubled in size, building on big-name companies like Motorola, which has been here since 1948, to attract small creative industry as well.

The cultural life of its cities attracts the well-educated technicians, people who like order and discipline, who are employed by Honeywell, McDonnell Douglas, Hughes and IBM. But Arizona, a state whose legislature has been notoriously laced with corruption, has also been steered by slippery operators. This is home to Charles Keating, savings and loan buccaneer. Phoenix, the capital city which boomed in the 1980s, is now one of the most overbuilt real estate markets in the country.

Boom to bust in the dust

Today about 40% of all American tribal lands are in Arizona. The western Apache, mounted on horses introduced by Spaniards, proved the most resistant to the incursion of white settlers. Led by warriors such as the great Cochise, they refused to yield Arizona's southern frontier until Geronimo surrendered in 1886. The discovery of precious metal in the valleys just north of the Mexican border built the copper country towns of Bisbee and Tombstone (site of the famous shoot-out at the OK Corral). Settlement accelerated with the arrival of the Southern Pacific Railroad.

The 20th century brought explosive growth to Arizona. Construction of the Roosevelt Dam in 1911 spurred rapid development of irrigated agriculture. During the second world war the state's vast deserts attracted airfields and prisoner-of-war camps (19 German submariners pulled off the biggest POW escape on American soil when they tunnelled out of an internment camp outside Phoenix in 1944). But nothing contributed to the growth of Arizona's desert cities as much as the development of modern air conditioning.

Phoenix sprouted from sleepy whistle stop to highrise-studded metropolis of 2 million with lots of money. Postwar industrial and urban expansion has severely strained the state's limited water supply. Dilapidated neighbourhoods lie within blocks of the city's skyscrapers, and poor stucco houses, vacant lots and garish roadside establishments dot the outskirts.

More sedate Scottsdale began as a refuge from the saloons and gambling halls of Arizona's boom towns. Its reputation as a centre for creative people was enhanced in 1938 when Frank Lloyd Wright built Taliesin West, a winter headquarters for his Wisconsin school and studio. The resort has flourished, but its development stops abruptly at the Salt River-Maricopa-Pima Indian Reservation.

Aside from the Grand Canyon, the west is mostly desert dotted with old mining towns, former "pinto" (conservative) Democrat country. Affluent retirees and family-minded migrants have taken its politics further rightward. But here, nearly 200 miles across desert to the southwest of Phoenix lies the state's agricultural centre. Yuma, perched on the banks of the Colorado river, is on many days the hottest place in America. Springing up improbably in the country's most barren landscape is also Lake Havasu City, proud owner of the transplanted London Bridge.

Drawing plans in the sand

Copper, once the mainstay of Arizona's economy, has been in eclipse since the 1970s as world prices slumped. Luckily for Arizona, thousands of high-tech and aviation jobs came in the early 1980s, but manufacturing accounts for a relatively small segment (12.7%) of the workforce; this is an economy heavily weighted toward commerce, with big retail and service sectors. Phoenix is the south-west's white-collar centre, but the city lost jobs when Digital, a major employer, closed shop in 1991. Credit card companies have begun to move in operations since regulations eased, but it will take time to make up for the loss of nearly 25,000 construction-related jobs since the building bust.

Arizona has been hard hit by recession and for the first time has been bowed to economic strategising. This requires a big adjustment in philosophy among developers imbued with the endless optimism of the West. Some continue to forecast an economic bonanza in the state by 1995, pointing out that employment growth remains faster than the national average. But state economists emphasise that growth in per person income levels has been pushed well below the national average, and they urge the importance of developing high quality jobs. If Arizona follows the plan strategists have mapped out for it, the state will augment high value-added activities in "clusters" such as agriculture, doing the packaging and distributing, not just the growing, of its year-round vegetables.

State facts

Date of statehood	14 February 1912	Total area	114,006 sq miles
Capital	Phoenix	Highest point ft	Humphreys Peak
Other cities	Tucson,		12,633
	Mesa, Glendale	Main rivers	Colorado,
			Little Colorado, Gila, Salt

Climate Clear and dry in the southern regions and northern plateau; high central areas have heavy winter snows.
Geography Colorado plateau in the north, containing the Grand Canyon; Mexican Highlands running diagonally north-west to south-east; Sonoran Desert in the south-west.
Time zone Mountain

People

			%
Population m	3.83	Under 18	27.4
% av. ann. growth 1980–92	2.9	Over 65	13.4
Pop. per sq mile	33.7	Urban	87.5
Birth rate per 1,000 pop.	18.8	Male	49.4
Death rate per 1,000 pop.	7.8	White	80.8
Families below poverty line %	11.4	Hispanic	18.8
Doctors per 100,000 pop.	197	Black	3.0
Hospital beds per 100,000 pop.	355	School spending per head	$4,750

The economy

GSP $m	65,306	Av. income per head $	17,119
No. of new corporations '000	9.8	% of national average	86

Structure of GSP	%		%
Construction	7.1	Manufacturing	12.7
Transportation, public utilities	9.2	Wholesale/retail trade	16.5
Services	19.5	Finance, insurance, real estate	17.5
Government	13.8	Other	3,7

Principal industries Manufacturing, tourism, mining, agriculture
Main crops Cotton, sorghum, barley, corn, wheat, sugar beets, citrus fruits

Politics

Senate Dennis DeConcini (D; term expires 1995), John McCain (R; term expires 1999)
House Bob Stump, Jon Kyl, Jim Kolbe (all R); Ed Pastor, Karan English (both D)

State government
Governor Fife Symington (R; term expires 1995)
State Legislature Senate 18R, 12D; House 35R, 25D
Total expenditure (1992) $7,463m

ARKANSAS

"Thank God for Arkansas" goes the refrain whenever Mississippians bemoan the relative poverty of their own state. Arkansas has grown faster than most states since the second world war, but a reputation for backwardness and ignorance has stuck. That is now increasingly unfair.

Arkansas is the smallest and least populated state in the South. It was created almost by default, as the land left over once Louisiana and Missouri had been carved from the Louisiana Purchase, and Oklahoma set aside as Indian territory. The state is divided by a line that runs south-west to north-east. Below the line lie lowland plains watered by the Arkansas river, the White river and, along the east, by the Mississippi Delta. Above are the uplands of the north-west, the Ozark and the Ouachita Mountains.

In the "hollers" of these mountains vestiges of an old, pioneer life are still seen and heard that have little in common with the Deep South. And, partly because the forests and swamps of the south-east had barely been cleared for cotton and slaves by the time of the Civil War, Arkansas initially voted in 1861 against seceding from the Union. It joined the Confederacy only once the first shots had been fired upon South Carolina's Fort Sumter.

Low-wage economy

The ravages of the war and of a bitter Reconstruction ensured that Arkansas would long remain a backwater. Timber and cotton were the state's only two significant activities until the 1920s. Then, Arkansas had an oil boomlet of its own. At around the same time manufacturing businesses began to sprout, mostly to process the state's raw products. Today, Arkansas is one of America's biggest lumber processors and is the country's biggest producer of poultry. The state is also the birthplace of the late Sam Walton's giant Wal-Mart chain. But most of these businesses are low-wage ones and Arkansas lacks any true metropolis to act as a magnet for wealth and investment. As a result, incomes in Arkansas are still about one-fifth below the national average.

In 1957 Arkansas became notorious for the "'57 Crisis", when Governor Orval Faubus called in the National Guard to prevent nine black students from attending the Central High School in Little Rock, the state capital. Bill Clinton, five times governor, knew that better schooling is Arkansas's path to higher wages and pushed hard for educational reform in his state. He has since successfully taken his message to a national audience.

State facts

Date of statehood	15 June 1836	Total area	53,182 sq miles
Capital	Little Rock	Highest point ft	Magazine
Other cities	Fort Smith,		Mountain 2,753
	North Little Rock, Pine Bluff	Main rivers	Mississippi, Arkansas

Climate Long hot summers, mild winters; generally abundant rainfall.
Geography Eastern delta and prairie, southern lowland forests, and north-western highlands, which include the Ozark Plateaus.
Time zone Central

People

			%
Population m	2.40	Under 18	26.2
% av. ann. growth 1980–90	0.5	Over 65	14.9
Pop. per sq mile	46.1	Urban	53.5
Birth rate per 1,000 pop.	15.5	Male	48.2
Death rate per 1,000 pop.	10.2	White	82.7
Pop. below poverty line %	19.1	Hispanic	0.8
Doctors per 100,000 pop.	150	Black	15.9
Hospital beds per 100,000 pop.	554	School spending per head	$3,770

The economy

GSP $m	37,169	Av. income per head $	15,439
No. of new corporations '000	5.3	% of national average	78

Structure of GSP	%		%
Construction	4.2	Manufacturing	25.0
Transportation, public utilities	11.3	Wholesale/retail trade	14.8
Services	13.5	Finance, insurance, real estate	14.1
Government	10.4	Other	6.7

Principal industries Manufacturing, agriculture, tourism, forestry
Main crops Soybeans, rice, cotton, tomatoes, water melons, grapes, blueberries, apples, commercial vegetables, peaches, wheat

Politics

Senate Dale L. Bumpers (D; term expires 1999), David Pryor (D; term expires 1997)
House Blanche Lambert, Ray Thornton (both D); Tim Hutchinson, Jay Dickey (both R)

State government
Governor Jim Guy Tucker (D; term expires 1995)
State Legislature Senate 30D, 5R; House 89D, 10R, 1 Ind
Total expenditure (1992) $5,579m

CALIFORNIA

California is famously supposed to be "like America – only more so". With 30m people and one of the ten biggest economies in the world, the state is certainly big enough to be compared with a country. Thanks to its high birth-rate and its ability to attract immigrants (both legal and illegal), the population is likely to increase to nearly 40m by 2005.

California's most obvious charm is its variety. Its geography includes the snow capped Sierra mountains, the Sahara-like desert of Death Valley, the Redwood forests, the vineyards of Napa Valley and a fine coastline. Its 30m people make up the most cosmopolitan mixture in America. Los Angeles alone is home to the biggest overseas communities of, among others, Mexicans, Koreans, Armenians and the Lebanese Druze.

According to the 1990 census, whites made up 69% of the state's population, but only slightly less than half of its school-age population. Within 50 years, the Hispanic population is likely to outnumber them. Until recently, this ethnic smorgasbord was hailed as one of the great socio-economic successes of the western world. But that was before the recent recession, which hurt California badly, and the 1992 Los Angeles riots and the 1994 earthquake. Once again the "Californian dream" is being questioned – and not just by its familiar critics in the East Coast press.

Tale of two cities

California is built on some of the most unpromising terrain in the world. Today, it is hard to believe that the miles of swimming-pooled suburbia in Southern California were, until relatively recently, desert. No modern city of its size in the world began with as few natural advantages as the dusty harbourless bowl of Los Angeles.

The state's early history is unclear. There are stories of Russian, Japanese and Chinese visitors sneaking across the Pacific in the late middle ages, but the first European to reach California was Juan Rodriguez Cabrillo in 1542. A few sea settlements sprang up, including the state's first capital, Monterey, but New Spain did not try to colonise California properly until the late 18th century. In 1831, ten years after Mexico achieved independence from Spain, the Californios, as they were known, revolted against the Mexican governor. In 1850, after a long tussle, it finally became part of the United States of America, a tiny western outpost with a population of only 93,000 people.

In 1859, its politicians passed a resolution splitting the state into two, but the Civil War intervened. All the same, the history of the state ever since has often seemed like a battle between the two halves: Northern and Southern California with their respective centres in Los Angeles and San Francisco.

For most of the 19th century San Francisco seemed such a natural centre for the West Coast that it was known simply as "the city" from Vancouver to San Diego. Many of its early fortunes came from the goldrush and the railroad. In 1870 Los Angeles numbered only 5,000 residents. The arrival of the Santa Fe railroad in 1886 helped give birth to a thriving agricultural industry, pushing Los Angeles' population up to 100,000, still only a quarter the size of San Francisco.

In 1906, an earthquake struck San Francisco, levelling some 26,000 buildings. Seven years later the Los Angeles aqueduct was completed: its water, carried some 250 miles from the Owens river, turned the city's most obvious disadvantage, its arid climate, into an advantage. Two of southern California's biggest industries, entertainment and aerospace, first came to the region for the sun. The jobs they offered, as well as the swimming pool and the glamorous lifestyle promoted by Tinseltown, lured millions of mid-Westerners to the city. In 1960 Los Angeles was often laughed at as "Iowa by the sea". In contrast, San Francisco seemed much more cosmopolitan, with its large Chinese, Italian and Irish communities.

That was before three decades of enormous immigration to Southern California from Asia and Central America, which has pushed the proportion of "Anglos" down from 85% to 50% in Los Angeles, and helped to make it the only first world city growing at a third world pace. The Bay Area around San Francisco has grown rapidly too, but not at the same pace. Los Angeles County is now home to some 9m people. In the south, San Diego has grown rapidly into America's fifth biggest city. During the 1980s, roughly 40% of the population growth happened in the interior of California as companies (and their employees) scrambled to escape the overcrowded and expensive coast.

Rich pattern

Unfortunately, California's government does not reflect its population: Hispanics, who make up a quarter of the state's population, account for less than a tenth of its elected officials; Asians, who account for a tenth of its population, account for only a fiftieth of its elected officials. Roughly 80% of the voting electorate is white.

The state's government fragments into 58 counties, 468

cities, 1,012 school districts and over 6,000 special districts which monitor everything from air quality to mosquito abatement. The city of Los Angeles, like those of Beverly Hills and Pasadena, is only one out of nearly 90 different districts within Los Angeles county.

While other states combine their political troops in Washington to ferret out federal help, California's enormous Congressional delegation rarely meets and never agrees. In so doing, the politicians may only be reflecting the desires of their electorate, which has a habit of voting for Republicans in presidential elections and Democrats in Congressional ones. The state embraces politicians with a sense of vision: its recent governors have included both the maverick Jerry Brown and Ronald Reagan. Areas such as San Francisco, Santa Monica and Hollywood house some of the most wealthy liberals in the country. Orange County, on the other hand, remains a conservative stronghold.

However, the most important political development in California in the past quarter century was the tax-payers' revolt of the late 1970s, which gave rise to the craze for voter propositions that appear on the ballot alongside candidates for office. Many of these initiatives remain extremely popular, but there is also a growing body of evidence that they add to the political confusion of the state.

Freeway economics driven by powerhouses

Nine out of ten Californians live in cities, most of them in suburban "edge cities", some of which are marked by little more than the meeting of two freeways. The state's economy has the same amorphous feel. California is home to less than 10% of the *Fortune 500* companies; instead its economy is founded on small and medium sized businesses, many of them family-owned. One in five of America's fastest growing companies are in California.

Nevertheless, the bulk of California's economy can be divided, a little crudely, into three powerhouses: southern California, the Bay Area and agriculture. The most important is the urban sprawl of southern California, which now stretches pretty well uninterrupted from Los Angeles to San Diego and is home to nearly two-thirds of the state's population. The Los Angeles-Riverside-Anaheim megalopolis alone contains nearly 15m people. Los Angeles is now America's biggest trading and manufacturing centre.

Southern California's most important industry is still defence. California sucks up roughly one out of every five dollars the Pentagon dispenses. The end of the cold war thus helped make the most recent recession particularly painful for southern California.

However, there are two reasons for optimism about the state's defence industry. First, while defence spending may decrease, it will not evaporate. And, second, the local economy is now so diversified that defence accounts for only around one-twentieth of the workforce. As well as Hollywood, Los Angeles also has enormous clothing and furniture businesses (both of which employ more people than Tinseltown). Southern California is also home to many fast growing technology businesses and, of course, trade. It has even managed to turn one of the region's supposed drawbacks – its tough environmental laws – into "Smog Valley", a network of environmental firms.

The other important urban region in the state is "the Bay Area" megalopolis which includes San Francisco, Oakland and San Jose, a region of some 6m people. This area includes San Francisco's big financial community (founded around the state's two banking giants, Bank of America and Wells Fargo) and the huge port of Oakland. But its most famous industry is Silicon Valley, the mecca of American high technology, where companies like Apple Computer have sprung out of garages to surprise the world. Thanks to cut-throat competition from Asia and Europe, computers are now viewed as commodity products by many businessmen, but the valley reigns supreme in the brainier parts of technology, particularly software.

The last economic powerhouse is California's $15 billion agriculture industry, which still ranks as the state's largest employer. The state grows just about every conceivable crop from rice to wine to the edible flowers which often appear in its cuisine. To grow such crops, the state's farmers drink up 80% of California's water, but account for less than 5% of its economic output. Worse, they receive their water at special subsidised rates. Reform is progressing slowly: farmers no longer flood their orchards as they once did and "water trading" laws, allowing the farmers to sell their allocations to the cities, are slowly being introduced.

Back to the future

Whatever the short-term problems, it is difficult not to be optimistic about California's economy. It is hard to think of another place in the world with so many industries of the future: from technology to electronics to health-care to aerospace (of the non-defence type) to entertainment. Even if some of these fail to live up to expectations, California will remain the conduit for America's trade with Asia.

The Pacific has long since passed the Atlantic as the route for most of America's trade. The North American Free Trade Act should give the state another boost, increasing trade with its southern neighbour, Mexico, and, hopefully, controlling the flow of illegal immigrants across the border. Unfortunately, unlike Texas, California has made very little effort to foster friendships across the border.

The deeper truth is that California's real problems are social and political and not economic. For example, Los Angeles' long-term problem is not likely to be creating jobs, but creating the right type of jobs. First-generation immigrants may be happy with jobs as valet parkers and maids; their children want the highly paid manufacturing jobs which are disappearing in favour of service-industry ones.

A still bigger challenge is government. Even libertarians, who used to rejoice in Californians' long distrust of politics, are beginning to see the bad side of political apathy. Only half the state's electorate bothers to vote: in the areas of Los Angeles that were worst affected by the riots, the figure for council elections is closer to 5%. Nearly all California's political institutions were founded earlier this century; the system of county and local government that has sprung up haphazardly since then is notoriously inefficient.

As more of the state's money has got choked by this bureaucracy or siphoned off by taxpayers, less has gone into the type of investment it needs to maintain its edge. Most of California's infrastructure dates back to the 1960s, which was also the last time that the state invested heavily in its schools and universities. That investment paid off handsomely, but now, after years of cuts, the state spends less per pupil than the national average, a dangerous policy in a state where the schools have to cope with roughly 200,000 new students a year. If California has a reason to worry about its future, it is in its classrooms.

House Dan Hamburg, Vic Fazio, Robert T. Matsui, Lynn Woolsey, George Miller, Nancy Pelosi, Ronald V. Dellums, Tom Lantos, Fortney H. Stark, Anna Eshoo, Norman Mineta, Don Edwards, Leon Panetta, Gary Condit, Rick Lehman, Calvin Dooley, Anthony Beilenson, Howard L. Berman, Henry A. Waxman, Xavier Becerra, Matthew G. Martinez, Julian C. Dixon, Lucille Roybal-Allard, Esteban Torres, Maxine Waters, Jane Harman, Walter Tucker, George Brown Jr, Mark Takano, Lynn Schenk, Bob Filner (all D); Wally Herger, John Doolittle, Bill Baker, Richard Pombo, Bill Thomas, Michael Huffington, Elton Gallegly, Howard McKeon, Carlos J. Moorhead, David Dreier, Steve Horn, Edward Royce, Jerry Lewis, Jay Kim, Al McCandless, Dana Rohrabacher, Robert Dornan, Christopher Cox, Ron Packard, Randy Cunningham, Duncan Hunter (all R)

State facts

Date of statehood	9 September 1850	Total area	163,707 sq miles
Capital	Sacramento	Highest point ft	Mt Whitney 14,494
Other cities	Los Angeles,	Main rivers	Sacramento,
San Diego, San Jose, San Francisco			San Joaquin

Climate Moderate temperatures and rainfall along the coast; extremes in the interior.
Geography Long mountainous coastline; central valley; Sierra Nevada on the east; desert basins in the southern interior; rugged mountains to the north.
Time zone Pacific

People

			%
Population m	30.87	Under 18	27.3
% av. ann. growth 1980–92	2.2	Over 65	10.5
Pop. per sq mile	197.9	Urban	92.6
Birth rate per 1,000 pop.	20.6	Male	50.1
Death rate per 1,000 pop.	7.2	White	69.0
Pop. below poverty line %	12.5	Hispanic	25.8
Doctors per 100,000 pop.	242	Black	7.4
Hospital beds per 100,000 pop.	340	School spending per head	$4,686

The economy

GSP $m	697,381	Av. income per head $	21,278
No. of new corporations '000	36.6	% of national average	107

Structure of GSP	%		%
Construction	4.8	Manufacturing	16.9
Transportation, public utilities	7.0	Wholesale/retail trade	16.1
Services	21.0	Finance, insurance, real estate	20.0
Government	11.2	Other	3.0

Principal industries Agriculture, manufacturing, services, trade
Main crops Grapes, cotton, flowers, oranges, nursery products

Politics

Senate Dianne Feinstein (D; term expires 1995), Barbara Boxer (D; term expires 1999)
House See list on page 65.

State government
Governor Pete Wilson (R; term expires 1995)
State Legislature Senate 23D, 15R, 2 Ind; House 47D, 33R
Total expenditure (1992) $83,743m

COLORADO

The red-rock country of this western mountain state earned Colorado its name, "ruddy" in Spanish. The Rockies mark the Continental Divide in the west, and the mountain range gives Colorado the highest mean elevation (6,800 feet) in the country. But the high grasslands in the east betray the fact that this self-consciously western state has one foot still in the Great Plains. Even Denver, the "mile-high" capital city, has never fitted the pattern of a typical western town.

Not two decades after it served as a campground for the Arapaho, the settlement bisected by the Platte river became a city of 35,000 when Colorado declared statehood in 1876. But since its rowdy gold-digging days Denver has been staid and smug about its growth, rejecting the 1972 and 1976 Olympics and ever-protective of its many military installations. Self-sufficient and self-contained, the city has a modest skyline with mountains in the distance.

In the arid west of the state lies the Colorado Plateau carved into spectacular canyons by the Colorado and Gunnison rivers. In the heart of the state stands Pike's Peak, where the view that sweeps from Denver to New Mexico inspired the hymn "America the Beautiful." The state motto is "nothing without providence", but Colorado has hardly left its fortunes to divine direction. High-tech, pro-environment, culturally liberal and economically moderate, Colorado was for years rated as the nation's foremost trend-setter. But for all its natural beauty and dogged determination, Colorado has fallen behind since 1990.

Built on the "geography of hope"

The cliff dwellings of Colorado's early inhabitants are preserved at Mesa Verde National Park in the south-west. Spain claimed the region comprising present-day Colorado in 1706. America acquired much of it in the Louisiana Purchase of 1803, but no American explorer had come within 1,000 miles of Colorado until three years later, when President Thomas Jefferson dispatched a team to discover what he had bought from Napoleon for $15 million.

The first permanent settlements in Colorado were clustered in the southern San Luis Valley on Mexican land grants. Fort Massachusetts was built to protect the small adobe villages from Indian raids. Kit Carson led American forces in a campaign to rout the native Ute, but the region remained largely unsettled until the 1870s, when prospectors struck gold and silver in the San Juan mountains.

Narrow gauge trains soon puffed over precarious mountain passes two-miles high along the "million-dollar highway" to reach boom towns such as Silverton and Telluride. Terrain was so steep that between Georgetown and Silver Plume, four and a half miles of track were required to cover two miles' distance with loops and overlaps. The incursion of miners provoked further conflicts with the Indians at Milk Creek and resulted in the Meeker massacre in 1879; soon afterwards the Ute were forcefully removed to Utah.

The small cities that sprang up along the river as gold was panned and mined along the South Platte tributary busted within a matter of months into just so many scattered ghost towns. The discovery of silver and lead stirred up another economic fury – at least for a time. In 1893 the government repealed the Sherman Act which had buoyed silver prices and the bottom fell out of the market, triggering a statewide depression in Colorado. The state's economy was saved with the discovery of new gold at Cripple Creek, where it was reported to "stick out of the rock like raisins out of a fruit cake". This time Colorado managed to sustain the economic revival by using the rush of prosperity to irrigate fields to grow sugar beet. It remained a mining and farming state until the 1950s, when manufacturing took over as Colorado's biggest earner.

Postwar growth

The second world war brought giddy growth to Colorado's urban centres and winter sports entrepreneurs built ski resorts and condominiums to draw young families equal to the rigours of the countryside. The affluent edge of the Baby Boom settled here and propelled into political office the anti-Vietnam, pro-environment Democrats of the early 1970s like Pat Schroeder and Gary Hart. But there is nothing one-dimensional about Colorado politics. The state is also home to free-market Republicans led by the Coors family who gave large majorities to Ronald Reagan; in 1988 Colorado voted against state-financed abortions and in favour of declaring English the state's official language. In 1992 it voted in favour of repealing gay rights legislation.

Denver's ring of affluent suburbs such as Englewood, Littleton and the neighbourhood of Cherry Hills are reliable Republican strongholds, but regional partisanship can be read also in the moderately-sized cities that dot the foothills. The Western Slope comprises both the Victorian houses and liberal politics of Aspen and Telluride, and the staunchly Republican affinities of the Gerald Fords and their ilk at Vail. The mining area around Grand Junction – rumoured to be crackling with radioactivity – is hostile to Colorado's environmentalists, while the largely Hispanic and Indian communities in the south vote Democratic.

Colorado is popular year-round with tourists, especially among skiers who flock each winter to the Rocky Mountains. Colorado Springs was already a tourist attraction 100 years ago. The area has since become an American military fortress. The Army's Fort Carson lies within city limits and the Air Force Academy is situated just to the north. Falcon Air Force Base, the central planning base for the Strategic Defence Initiative (SDI) is just a short distance away and NORAD patrols the skies for ballistic missiles from its underground headquarters at Cheyenne Mountain. The defence-related jobs provided a boon to Colorado Springs, but the region has since been pinched; the Challenger disaster delayed development of the Consolidated Space Operations Center it was chosen to host and there have been defence cuts.

No stranger to disappointment

The national energy crisis of the 1970s benefited Colorado's coal and petroleum industries. In 1973 Denver became the centre of oil exploration and mineral development for the whole Rocky Mountain area. But the collapse of oil prices in the 1980s had drillers and plungers pouring back out of the state, at around the same time as the city's renowned "Brown Cloud" settled in over the metropolis.

Colorado is host to US West, the Baby Bell, which is the state's biggest employer. But Colorado has not generated growth of small creative firms such as those drawn to Oregon, Massachusetts or even New Jersey. Many big businesses in the state have seen hard times: after United bought Frontier Airlines in 1986, Colorado lost 4,000 jobs; Manville Corporation has been tangled for years in asbestosis law suits; numerous safety violations shut down the government's plutonium plant at Rocky Flats in 1989.

At 5.9%, the state unemployment rate was below the national average, and Colorado had seen moderate job growth that outpaced negative national rates. Growth in services accounts for most of the new jobs, but housing starts were up by 45% over 1990 as the residential market expanded in Denver and Colorado Springs suburbs. Apple and a flurry of religious organisations have brought significant employment to the state. The new Stapleton airport with a strip a half-hour drive north-east of downtown is another scheme to boost the state's economy, but it needs to overcome its considerable teething problems.

State facts

Date of statehood	1 August 1876	Total area	104,100 sq miles
Capital	Denver	Highest point ft	Mt Elbert 14,443
Other cities	Colorado Springs,	Main rivers	Colorado, S. Platte,
	Aurora, Lakewood		N. Platte, Rio Grande, Arkansas

Climate Low relative humidity, abundant sunshine, wide daily, seasonal temperature ranges; alpine conditions in the high mountains.

Geography Eastern dry high plains; hilly to mountainous central plateau; western Rocky Mountains of high ranges, broad valleys and deep, narrow canyons.

Time zone Mountain

People

			%
Population m	3.47	Under 18	26.2
% av. ann. growth 1980–92	1.5	Over 65	10.0
Pop. per sq mile	33.5	Urban	82.4
Birth rate per 1,000 pop.	16.2	Male	49.5
Death rate per 1,000 pop.	6.6	White	88.2
Pop. below poverty line %	11.7	Hispanic	12.9
Doctors per 100,000 pop.	211	Black	4.0
Hospital beds per 100,000 pop.	395	School spending per head	$5,259

The economy

GSP $m	66,180	Av. income per head $	20,124
No. of new corporations '000	13.6	% of national average	101

Structure of GSP	%		%
Construction	4.2	Manufacturing	13.1
Transportation, public utilities	11.0	Wholesale/retail trade	16.6
Services	20.6	Finance, insurance, real estate	15.5
Government	14.2	Other	4.8

Principal industries Manufacturing, government, tourism, agriculture, aerospace, electronics equipment

Main crops Corn, wheat, hay, sugar beets, barley, potatoes, apples, peaches, pears, dry edible beans, sorghum, onions, oats

Politics

Senate Hank Brown (R; term expires 1997), Ben Nighthorse Campbell (D; term expires 1999)

House Scott Mcinnis, Wayne Allard, Joel M. Hefley, Dan Schaefer (all R); Pat Schroeder, David E. Skaggs (both D)

State government

Governor Roy Romer (D; term expires 1995)

State Legislature Senate 19R, 16D; House 34R, 31D

Total expenditure (1992) $6,043m

CONNECTICUT

Neat-as-a-pin Yankee Connecticut is the southernmost state of New England and is the richest in the country. A rectangle of 90 x 55 miles bisected by New England's longest river, the eponymous Connecticut, the state forms a buffer between the Boston-centred north-east and New York city. Its southernmost towns, Greenwich, Stamford and Darien, are little more than dormitories for New York city executives. To the north lie the picture-book white-clapboard colonial villages that line the gentle, wooded valleys of inland Connecticut. Eastwards along the inlets of Long Island Sound is a ribbon of small but historical industrial and harbour towns such as Bridgeport, New Haven (home of Yale University) and New London.

It is Mark Twain and John Cheever country: well-heeled; well-schooled; and well-kept. Connecticut, it is unkindly said, always looks as if the maid has just finished.

Conservative and commercial-minded

Algonquin Indians had lived in what is now Connecticut for two centuries before English settlers first arrived in 1635, seeking both farmland and escape from the autocratic Puritanism of the Massachusetts Bay colony. A constitution proclaiming independence for "the Hartford colony" was drawn up in 1639. It is said to be the world's first written constitution, and grandfather to the United States' constitution of 1788. Connecticut calls itself "The Constitution State".

Except for the tobacco-growing upper Connecticut valley, Connecticut's soil proved too poor to farm well. It was from the sea, commerce and inventive industry that the prosperity which has never left the state first came. Today its 3.28m residents have the highest average per person income of any state in the nation.

They owe their collective inheritance to Eli Whitney, inventor of the cotton gin and a New Haven gunsmith who invented making weapons from standard parts. In the 19th century, mass-produced weapons, clocks, tools and housewares poured out of Connecticut factories. Yankee pedlars carried them across the length and breadth of the young and expanding United States. Yankee clippers from New Haven, New London and Mystic plied the China and Indies runs. New London was one of New England's three biggest whaling ports.

Manufacturing remains a staple of the state's economy. It accounts for one-fifth of state domestic product and more than one job in five. General Electric, United Technologies and Xerox, three of the largest *Fortune 500* companies, have headquarters there.

Two-thirds of that manufacturing is defence-related. The gunsmiths of old became today's armament-makers and defence contractors. United Technologies is the state's largest private-sector employer. Sikorsky helicopters and Pratt & Whitney aero-engines are made in Connecticut. So are Seawolf nuclear submarines at General Dynamics' Electric Boat yard at Groton.

There is a considerable white-collar sector, particularly financial services. The insurers who wrote policies for the early shipowners grew into some of America's largest insurance companies, such as Travelers. The state capital, Hartford, is home to some 40 insurance firms. It reckons itself the nation's insurance capital.

More recently other financial services, notably fund management firms, have moved north to Connecticut to escape New York's high costs and hassles. There is perennial talk of a big Wall Street firm following them. In all, finance, insurance and real estate is the second largest sector of the Connecticut economy, accounting for 20.9% of GSP.

Battered by winds of peace

Like those of its neighbours, Connecticut's economy boomed in the 1980s. It now shares with the rest of New England many of the same problems. The north-east's industrialised economies are coming face to face with the arrival of the information age and the growth of lower wage manufacturing centres elsewhere.

The recession, which was more severe in the region than in the rest of the country, has only served to throw the challenges into sharper relief. Connecticut has lost more than 100,000 manufacturing jobs from a peak of 450,000 in 1988. This has also hit hard the state's revenue, 40% of which came from sales taxes. The resultant ballooning budget deficits and fiscal crisis forced the state's maverick independent governor, Lowell Weicker, to introduce a highly controversial state personal-income tax in 1992.

Longer term, Connecticut has to adapt to leaner times for two of its lynch-pin industries, defence contracting and insurance. For years Connecticut was the Pentagon's biggest supplier. Since the end of the cold war, national defence spending has been cut. The insurance industry, too, is seeing a contraction in employment after rapid growth in the 1980s because of the continuing automation of clerical jobs and flattening of management.

State facts

Date of statehood	9 January 1788	Total area	5,544 sq miles
Capital	Hartford	Highest point ft	Mt Frissell 2,380
Other cities	Bridgeport,	Main rivers	Connecticut,
	New Haven, Waterbury		Housatonic, Quinnipiac

Climate Moderate; winters average slightly below freezing, warm and humid summers.

Geography Western uplands, the Berkshires, in the north-west, highest elevations; narrow central lowland north–south; hilly eastern upland drained by rivers.

Time zone Eastern Standard

People

			%
Population m	3.28	Under 18	23.5
% av. ann. growth 1980–92	0.5	Over 65	13.9
Pop. per sq mile	677.2	Urban	79.1
Birth rate per 1,000 pop.	15.2	Male	48.5
Death rate per 1,000 pop.	8.4	White	87.0
Pop. below poverty line %	6.8	Hispanic	6.5
Doctors per 100,000 pop.	305	Black	8.3
Hospital beds per 100,000 pop.	430	School spending per head	$8,299

The economy

GSP $m	88,863	Av. income per head $	26,979
No. of new corporations '000	8.5	% of national average	136

Structure of GSP	%		%
Construction	4.8	Manufacturing	21.2
Transportation, public utilities	7.6	Wholesale/retail trade	16.7
Services	19.3	Finance, insurance, real estate	20.9
Government	8.2	Other	1.3

Principal industries Manufacturing, retail trade, government services, finances, insurance, real estate

Main crops Nursery stock, vegetables, sweet corn, tobacco, apples

Politics

Senate Christopher J. Dodd (D; term expires 1999), Joe Lieberman (D; term expires 1995)

House Christopher Shays, Gary Franks, Nancy Johnson (all R); Barbara B. Kennelly, Rosa Del auro, Sam Geidenson (all D)

State government
Governor Lowell P. Weicker Jr (Ind; term expires 1995)
State Legislature Senate 20D, 16R; House 87D, 64R
Total expenditure (1992) $9,117m

DELAWARE

Plenty of heavy industrial states had their manufacturing bases rocked by the oil shocks and recessions of the 1970s and early 1980s, and then failed to jump the hurdle to more modern, service-based economies. But not tiny Delaware. In the past decade banks and insurance companies have flooded the state with jobs, throwing up smoked glass cages between the old, dead smokestacks. Not that manufacturing itself is dead: Delaware's plants today are amongst the country's most modern and productive.

Delaware has skilfully sought peace and prosperity since the first, Dutch, settlement in 1631. Few violent incidents occurred between the settlers and the fur-trapping Lenni Lenape and Nanticoke tribes. Farming, milling and shipping thrived. The Revolutionary war passed most of Delaware by. It was only in 1776 that Delaware's three counties formally broke from Pennsylvania to form a separate state. A youthful eagerness then helped the legislature to become the first to ratify the Constitution. Thus Delaware earned its moniker, the First State.

Maintaining a prosperous record

Delaware's industrial revolution began at about the same time. The inventions of Oliver Evans improved the automation of the state's flour milling, and new mills sprang up along the Brandywine valley, north of the port of Wilmington. In 1799 the state's future prosperity was assured by the arrival from revolutionary France of Iréné Du Pont. His gunpowder mill on the Brandywine grew into a munitions and chemicals company which prospered anew with every war. By the 1920s the Du Pont company was powerful enough to control General Motors for three decades.

Today chemical manufacturing is still a prop of Delaware's economy. This is capital-intensive business, yet employs one in every ten of the state's workers. Manufacturing is only one reason why the number of jobs in Delaware jumped by two-fifths in two decades. During the 1980s Delaware liberalised its banking laws to attract out-of-state banks. These brought in 14,000 jobs; the number of finance jobs doubled. Lastly, the state's laws of incorporation, which favour the powers of managers and owners of companies over outside shareholders, have brought firms rushing to incorporate in Delaware.

Most businesses, and two-thirds of the state's population, are in Delaware's northern county. That has left the attractive southern two counties to orchards, farming and the country-house whims of rich industrialists.

State facts

Date of statehood	7 December 1787	Total area	2,489 sq miles
Capital	Dover	Highest point ft	On Ebright Road 442
Other cities	Wilmington, Newark, Milford	Main rivers	Delaware, Christina, Appoqinimink, Leipsic

Climate Moderate
Geography Piedmont plateau to the north, sloping to a near sea level plain.
Time zone Eastern Standard

People

			%
Population m	0.69	Under 18	25.0
% av. ann. growth 1980–92	1.2	Over 65	12.3
Pop. per sq mile	352.5	Urban	73.0
Birth rate per 1,000 pop.	16.7	Male	48.5
Death rate per 1,000 pop.	8.6	White	80.3
Pop. below poverty line %	8.7	Hispanic	2.4
Doctors per 100,000 pop.	199	Black	16.8
Hospital beds per 100,000 pop.	406	School spending per head	$6,080

The economy

GSP $m	15,418	Av. income per head $	21,451
No. of new corporations '000	29.9	% of national average	108

Structure of GSP	%		%
Construction	4.7	Manufacturing	28.7
Transportation, public utilities	8.0	Wholesale/retail trade	12.9
Services	15.9	Finance, insurance, real estate	17.2
Government	10.5	Other	2.1

Principal industries Chemistry, agriculture, finance, poultry, shellfish, tourism, auto assembly, food processing, transportation equipment
Main crops Soybeans, potatoes, corn, mushrooms, lima beans, green peas, barley, cucumbers, snap beans, water melons, apples

Politics

Senate William V. Roth Jr (R; term expires 1995), Joseph Biden Jr (D; term expires 1997)
House Michael Castle (R)

State government
Governor Tom Carper (D; term expires 1997)
State Legislature Senate 15D, 6R; House 23R, 18D
Total expenditure (1992) $2,618m

DISTRICT OF COLUMBIA

Few lived around Washington, DC when a young federal government decided upon a capital for itself at the swampy confluence of the Potomac and Anacostia rivers in 1790. The Founding Fathers had looked with horror upon the mob terrorism of London and Paris, and this more than anything led them to wish for a capital under federal control. George Washington persuaded Virginia and Maryland to cede a ten-mile square for a new federal enclave.

Washington commissioned Pierre L'Enfant, a French engineer, to plan the future city, and L'Enfant had a grand vision. Superimposed upon that most practical of American accomplishments, the urban grid, L'Enfant envisaged a series of baroque avenues. These would not merely open up great views across the town and allow for civic squares and circles where they crossed. They would also get people quickly from Washington's edge to its (and the country's) centre: the Capitol, the president's house and the federal buildings.

Capital matters

That vision, in essence, is the Washington of today. Yet the seat of federal power has an influence, both nationally and internationally, about which even the most ardent federalist amongst the Founding Fathers would be horrified. Such power has been established only comparatively recently, thanks to two world wars and to the New Deal social programmes of the 1930s, which increased federal control at the expense of the states. Before that, Washington's claim to speak for America was never so certain.

In the early 1800s many more buildings were put up than occupied, and almost all of those were burnt by the British in the war of 1812. Later, Charles Dickens described "spacious avenues that begin in nothing and lead nowhere … public buildings that need but a public to be complete". And in the late 19th century the calls were strong for the capital (long home to a large black population) to be moved to Chicago, St Louis and even Kansas City. Under Alexander "Boss" Shepherd, Washington launched a huge public-works programme in the 1870s to cement, literally, its claim to the capital. Shepherd bankrupted the city in the process.

Mistrusting majority

That also ended a brief spell of self-government for the District of Columbia which reinforced a mutual mistrust which exists still between the federal government and the town over which it has near-total control. The roots of the mistrust are plain:

since 1790 Washington's population has been at least a quarter black; now it is nearer three-quarters black.

Long a home to freed slaves, blacks flooded to Washington after the Civil War. A black college, Howard University, was founded in 1867, and a black middle class sprang up, albeit an indigent one. The collapse of self-government in 1874 revived racial antagonisms which still have not been stamped out. The riots that burnt a swathe of the city on the news of Martin Luther King's killing had as their precedent the race riots of 1919. In 1922 blacks who wanted to watch the unveiling of the memorial to their white hero, Abraham Lincoln, watched from behind a cordon across the street.

After the civil rights revolution of the 1960s, home rule for Washington became irresistible. Until 1968 Washingtonians could not vote for a president. Only in 1971 could they send a Representative to Congress, who may not vote. Though the offices of mayor and city council were granted in 1974, Congress still has the final say over District affairs.

The politics of irony

Scant democracy has denuded local life of a political tradition – an irony in this, the federal seat. The politics of the town are immature, the city government America's most inept. Washington is the most overwhelmingly Democratic part of the country; 83% voted for Michael Dukakis in 1988, compared with 46% nationwide. The town's local politicians have, with few exceptions, proved dismal. As mayor, Marion Barry, a housecleaner's son, could have been a model for the city's troubled young blacks. Instead he corrupted local government and took drugs. Only in Washington could a Marion Barry come back to win a seat on the council and contemplate another tilt at the mayor's office. Statehood, much willed by the District's residents, is unlikely.

Not so bad

Although the south-east section of Washington is poor, drug-ridden and dangerous, most of the north-west is affluent and the average income for the city as a whole is above the national average. The contrast is also stark between the town and the sprawling Virginia and Maryland suburbs that house the region's commuters. During the 1980s Arlington and Fairfax counties in Virginia leapt to become the second and third richest in the country. This is all thanks to the growth of federal government, and in particular to Ronald Reagan's high-tech defence build-up.

Facts

Date of statehood	n/a	Total area	68 sq miles
Capital	n/a	Highest point ft	Tenleytown 410
Other cities	n/a	Main rivers	Potomac, Anacostia, Rock Creek

Climate Mild and equable.
Geography Co-extensive with city of Washington on the Potomac river on west central edge of Maryland, opposite Virginia.
Time zone Eastern Standard

People

			%
Population m	0.59	Under 18	19.9
% av. ann. growth 1980–92	-0.7	Over 65	13.1
Pop. per sq mile	9,649.5	Urban	100.0
Birth rate per 1,000 pop.	19.5	Male	46.6
Death rate per 1,000 pop.	11.7	White	29.6
Pop. below poverty line %	16.9	Hispanic	5.4
Doctors per 100,000 pop.	615	Black	65.8
Hospital beds per 100,000 pop.	1,271	School spending per head	$8,116

The economy

GSP $m	39,363	Av. income per head $	26,360
No. of new corporations '000	2.3	% of national average	133

Structure of GSP	%		%
Construction	6.9	Manufacturing	3.3
Transportation, public utilities	5.8	Wholesale/retail trade	5.3
Services	29.4	Finance, insurance, real estate	8.2
Government	41.1	Other	–

Principal industries n/a
Main crops n/a

Politics

Senate Jesse Jackson (D; known as the Shadow Senator – non-voting)
House Eleanor Holmes Norton (D; non-voting delegate)

Government
Governor Mayor Sharon Pratt Kelly (D; term expires 1995)
State Legislature n/a
Expenditure (1991) n/a

FLORIDA

Plenty of its residents, when they think about it at all, imagine the fourth most populous state to be a quintessentially American discovery, and then some time around the turn of this century. Florida, though, is the region of North America longest settled by Europeans, and this because of the Spanish and French rather than the English and Americans.

The first to explore Florida was a Spaniard, Juan Ponce de Leon, a one-time shipmate of Christopher Columbus who landed in April 1513. The country he saw was covered in flowers; it being Easter time (in Spanish, Pascua Florida), the name for the region stuck. Less permanent were Florida's earliest Spanish settlements, which came to nought. But then a French Huguenot, Jean Ribault, established a colony in 1562 at Fort Caroline, at the mouth of the St John's river in present-day Jacksonville; he claimed the whole region for France. At that, the Spanish crown dispatched Pedro Menendez de Aviles, who landed south of Fort Caroline on the feast day of St Augustine in 1565. Menendez marched north to the fort and slaughtered the women and children. He meted the same to the men when he came upon them at present-day Matanzas (Spanish for "killings"). Menendez's landing-point, named St Augustine, is North America's longest settled city.

European exchanges

During the 17th century the Spanish were pre-eminent in Florida (which in those days stretched west all the way to New Orleans). They built a series of Franciscan missions and a set of remarkable coastal fortresses upon both the Gulf of Mexico and the Atlantic coasts. To this day three such forts bear testimony to a power which was not yet rivalled by England: San Marcos de Apalache, just south of Tallahassee; Fort Matanzas, built in 1742; and the earlier Castillio San Marcos at St Augustine, a massive feat of military architecture which stands upon the site of nine previous Spanish forts.

During most of the 18th century, though, Spanish power was on the wane, just as Britain's influence in the Caribbean economy, of which Florida formed an outcrop, was growing. Both the British and the Creek nation of Indians had made inroads into northern Florida. The region became a counter in colonial power games between the Spanish, French and English. In 1763 Britain won Florida from the Spanish in exchange for Havana; Britain swapped it back in 1783 for the Bahamas. In 1814 and 1818 the Americans under Andrew Jackson made two incursions into Florida against the Seminole Indians (a branch of the Creek who, along with escaped black slaves, had drifted into Florida). Finally, in 1822, the Americans pressured the Spanish into selling Florida to them. It became a state of the union in 1845.

As a footnote, the Seminoles bravely resisted the influx of American settlers who demanded their deportation. They held out for two years in the Seminole War of 1835, defeated in the end by General (later President) Zachary Taylor by Lake Okeechobee. Some tribal members held out after that far into the Everglades; a treaty was not formally signed until 1934.

In comparison with northern Florida, though, most of the south is young. At the turn of this century Miami was a tiny village with no postman. When there were exceptions to this immaturity, it was for unorthodox reasons. Until the early 19th century Key West, 100 miles down the Florida Keys from the mainland peninsula, was home to freebooters and buccaneers. The town then turned for its living to salvaging the many boats that ran afoul of the Florida Reef. By 1830 the townspeople were reputed to have the highest per person income in the country. Their prosperity grew with the cigar-packing industry and the presence of the American navy.

Sunshine state

It was at around this time that the first attempts were made to sell the dream whose outcome is now modern Florida, a land of fabled pleasures drained from the dismal swamps. During the 1880s two millionaires, Henry Flagler and Henry Plant, saw in southern Florida's climate and beaches a mecca for Yankees yearning to escape the northern winters. They laid railroads and built resort hotels across to Tampa and down to Palm Beach, Miami and down to Key West. Today, northerners have flooded to southern Florida, and not just the retirees of conventional wisdom. Only 35% of Floridians are native-born, yet the state has one of the fastest rising rates of schoolchildren. Florida's median age is just 36.

This is proof, for many still demand it, of some permanence to Florida's economy. Service-sector, high-technology and white-collar jobs have sprouted over the past two decades. Nowhere more so than in Brevard County, home to the Cape Canaveral space programme. There, the population has grown from 20,000 in the 1940s to 400,000 today.

Winds of change

Yet Florida's growth was – and still is – far from even. A huge Florida land boom went wildly bust in 1926, after a hurricane reminded thousands of speculators that they were seeking profits in inhospitable territory. Likewise, Hurricane Andrew in 1992 was the country's worst ever; it will do much to remind Americans that Florida's elemental nature is never far from view. North-eastern retirees who anyway are having trouble selling their homes in a bust property market may decide to stay put.

Florida, though, will continue to exert a pull upon America, because it has long been seen as that country's future. Long before the rest of the United States, Florida had laid out strip malls and four and eight-lane highways to reach them. Florida has no centre, which is now also quintessentially American. (Miami, its biggest city and two-fifths Cuban, is culturally and geographically apart from the rest of the state, but it is increasingly economically important as a centre for business with Latin America.) And Florida, which attracts over 40m tourists a year, many to the Universal and Disney World theme parks and movie lots near Orlando, leads the country in creating tourism-as-employment – life imitating art imitating life again.

Time to grow up

If Florida is America's future, it is not all good. Especially outside the northern panhandle (which resembles the Baptist south of Georgia and Alabama more than it does southern Florida, and still has a Dixiecrat flavour), there is a woeful lack of local elites. Politics is weak and fragmented, and there is little commitment by Floridians to civic bodies. Public education is poor. Violent crime is a concern even among the most affluent and protected of retirement communities, which are strongly for capital punishment. It also deters tourists. Lastly, Florida is the natural home to the sharp operator – be it a lawyer, a savings-and-loan owner, or a property developer. The boom years of the 1980s have left evidence aplenty of their activities: overdevelopment is just the most obvious example. So long as Florida has some of the mentality of the wild frontier, it will remain an immature state.

State facts

Date of statehood	3 March 1845	Total area	65,758 sq miles
Capital	Tallahassee	Highest point ft	Sec. 30, T6N, R20W
Other cities	Jacksonville,		345
	Miami, Tampa	Main rivers	St Johns, Suwannee, Apalachicola

Climate Sub-tropical north of Bradenton – Lake Okeechobee – Vero Beach.
Geography Land is flat or rolling: highest point is in the north-west.
Time zone Eastern Standard

People

			%
Population m	13.49	Under 18	23.0
% av. ann. growth 1980–92	2.7	Over 65	18.4
Pop. per sq mile	249.8	Urban	84.8
Birth rate per 1,000 pop.	15.4	Male	48.4
Death rate per 1,000 pop.	10.2	White	83.1
Pop. below poverty line %	12.7	Hispanic	12.2
Doctors per 100,000 pop.	208	Black	13.6
Hospital beds per 100,000 pop.	466	School spending per head	$5,639

The economy

GSP $m	226,964	Av. income per head $	19,397
No. of new corporations '000	81.1	% of national average	98

Structure of GSP	%		%
Construction	6.9	Manufacturing	10.2
Transportation, public utilities	8.8	Wholesale/retail trade	19.1
Services	22.6	Finance, insurance, real estate	16.7
Government	12.4	Other	3.3

Principal industries Services, trade, government, manufacturing, tourism
Main crops Citrus fruits, vegetables, potatoes, melons, strawberries, sugar cane

Politics

Senate Bob Graham (D; term expires 1999), Connie Mack (R; term expires 1995).
House Tillie Fowler, Clifford B. Stearns, John Mica, Bill McCollum, Michael Bilirakis, Bill Young, Charles Canady, Dan Miller, Porter J. Goss, Tom Lewis, Ileana Ros Lehtinen, Lincoln Diaz-Balart, E. Clay Shaw Jr (all R); Earl Hutto, Pete Peterson, Corrine Brown, Karen Thurman, Sam M. Gibbons, Jim Bacchus, Carrie Meek, Harry A. Johnston II, Peter Deutsch, Alcee Hastings (all D)

State government
Governor Lawton Chiles (D; term expires 1995)
State Legislature Senate 20D, 20R; House 71D, 49R
Total expenditure (1992) $28,870m

GEORGIA

No state can rival the claim of Georgia, the last of England's original 13 colonies, as the heart of the South. The colony was founded in 1733, when James Oglethorpe landed on the eastern seaboard and set about building Savannah, a stunning town which bears much of his original stamp. Oglethorpe was a philanthropist and an idealist. He had persuaded King George II to grant a charter for debtors, oddballs and the poor to work the land without slaves and without alcohol. These constraints predictably did not last long, but Georgian whites then prospered and not only because of slave labour. It was Georgia which linked the coastal plains of Virginia and the Carolinas with the cotton plantations of the deep South. And for as long as the Appalachians acted as a natural frontier, it was through Georgia that anyone headed west had to travel.

Gone with the wind

As went Georgia, so did its main metropolis, Atlanta. The state capital has prospered by making itself indispensable as the hub of southern commerce. This William Tecumseh Sherman well understood in 1864, when Atlanta was a mere junction town for the Western & Atlantic Railroad. As the natural supply centre for the Confederate army, General Sherman flattened Atlanta; he then destroyed a 60-mile-wide swathe of land on his famous march to the sea. Sherman thereby sealed victory in the Civil War for the Union side, and instilled in the South a terrible and long-lasting sense of defeat which reached its celluloid expression in *Gone With the Wind*.

Bouncing back

Yet Atlanta sprang back: within two decades it was several times larger than it was at the start of the Civil War. It established itself not just as the centre of white-based commerce, but as the cultural centre for blacks. Over a dozen black colleges were founded, and with a strong black middle class and intelligentsia, it is no coincidence that Atlanta became the "cradle" of the civil-rights movement and home to Martin Luther King. "The City Too Busy To Hate" Atlanta liked to call itself. This label stretched the truth somewhat: blacks to this day lack commercial clout in this, the South's financial centre, even if they have won political power. And there is a black underclass as lamentable as in any other big city. Yet no other southern city comes close to claiming the label.

And Atlanta was never as busy as during the Reagan and Bush years which followed the presidency of Georgia's own Jimmy Carter. In the 1980s, the Atlanta region grew by a third. It was not just old businesses that prospered. (Coca-Cola, as a visitor cannot fail to notice, has its headquarters here.) New businesses flocked to take advantage of Atlanta's position at the hub of southern activity. The financial sector boomed. The city's airport claimed to be the world's busiest ("Atlanta exists only for changing planes", said those who were sceptical of the city's boosters). It has bred a cluster of innovative electronics and aviation companies around it. The malls in the city's northern suburbs are unparalleled in size and opulence anywhere in the South. And with the rise of Ted Turner's Cable News Network, Atlanta can now with some justification claim to be the world's news capital, too. All the city needs to establish its credentials is an Olympics. It will host the 1996 summer games.

Much more than dominant Atlanta

Atlanta is important because it dominates Georgia as few other cities dominate their state, but it does not overwhelm it, as the Southern-style alligator boots of the state legislators attest. Indeed, Georgia's regions are surprisingly varied, from the predominantly white Piedmont in the north to the strongly black counties in the flat south. Along the eastern seaboard, the region around Savannah has thrived with the kind of development during the 1980s that affected the rest of the mid-Atlantic. Yet still there exist on the nearby Sea Islands the remains of a black culture and patois, Gullah, that have discernible roots in West Africa.

Manufacturing may play only a small part in the Atlanta metropolis, but it is far from unimportant in the rest of the state. Low-wage industries such as textile mills, pulp plants and sawmills account for two-fifths of all jobs outside the Atlanta region. These jobs will not disappear rapidly. Georgia is not short of natural resources (it has pipped Oregon to become the number one lumber producer, partly because few environmentalists value the cheap pine that grows in Georgia). The state's rural regions are fairly poor, and it will be a long time before Atlanta's prosperous ripples reach the farthest corners of the state.

State facts

Date of statehood	2 January 1788	Total area	59,441 sq miles
Capital	Atlanta	Highest point ft	Brasstown Bald
Other cities	Columbus,		4,784
	Savannah, Macon	Main rivers	Savannah, Ocmulgee,
			Flint, Chattahoochee, Oconee,
			Suwannee

Climate Maritime tropical air masses dominate in summer; continental polar air masses in winter; east central area drier.

Geography Most southerly of Blue Ridge Mountains cover north-east and north central; central Piedmont extends to the fall line of rivers; coastal plain levels to the coast flatlands.

Time zone Eastern Standard

People

			%
Population m	6.75	Under 18	26.7
% av. ann. growth 1980–92	1.8	Over 65	10.1
Pop. per sq mile	116.6	Urban	63.2
Birth rate per 1,000 pop.	17.4	Male	48.5
Death rate per 1,000 pop.	8.0	White	71.0
Pop. below poverty line %	14.7	Hispanic	1.7
Doctors per 100,000 pop.	175	Black	27.0
Hospital beds per 100,000 pop.	524	School spending per head	$4,720

The economy

GSP $m	129,776	Av. income per head $	18,130
No. of new corporations '000	18.1	% of national average	91

Structure of GSP	%		%
Construction	4.6	Manufacturing	19.2
Transportation, public utilities	10.9	Wholesale/retail trade	18.7
Services	16.3	Finance, insurance, real estate	15.2
Government	12.6	Other	2.5

Principal industries Manufacturing, forestry, agriculture, chemicals

Main crops Soybeans, peanuts, hay, corn, cotton, wheat

Politics

Senate Sam Nunn (D; term expires 1997), Paul Coverdell (R; term expires 1999)

House Sanford Bishop, John Lewis, Buddy Darden, J. Roy Rowland, Nathan Deal, Don Johnson, Cynthia McKinney (all D); Jack Kingston, Mac Collins, Newt Gingrich, John Linden (all R)

State government

Governor Zell Miller (D; term expires 1995)

State Legislature Senate 41D, 15R; House 128D, 52R

Total expenditure (1992) $13,717m

HAWAII

From Polynesian settlement to America's 50th state, Hawaii has had many lives. The tropical archipelago was born 30m years ago when magma oozed through cracks in the ocean floor and started massing into a range of submerged mountains. Scattered volcanic summits surrounded by coral reef, Hawaii is a tourist's paradise and America's haven between the Pacific Rims.

In most minds Hawaii connotes Waikiki's postcard-familiar beaches or the sleek shops and high-rises of Honolulu. But the distinct personality of the state comes from the combination of Oahu's neighbour islands. To the west is unspoilt Kauai, to the east, resort-minded Maui. Between them lie little Lanai – literally "land hump" – where pineapples grow on terrain that once grazed cattle, and Molokai, a refuge for leprosy sufferers since 1860.

Hawaii has more ethnic groups than any other state, and the eponymous "Big Island" at the south-east of the chain reflects its long history of immigration. Here live descendants of cowboys who came from the Philippines and Latin America to ranch, of the Chinese and Japanese labourers who worked the sugar plantations, and of the Portuguese, Germans and Puerto Ricans who arrived later to inhabit the modest trading centre of Hilo.

Came to do good, stayed to do well

Captain James Cook named them the Sandwich Islands when he first set foot on the atolls in 1778, but he landed in a region wracked by warring factions. He paid the price, being eaten by cannibals. Peace came to the islands after King Kamehameha I ended decades-long rivalries among native chiefs by unifying them under his sovereignty in 1810. His hospitality to foreigners permitted a period of prosperity until diseases introduced by American and European traders devastated the native population. Missionaries found their work easy when they arrived in 1820, just one year after the Hawaiian king had abolished the native *kapu* system; the islanders embraced Christianity.

The mainlanders swiftly transplanted their economic system to the islands as well, sometimes with awkward result; on Maui devout Boston Congregationalists keen on building plantations clashed with whalers, with whom they differed as much over economics as they did on matters of morality. Steamship service from San Francisco provided a boon in the 1860s to trade and the nascent tourist industry. Mark Twain, Jack London and Robert Louis Stevenson were among the early visitors. But Hawaii's "Big Five" sugar agents, all headquartered in Honolulu and run by old missionary families, dominated the state's economy.

Its monarchy overthrown in 1893, Hawaii was annexed five years later and in 1900 became an American territory. America held the Philippines and Guam firmly in its grasp, but was sentimental about China and anxious about Japan; Hawaii presented a key to maintaining a military presence in the Pacific. It soon became a key military outpost and defence installations remain crucial to the state's economy. A surprise attack on the American naval base at Pearl Harbour by Japanese aircraft on December 7th 1941 hurled America into the second world war – and remote Hawaii into the mainstream. By 1959 it achieved statehood.

The native and royal heritage of Hawaii has bizarrely affected land ownership in the islands; about 40 people own more than 70% of the state. This simplifies long-term planning, but because Hawaii has been controlled by the same Democratic political machine since 1962, Republicans complain of a one-party state.

Relaxing and relaxed

On the north-west coast of Hawaii's Waiulua Bay sprawls one of the world's most expensive resorts ever built. The Hyatt Regency Waikoloa, complete with 62-acre tropical garden, cost $360m to construct; it is a fitting monument to the industry which is the state's mainstay. Half of Hawaii's jobs are in services. It is the one state that thrives when the dollar drops against the yen, and in 1990 when the mainland economy slowed, Hawaii's surged.

Hawaii's big boom of the late 1980s is clearly over. Growth rates have slowed and only modest rates are forecast. The service jobs Hawaii depends on are mostly low-wage in a market where prices have been bid up by wealthy buyers from Japan and east Asia. But at 7.5% Hawaii's growth in personal income in 1991 was double the national rate, and unemployment remains low.

Obvious possibilities exist for diversification of Hawaii's economy into areas such as ocean research, astronomy and securities markets (it is daytime here during the four hours between the close of New York's business day and the beginning of Tokyo's). But there is little concerted motion in those directions. Ever-dependent on tourism and defence, Hawaii has gotten comfortable as the Pacific purveyor of beaches and bases. Maybe a bit too comfortable.

State facts

Date of statehood	21 August 1959	Total area	10,932 sq miles
Capital	Honolulu	Highest point ft	Mauna Kea 13,796
Other cities	Hilo, Kailua, Kaneohe		

Climate Sub-tropical, with wide variations in rainfall; Waialeale, on Kauai, wettest spot in USA (annual rainfall 444 in).
Geography Islands are tops of a chain of submerged volcanic mountains; principal active volcano is Kilauea.
Time zone Pacific

People

			%
Population m	1.16	Under 18	25.2
% av. ann. growth 1980–92	1.5	Over 65	11.4
Pop. per sq mile	180.5	Urban	89.0
Birth rate per 1,000 pop.	18.5	Male	50.9
Death rate per 1,000 pop.	5.9	White	33.4
Pop. below poverty line %	8.3	Hispanic	7.3
Doctors per 100,000 pop.	236	Black	2.4
Hospital beds per 100,000 pop.	353	School spending per head	$5,453

The economy

GSP $m	25,755	Av. income per head $	21,218
No. of new corporations '000	3.8	% of national average	107

Structure of GSP	%		%
Construction	8.7	Manufacturing	4.3
Transportation, public utilities	9.8	Wholesale/retail trade	4.1
Services	21.7	Finance, insurance, real estate	16.8
Government	21.0	Other	13.6

Principal industries Tourism, defence and other government, sugar refining, pineapple and diversified agriculture, aquaculture, fishing, motion pictures
Main crops Sugar, pineapples, macadamia nuts, fruits, coffee, vegetables, melons, floriculture

Politics
Senate Daniel K. Inouye (D; term expires 1999), Daniel Akaka (D; term expires 1995)
House Neil Abercrombie, Patsy Mink (both D)

State government
Governor John Waihee (D; term expires 1994)[a]
State Legislature Senate 22D, 3R; House 47D, 4R
Total expenditure (1992) $5,540m

a December.

IDAHO

Idaho is gems, potatoes and winter sports. Separated from the Pacific by Washington and Oregon and from the plains by Montana and Wyoming, the state is an 84,000 square mile wedge of raw, mineral-rich mountain ranges stretching south along the continental divide from the Canadian border through the potato-growing Snake river plain to Nevada and Utah.

Idaho was acquired by the United States in 1803 under the Louisiana treaty, but its boundaries were not settled until the Oregon treaty of 1846. The first Americans to settle were Mormon missionaries sent from neighbouring Utah in 1855. These pioneers set up farms and irrigation systems which set Idaho on the way to becoming the Potato state. The discovery of gold at Orofino Creek in northern Idaho in 1860 triggered a gold rush, but Idaho remained mostly frontier and Indian territory until the railways arrived towards the end of the century. Statehood come in 1890. Politically the state has been a rare Republican stronghold in the north-west, but this is changing.

Spuds, snow and semiconductors

Mining accounts for only a sliver of the state economy today, although Idaho mines one-fifth of America's silver and is a leading source of a dozen minerals and metals from antimony to zinc. The state has been farmed from the early days – Idaho still grows one in four of America's potatoes and 18% of the state's 1m residents make their living from family farms – but it was the second world war that made food processing big business, particularly potato freezing and dehydrating. The cold war prompted a nuclear industry. More recently, cheap hydropower and a clean atmosphere has brought electronics. However, the state's biggest dollar-earner has become tourism. Resorts such as Sun Valley draw hundreds of thousands of winter-sports enthusiasts; its elk herds draw hunters; its mountain streams and lakes, fishermen.

Like other mountain states, Idaho had a mild ride through the early 1990s recession. Its economy grew, creating new jobs faster than nearly all other states, especially in service industries. Personal income and the population rose, but the state's property market suffered none of the ravages seen in the coastal states. Though always vulnerable to the fluctuations of world commodity prices, diversification has provided a solid foundation for continued growth, but the state needs to keep developing export markets for both its manufactures and raw and processed foods.

State facts

Date of statehood	3 July 1890	Total area	83,574 sq miles
Capital	Boise	Highest point ft	Borah Peak 12,662
Other cities	Pocatello,	Main rivers	Snake, Salmon,
	Idaho Falls, Nampa		Clearwater

Climate Tempered by Pacific westerly winds; drier, colder, continental clime in SE; altitude an important factor.

Geography Snake river plains in the south; central region of mountains, canyons, gorges (Hells Canyon, 7,900 ft, deepest in North America).

Time zone Mountain

People

			%
Population m	1.07	Under 18	30.4
% av. ann. growth 1980–92	1.0	Over 65	11.9
Pop. per sq mile	12.9	Urban	57.4
Birth rate per 1,000 pop.	16.3	Male	49.8
Death rate per 1,000 pop.	7.5	White	94.4
Pop. below poverty line %	13.3	Hispanic	5.3
Doctors per 100,000 pop.	125	Black	0.3
Hospital beds per 100,000 pop.	374	School spending per head	$3,528

The economy

GSP $m	16,339	Av. income per head $	16,067
No. of new corporations '000	1.9	% of national average	81

Structure of GSP	%		%
Construction	2.5	Manufacturing	18.4
Transportation, public utilities	9.8	Wholesale/retail trade	15.3
Services	15.8	Finance, insurance, real estate	14.1
Government	11.9	Other	12.2

Principal industries Agriculture, manufacturing, tourism, lumber, mining, electronics

Main crops Potatoes, peas, sugar beets, alfalfa seed, wheat, hops, barley, plums and prunes, mint, onions, corn, cherries, apples, hay

Politics

Senate Larry Craig (R; term expires 1997); Dirk Kempthorne (R; term expires 1999)

House Larry LaRocco (D); Michael Crapo (R)

State government

Governor Cecil D. Andrus (D; term expires 1995)

State Legislature Senate 23R, 12D; House 50R, 20D

Total expenditure (1992) $2,171m

ILLINOIS

The Prairie State lives up to its nickname. It is 56,000 square miles of rolling prairie and fertile plain hanging off the south-western end of Lake Michigan. To the north is Wisconsin. To the west, beyond the Mississippi river, are Iowa and Missouri. Kentucky is to the south, beyond the Ohio river. To the east is Indiana with the Wabash river forming the southern end of both states.

Illinois has America's largest prehistoric earthworks, suggesting occupation as far back as 5,000 BC. The first European exploration in the area was undertaken by the Frenchmen Louis Joliet and Jacques Marquette, who canoed the Illinois and Mississippi rivers in 1673. Robert Cavelier de La Salle established a fort, Crève Coeur, in 1680 near present-day Peoria. The first French settlements, on the Illinois river, came twelve years later. The area passed into British hands after 1763 following the French and Indian War. Frontier fighting persisted intermittently if fiercely until the Indian defeat in 1832 in the Black Hawk war.

The United States gained sovereignty over the region in 1783 following the Revolutionary war. The US army set up Fort Dearborn in 1803 on a muddy swamp where Chicago stands today. Illinois became the 21st state in 1818. Widespread settlement did not come until the opening of the Erie canal in New York in 1825 opened the Mid-West to migration from the east, though southern Illinois was settled from Kentucky and Tennessee. The coming of the railways in the 1850s brought boom times to the state. By 1870 Illinois's population was approaching 2m.

Illinois has been closely linked with national politics since Abraham Lincoln rose from being an Illinois country lawyer and legislator to president of the union during the Civil War. Breadbasket Illinois tends to vote Republican while Cook County, which is Chicago, is famous for colourful Democratic city bosses. One of these, Mayor Richard Daley, ran the greatest party machine of them all. It was in Chicago that anti-war demonstrators clashed with police outside the 1968 Democratic convention. In 1992 Illinois elected the first black woman senator, Carol Moseley Braun.

Famous windy city

Chicago, America's second city though it is the third largest, is an endearing mix of cosmopolitan sophistication and the down-to-earth Mid-West. For a port city, it has a stunning waterfront of marinas, beaches and parks. The city was largely destroyed by fire in 1871, the first in a series of great disasters to hit the city over the years, including 1992's flooding of the downtown "Loop". The first re-building spawned the Chicago school of architecture, the skyscrapers of Louis Sullivan and the Prairie homes of Frank Lloyd Wright. The city was later home to Mies van der Rohe. The world's tallest building, the 110-story Sears Tower, opened in Chicago in 1974.

In the Prohibition era Chicago was the domain of Al Capone, who cut his teeth in the city's bloody newspaper circulation wars. As well as great gangsters, the city has a reputation for great newspapermen and jazzmen.

Big and reborn

Illinois is the fourth largest state economy, accounting for about 5% of the national total. Its economy is larger than Australia's, Holland's, South Korea's or Mexico's and would rank 13th in the world if it were an independent country. Since 1982, it has been growing at a real rate of 3% a year. It is widely diversified in manufacturing, coal mining, agriculture, trade and services. Chicago is the centre of America's grain markets and of the world's financial futures markets. Thanks to its position as the transport hub of the Mid-West, it is also frequently America's biggest exporting state. Seven of America's largest exporting firms have their head office in Illinois, including Caterpillar and Motorola. One job in 16 in the state is export-related.

Like other mid-western states that went through painful restructuring in the 1980s, Illinois escaped relatively unscathed in the recession of the early 1990s. Its residents' average income per person rose from twelfth-highest in 1989 to ninth the following year, a fifth faster increase than the national average.

Manufacturing still drives the economy but one in three manufacturing jobs has gone since the days of peak employment in the early 1970s. Manufacturing accounted for barely 17% of jobs in 1991 (when more than half of the 68,000 jobs lost were in manufacturing), down from more than 25% in 1976, with the biggest job losses being in durable-goods manufacturing. The silver lining is that manufacturing productivity has increased by 40% since the early 1980s. That is mostly thanks to the closing of some large smokestack plants and average hourly earnings falling from 9% above the national average in the first half of the 1980s to only 4% above.

Chicago and the polluted, industrial sprawl south along the shore of Lake Michigan towards Indiana was long part of the Mid-West's great iron and steel producing area. Steel making is a much diminished industry, but Illinois remains in the top four nationally for chemicals output, electronics, machinery, and rubber and plastics production. It is the fifth largest oil refining state, and in the top ten for paper products and motor-industry assembly. The range of Illinois industrial and consumer manufactures runs from farm equipment to surgical appliances. Of America's biggest manufacturing companies, 10% have their headquarters in Illinois.

Post-smokestack attractions

While Illinois is shedding its smokestack industries, it is attracting foreign direct investment in its place. It ranks third among states in the value of inward foreign investment. Japanese and Dutch firms account for more than two-fifths of the manufacturing part of that. Foreign-owned companies have created more than 200,000 jobs, more than in any other old Rustbowl state.

Illinois is also attracting increasing numbers of high-tech-based manufacturing industries, although it still only ranks eighth nationally. It has the fourth highest concentration of electronics firms and software companies in the country. It has the sixth-highest number of boffins and engineers. It ranks third in corporate R&D facilities and seventh in private industrial and university-based R&D. It is the leading centre of academic R&D in the Great Lakes region, with top-flight universities such as the University of Chicago, Northwestern and the state university, which is host to the country's national supercomputing centre. Data Resources forecast that of all America's big cities, Chicago will create the third highest number of new technical jobs in the first half of the 1990s.

High on the hog

Chicago was once the railhead and meat market of the Mid-West. Today the cattle yards are gone (the site is an industrial park), but Illinois remains one of America's top three exporters of farm produce. Some 8% of America's farm exports come from Illinois, one seventh of the exports of feed grains, and soybeans and soybean products. The state is the nation's leading grower of soybeans and only Iowa exceeds its corn crop. Other bounteous crops are hay, grain, sorghum and oats. The state ranks second in the production of hogs and is an important cattle, dairy, poultry and vegetable-growing state. Cash receipts from farming are in excess of $7 billion a year. Illinois has the second-largest food-processing industry in the country.

Services strength, primary power

Services account for more than one job in four now, a share which is expected to increase throughout the 1990s. The state has the second-highest concentration of *Fortune 500* company head offices, with nearly 50. Tourism is fast growing with spending rising by two-thirds between 1985 and 1990, and travel-related jobs increasing by 50%. Illinois ranks fifth in domestic tourism spending, at $15 billion. Foreign tourists, led by the unlikely combination of Japanese and British visitors, contribute a further $2.6 billion to the state's economy. Illinois is also becoming a popular location for film-makers, who contribute $40m a year to the local economy.

Retailing and wholesaling are very important to Illinois. The state is the fifth largest retail market in the country. Chicago is home of some of America's best-known retailers, including Sears, Roebuck and Marshall Field.

Financial services revolve around Chicago's financial futures markets and the commodities exchanges, though there is also a sizeable fund management community. Some 5% of America's venture capital is managed out of Chicago.

Illinois is a big energy state. It is the leading generator of nuclear power, accounting for half the state's generating capacity. It is the fifth leading coal producer and also has crude oil deposits.

Can it keep it up?

With a relatively healthy and more diversified economy which has generated more new manufacturing jobs in recent years than any other state in the Great Lakes region, the main challenge facing Illinois is to sustain manufacturing productivity growth, which has started to lag behind the national improvement in productivity. Most worrying is whether capital investment is being made at sufficiently high levels. It also needs to expand export markets for its growing number of services firms to absorb the labour that has been permanently displaced from manufacturing. A nagging concern is the state's finances. Illinois's bonds were downgraded by the rating agencies in 1992 because of its budgetary weakness. Like all big cities Chicago will require considerable spending on infrastructure renewal and public services in the 1990s.

State facts

Date of statehood	3 December 1818	Total area	57,918 sq miles
Capital	Springfield	Highest point ft	Charles Mound
Other cities	Chicago, Rockford,		1,235
	Peoria	Main rivers	Mississippi, Illinois, Ohio, Wabash

Climate Temperate, typically cold, snowy winters, hot summers.
Geography Prairie and fertile plains throughout; open hills in the southern region.
Time zone Central

People

			%
Population m	11.63	Under 18	26.0
% av. ann. growth 1980–92	0.1	Over 65	12.6
Pop. per sq mile	209.2	Urban	84.6
Birth rate per 1,000 pop.	17.1	Male	48.6
Death rate per 1,000 pop.	9.0	White	78.3
Pop. below poverty line %	11.9	Hispanic	7.9
Doctors per 100,000 pop.	212	Black	14.8
Hospital beds per 100,000 pop.	491	School spending per head	$5,248

The economy

GSP $m	256,478	Av. income per head $	21,608
No. of new corporations '000	20.1	% of national average	109

Structure of GSP	%		%
Construction	4.7	Manufacturing	19.9
Transportation, public utilities	10.1	Wholesale/retail trade	17.1
Services	19.4	Finance, insurance, real estate	17.4
Government	9.0	Other	2.4

Principal industries Manufacturing, services, travel, wholesale and retail trade, finance, insurance, construction, government, healthcare, agriculture
Main crops Corn, soybeans, wheat, oats, hay

Politics

Senate Paul Simon (D; term expires 1997); Carol Moseley Braun (D; term expires 1999)
House Bobby Rush, Mel Reynolds, William Lipinski, Luis Gutierrez, Dan Rostenkowski, Cardiss Collins, Sidney R. Yates, George Sangmeister, Jerry Costello, Lane Evans, Glenn Poshard, Richard J. Durbin (all D); Henry J. Hyde, Philip M. Crane, John E. Porter, Harris Fawell, Dennis Hastert, Thomas Ewing, Donald Manzullo, Robert H. Michel (all R)

State government
Governor Jim Edgar (R; term expires 1995)
State Legislature Senate 32R, 27D; House 67D, 51R
Total expenditure (1992) $22,528m

INDIANA

Indiana calls itself the Crossroads of America. As an eastern north-central state it is so geographically·in many ways, but in a metaphorical sense it is even more so. It is Rustbowl America trying to shine again and farmbelt America glowing.

The Hoosier state stretches south from a narrow 41-mile strip of Lake Michigan shoreline near Gary, which was once one of the great industrial centres of America. The centre of the state is fertile plain which raises corn, soybeans, hogs and basketball players. Southern Indiana is covered with hilly forest, beyond which is the Ohio river, which forms the state's southern boundary, with Kentucky. Ohio lies to Indiana's east; Illinois to its west.

The area was ceded by the French to the British after the French and Indian war in 1763, and then by the British to the United States in 1783. Indiana witnessed some of the bitterest frontier fighting in the Revolutionary war. A series of subsequent Indian uprisings, which included two defeats for the United States army, were not finally quelled until General William Harrison defeated Tecumseh's Indian confederation at the Battle of Tippecanoe in 1811. Statehood followed in 1816. Indianapolis was made the state capital four years later. Like much of the Mid-West, Indiana was largely settled in the 19th century by German immigrants after the opening of the Erie canal opened up the way for the influx of European migrants into New York to head west.

Smokestacks stilled

Indiana's industrial history started in 1906, when US Steel founded Gary on the shores of Lake Michigan. That spawned mills and factories from which spewed the iron, steel and oil products needed by the burgeoning regional motor industry and the growing manufacturing city of Chicago, 30 miles up the coast. For decades Indiana was a central part of the industrial Mid-West, not only metal bashing but also in electrical engineering and the new phonographic and television industries. Conservative Republican government kept the state friendly to industry with low taxes and a hands-off approach.

Like the rest of smokestack America Indiana was hit hard by the recession of the early 1980s, which exposed how uncompetitive much of American manufacturing had become in the previous decades. An early warning in Indiana had been the closure of the the Studebaker plant at South Bend in 1962, causing a ripple of unemployment through the plant's local sub-contractors. Over the next two decades that cause and effect would be repeated again and again as large manufacturing companies shut down local operations, often moving to the Sunbelt for lower labour and utilities costs in a bid to stay competitive with foreign rivals.

Motoring on

Compared with neighbouring mid-western states, traditionally laissez-faire Indiana was slow to respond to the devastation being wreaked on its manufacturing employment by buying in jobs with subsidies. However, it started to do so in the 1980s, attracting both Japanese and European investment, which has helped to restore productivity.

Manufacturing still accounts for almost one-third of Indiana's economy, though its share of employment has fallen to one-quarter. Leading industries include electronics, steel, chemicals, machinery-making, transport equipment, rubber and plastics, petroleum products and pharmaceuticals. Much of it is related to the motor industry, which accounts directly for about one-third of the state's manufacturing output by value. Indiana ranks fourth in the nation in vehicle production, although its position is increasingly challenged by the presence of Japanese transplant factories in Tennessee and Ohio. Symbolically, the state capital has been the home to the "Indy 500" motor race since 1911.

Food and rocks

Indiana is a big farm state. Its main crops are corn and soybeans. Cattle and hogs are raised. Indiana's poultry farmers rank second in the country in egg production. It is also the fourth-leading tomato-growing state in America.

Much of the limestone used by American builders is quarried in southern Indiana. Some 4,000 are still employed in mining the coal fields. Indiana's energy-use laws are protective of the state's coal industry.

Dented future

Indiana's challenges remain fourfold: to make sure that the new industrial jobs that the state creates or lures with incentives are high-value added ones that will not easily flee south or east just because of cheaper labour costs; to develop service industries that can soak up the labour that such higher-value manufacturing jobs will make redundant; to develop export markets; and to deal with the closing of the state's several military bases, which will leave a $500 million-a-year dent in the state's economy.

State facts

Date of statehood	11 December 1816	Total area	36,420 sq miles
Capital	Indianapolis	Highest point ft	Franklin Township
Other cities	Fort Wayne,		1,257
	Evansville, Gary	Main rivers	Wabash, Ohio

Climate Four distinct seasons with a temperate climate.
Geography Hilly southern region; fertile rolling plains of central region; flat, heavily glaciated north; dunes along Lake Michigan shore.
Time zone Central

People

			%
Population m	5.66	Under 18	25.8
% av. ann. growth 1980–92	0.3	Over 65	12.7
Pop. per sq mile	157.8	Urban	64.9
Birth rate per 1,000 pop.	15.6	Male	48.5
Death rate per 1,000 pop.	9.2	White	90.6
Pop. below poverty line %	10.7	Hispanic	1.8
Doctors per 100,000 pop.	157	Black	7.8
Hospital beds per 100,000 pop.	459	School spending per head	$5,429

The economy

GSP $m	105,314	Av. income per head $	18,043
No. of new corporations '000	10.2	% of national average	91

Structure of GSP	%		%
Construction	5.0	Manufacturing	28.9
Transportation, public utilities	9.5	Wholesale/retail trade	15.4
Services	14.2	Finance, insurance, real estate	14.8
Government	9.0	Other	3.2

Principal industries Manufacturing, wholesale and retail trade, agriculture, government, services
Main crops Corn, sorghum, oats, wheat, rye, soybeans, hay

Politics

Senate Richard Lugar (R; term expires 1995), Dan Coats (R; term expires 1999)
House Peter J. Visclosky, Philip Sharp, Tim Roemer, Jill Long, Frank McCloskey, Lee H. Hamilton, Andrew Jacobs Jr (all D); Steve Buyer, Dan Burton, John T. Myers (all R)

State government
Governor B. Evan Bayh III (D; term expires 1997)
State Legislature Senate 28R, 22D; House 55D, 45R
Total expenditure (1992) $10,198m

IOWA

In Iowa, the corn really does grow as high as an elephant's eye and the people are down-to-earth. Many of these mid-westerners are of German ancestry and they live longer than nearly any other Americans.

The Hawkeye state is 56,000 square miles of some of the most fertile soil in the world, on the plain between the Mississippi river which forms Iowa's eastern boundary and the Missouri river which forms the western one. Minnesota and Missouri are north and south respectively.

Inhabited since prehistory, the area became part of the United States through the Louisiana Purchase of 1803. Three fierce wars were fought between American settlers and the Black Hawk Indians in the 1830s before Iowa became a state in 1846. Since the early 1970s, the state's political caucuses have had national attention in presidential election years as early tests of candidates' support. Iowan voters are as unpredictable as the weather, though in many ways the state is average America.

Fabulous farming

Iowa grows 10% of America's food. Iowa ranks first in the nation in corn, oats and pig and hog production. Only California's farms earn more. Yet manufacturing output is worth twice as much. Much of that is farm related: chemicals; fertilisers; farm machinery and equipment; and food processing; but there is also electronics and office-furniture making.

Iowa suffered horribly in the farmbelt bust of the 1980s. Drought and debt turned the state into what looked like a huge farm foreclosure. But that spared Iowa the speculative excesses of the decade. Like the rest of the Mid-West, it rode out the early 1990's recession relatively comfortably.

Its manufacturers had already become more productive. The relatively few laid-off manufacturing workers were absorbed by service industries. These have been increasing jobs by 10% a year, almost half as fast again as the national average. Des Moines has become a centre for insurance firms, transforming the city's skyline with office towers and the pedestrian Skywalk that connects them.

The risks to Iowa's recent steady economic performance are that the prolonged downturn in commodity prices could again trigger the over-indebtedness which was so disastrous in the early 1980s. The challenge is to keep increasing productivity in both farming and manufacturing to offset the state's population loss, and to keep finding export markets for its goods and produce.

State facts

Date of statehood	28 December 1846	Total area	56,276 sq miles
Capital	Des Moines	Highest point ft	Sec 29, T100N,
Other cities	Cedar Rapids,		R41W (1,670)
	Davenport, Sioux City	Main rivers	Mississippi, Missouri

Climate Humid, continental.
Geography Watershed from north-west to south-east; soil especially rich and land level in the north central counties.
Time zone Central

People

			%
Population m	2.81	Under 18	26.1
% av. ann. growth 1980–92	-0.3	Over 65	15.4
Pop. per sq mile	50.3	Urban	60.6
Birth rate per 1,000 pop.	14.2	Male	48.4
Death rate per 1,000 pop.	9.3	White	96.6
Pop. below poverty line %	11.5	Hispanic	1.2
Doctors per 100,000 pop.	151	Black	1.7
Hospital beds per 100,000 pop.	605	School spending per head	$4,949

The economy

GSP $m	52,574	Av. income per head $	18,287
No. of new corporations '000	4.5	% of national average	92

Structure of GSP	%		%
Construction	3.4	Manufacturing	21.7
Transportation, public utilities	7.9	Wholesale/retail trade	15.1
Services	14.8	Finance, insurance, real estate	18.1
Government	10.0	Other	9.0

Principal industries Insurance, manufacturing, agriculture
Main crops Silage and grain, corn, soybeans, oats, hay

Politics

Senate Charles E. Grassley (R; term expires 1999), Tom Harkin (D; term expires 1997)
House Jim Leach, Jim Nussle, Jim Lightfoot, Fred Grandy (all R); Neal Smith (D)

State government
Governor Terry E. Branstad (R; term expires 1995)
State Legislature Senate 26D, 24R; House 51R, 49D
Total expenditure (1992) $8,399m

KANSAS

The history of Kansas since European settlement was long a stormy one. For the first part of the 19th century what was called the Kansas Territory became home to a complex and often fractious demography of Indian tribes. Hope of stability, however, was shattered by the Kansas-Nebraska Act of 1854. This act had the effect of driving nearly all Indians to reservations in Oklahoma. It also precipitated the Civil War.

The act let the territories of Kansas and Nebraska into the union. In so doing, it repealed the Missouri Compromise of 1820. This earlier legislation, by decreeing the slave states and free states had to join the union in equal numbers, was an attempt to keep pro- and anti-slavery advocates from each other's throats.

Bleeding state

The Kansas-Nebraska Act declared that the issue should henceforth be settled by the popular sovereignty of territorial residents. The race was on between opposing forces to be the first to settle Kansas. Pro-slavery settlers poured in from Missouri, a slave state. East-coast opponents of slavery arranged for German immigrants and others to claim land in the new territory. A nasty guerrilla campaign raged between the pro-slave "bushwhackers" and the free-soil "jayhawkers" during the 1850s. These were known as the border wars (a training ground for the hoodlums and outlaws that long plagued the region), and the new state earned the moniker of Bleeding Kansas. That name was reinforced by the Civil War. Kansas sent the highest proportion of its men to the war of any state; an even higher proportion was killed.

Railroading influences

The period after the Civil War delivered some of the prosperity that its earlier settlers had dreamt of. The course of the two major railroad companies, the Missouri, Kansas and Texas, and the Atchison, Topeka and Santa Fe, determined the sites of the towns that are scattered over Kansas today. The railroad companies received vast tracts of land – 10m acres – from the federal government to encourage the building. The rail companies in turn recruited immigrants to the American dream, using heavy publicity in Europe and on the east coast. As a result, the state is ethnically diverse, if overwhelmingly white. Even so, Kansas has a higher proportion of blacks than most plains states, because of its symbol as a free state. In the second half of the 19th century what was known as the Kansas Fever Exodus brought

"Exodusters" up from the Deep South – blacks who sought manual labour in a less hostile land.

Cattle and corn

Until the 1880s, this was a land of pronghorn cattle and their drovers up from Texas. Then German-Russian new-comers brought from the steppes the techniques of dry-land farming, which they first applied by cutting down the waist-high prairie grass that covered the third of the state east of the 98th parallel that sees most rain. Drought-resistant strains of wheat were introduced.

Not everything went well: farmers were plagued by grasshoppers, tornadoes and more drought than they bargained for. Hard times in Kansas spawned the agrarian Populist movement, which, among other things, pushed for the repudiation of farmers' debts. One Populist orator, Mary Ellen Lease, summed it up: "Raise less corn and more hell." Echoes of these sentiments could be heard during the farm crisis of the 1980s. Nevertheless, Kansas farmers have long been the biggest – and richest – producers of American wheat, and today are amongst the most productive farmers in the world.

Middle America's metropolitanisation

It is this now-tamed land of neat, white towns and regular farms which is the epitome of Middle America, the Kansas of the Wizard of Oz. Yet the rural counties tied to the farm economy are playing an ever smaller, if still substantial, part in the state's economy. Only 53,900 people these days count farming as their main job. Between 1980 and 1990 the number of farmers fell by over 17%, so concentrating the business in the hands of the larger (and better-subsidised) operations.

A number of people equivalent to one-quarter of Kansas's total population lives not in Kansas at all, but across the state line in Kansas City, Missouri. Even so, 600,000 Kansans live in the Kansas City metropolitan area, which includes Kansas City, Kansas, a meatpacking town with smart suburbs which grew during the 1980s on the back of a services boom. Wichita, on the other hand, is the state's biggest freestanding city, built on wheat and oil. Long the quintessential "flyover city" where planes stopped only to refuel between the east and west coasts, Wichita today is home to three aircraft makers: Beechcraft, Cessna and Learjet.

State facts

Date of statehood	29 January 1861	Total area	82,282 sq miles
Capital	Topeka	Highest point ft	Mt Sunflower 4,039
Other cities	Wichita, Kansas City, Overland Park	Main rivers	Kansas, Missouri, Arkansas

Climate Temperate but continental, with great extremes between summer and winter.

Geography Hilly Osage Plains in the east; central region level prairie and hills; high plains in the west.

Time zone Central

People

			%
Population m	2.52	Under 18	26.9
% av. ann. growth 1980–92	0.5	Over 65	13.9
Pop. per sq mile	30.8	Urban	69.1
Birth rate per 1,000 pop.	15.7	Male	49.0
Death rate per 1,000 pop.	9.0	White	90.1
Pop. below poverty line %	11.5	Hispanic	3.8
Doctors per 100,000 pop.	175	Black	5.8
Hospital beds per 100,000 pop.	611	School spending per head	$5,131

The economy

GSP $m	48,829	Av. income per head $	19,376
No. of new corporations '000	3.9	% of national average	97

Structure of GSP	%		%
Construction	3.6	Manufacturing	18.5
Transportation, public utilities	12.1	Wholesale/retail trade	15.6
Services	15.1	Finance, insurance, real estate	16.3
Government	12.3	Other	6.5

Principal industries Manufacturing, finance, insurance, real estate, services

Main crops Wheat, sorghum, corn, hay, soybeans

Politics

Senate Bob Dole (R; term expires 1999), Nancy Kassebaum (R; term expires 1997)

House Pat Roberts, Jan Meyers (both R); Jim Slattery, Dan Glickman (both D)

State government

Governor Joan Finney (D; term expires 1995)

State Legislature Senate 26R, 14D; House 66R, 59D

State expenditure (1992) $5,512m

KENTUCKY

It is hard to think of a state that has changed less this century than the Bluegrass state. Those activities upon which it depended at the time of the first world war – coal, heavy manufacturing, tobacco, whiskey and thoroughbreds – are predominant today. At the same time, Kentucky's population has grown less than most in recent years; indeed, numbers have risen by less than a third in the past half-century. Even today Kentucky's metropolitan areas, such as Louisville and Lexington, account for less than half of the state's population.

Rural variety

If Kentucky is rural, it is also varied. Like Tennessee, fertile alluvial plains run west to the Mississippi. This area is known as the Purchase since Andrew Jackson forced its sale by the Chickasaw Indians in 1818. The river and the railroad were long its commercial links to the world. In the centre of the state is the rolling bluegrass country for which the state is famous. The region's limestone not only produces lush grass (that flowers blue in late spring); it builds the bones of young racehorses. Here, too, is the famous Kentucky style: a class structure to rival England's and a southern courtesy learnt from the Virginia gentleman.

All this, however, is a far cry from the Appalachian hollows of eastern Kentucky. Mountaineers came here around the turn of the century to build the railroads and work the newly opened coal mines. They were a hardy and violent bunch: it is here that the Hatfield-McCoy family feud took 50 lives over 14 years. Later, during the union strikes of the 1930s, miners were bloodily suppressed. Today, many of the company towns have emptied, the coals seams mined. The region is still poor and backward. Some counties have a murder rate to rival any northern city; signs hang outside bars that order customers to leave their guns outside.

Horsepower

Not that Kentucky is mired in the past. The bloodstock business on the white-fenced farms around Lexington has become as international as any, though the great thoroughbred boom went spectacularly bust in 1985. More importantly for Kentucky's future is the $2 billion Toyota plant at Churchill, just outside Lexington. This is the kind of business Kentucky will do almost anything to lure. And Kentucky is the kind of place that looks aghast at the vandalism that is annually meted out to the Japanese models at the Detroit car show.

State facts

Date of statehood	1 June 1792	Total area	40,411 sq miles
Capital	Frankfort	Highest point ft	Black Mountain
Other cities	Louisville,		4,139
	Lexinton-Fayette, Owensboro	Main rivers	Mississippi, Ohio, Green, Kentucky,Tradewater, Licking

Climate Moderate, with plentiful rainfall.
Geography Mountainous in east; rounded hills of the Knobs in the north; Bluegrass, heart of state; wooded rocky hillsides of the Pennyroyal; Western Coal Field; the fertile Purchase in the south-west.
Time zone Central

People

			%
Population m	3.76	Under 18	25.7
% av. ann. growth 1980–92	0.2	Over 65	12.7
Pop. per sq mile	94.5	Urban	51.8
Birth rate per 1,000 pop.	14.8	Male	48.4
Death rate per 1,000 pop.	9.5	White	92.0
Pop. below poverty line %	19.0	Hispanic	0.6
Doctors per 100,000 pop.	168	Black	7.1
Hospital beds per 100,000 pop.	508	School spending per head	$4,616

The economy

GSP $m	65,858	Av. income per head $	16,354
No. of new corporations '000	6.8	% of national average	82

Structure of GSP	%		%
Construction	5.1	Manufacturing	23.5
Transportation, public utilities	8.9	Wholesale/retail trade	13.8
Services	13.5	Finance, insurance, real estate	15.4
Government	11.7	Other	8.1

Principal industries Manufacturing, coal mining, construction, agriculture
Main crops Tobacco, soybeans, corn

Politics

Senate Wendell H. Ford (D; term expires 1999), Mitch McConnell (R; term expires 1997)
House Tom Barlow, William H. Natcher, Romano L. Mazzoli, Scotty Baesler (all D); Jim Bunning, Harold Rogers (both R)

State government
Governor Brereton Jones (D; term expires 1995)[a]
State Legislature Senate 25D, 13R; House 72D, 28R
Total expenditure (1992) $10,595m

a December.

LOUISIANA

Thirty years ago A.J. Liebling compared Louisiana's population to two tectonic plates that met only under great stress. In the northern hinterland a culture prevails that is anglo, conservative and Protestant in nature. To the south, a Catholic culture with a Latin bent for corruption and lazy authoritarianism. At this culture's heart lies New Orleans, a city of many and mixed races that horrifies Louisiana's north. And it is true that New Orleans still has as much in common with the Latin American societies across the Gulf of Mexico as it does with the rest of America.

Cultural tectonics

These tectonic plates, as Liebling pointed out, mean that politics in Louisiana are matched in complexity only by that of Lebanon, as the two cultures vie for political supremacy. Louisiana's politics is therefore not only volatile; it can swiftly lead to extremism. A case in point was the 1991 governor's race, which a former Ku Klux Klan leader and neo-Nazi, David Duke, came perilously close to winning. The victor was a cajun, Edwin Edwards, the charmingly corrupt epitome of the gambling, womanising pol (and former governor) of which Louisiana has increasingly become ashamed. But as the bumper stickers ran: "Vote for the crook: it's important."

Poor relation

One reason why Louisiana's politics is, by American standards, so undeveloped is that the state's economy is America's most immature. Louisiana lies at the bottom of state income tables because, like a third-world country, exporting raw materials and primary products has always been its staple. Louisiana brings in a quarter of all America's seafood. Its lumber provides half of the country's matches. And the state still grows the staples of the antebellum years – cotton, rice and sugar – that were shipped down the Mississippi in flatboats. New Orleans to this day is one of America's biggest ports: it and Louisiana's other ports ship two-fifths of all American grain exports. Yet this is typical of Louisiana's economy: the shipping adds little value to the raw product, which is where the state's future lies.

Oil matters …

By far the biggest of Louisiana's raw products, though, is oil. It was first discovered in 1901 just across the Texan border, and then along the Louisiana coast west of New

Orleans. Exxon's vast oil refinery dominates the skyline of the state capitol, Baton Rouge. For 60 years Louisiana's fortunes have risen and fallen with those of Big Oil. In the 1930s the political machine of governor Huey Long forced the oil companies to cough up revenues that built the state's public roads and schools. In 1980 oil still made up two-fifths of all state revenues. But with the subsequent collapse in its price, oil accounted for less than a tenth of all revenues just ten years later.

... but less than it did

In 1986, when oil prices were low, Louisiana had the country's highest rate of unemployment. But there are now signs that the state is kicking off its unhealthy dependence upon the black stuff (it is certainly insisting at last that the industry be cleaner.) For instance, Shreveport, a petrochemical town in the state's north-west is attracting more sophisticated manufacturing business, from General Electric among others. And though northern Louisianans may see little of it, tourism now brings in $4 billion in revenues a year. Thanks partly to that, Louisiana was one of the states least affected by the national recession of 1990–91; however, unemployment is above the national average.

Yet, like an attractive third-world country, tourism will long remain an important part of the economy: and with good reason, for Louisiana is one of America's most attractive and fascinating states with its mix of musics, its French Cajun culture and language to the west of New Orleans, and with great New Orleans itself.

Preservation row

New Orleans was acquired by the United States in 1803 as part of the Louisiana Purchase (the dubious legality of which was overlooked by Jefferson in the country's dealings with Napoleon). But French and Spanish influence is still strong, particularly in the cuisine and in the city's heart, the French Quarter (which architecturally would better be called Spanish). Not that American influence is not clear: in the 19th and early 20th centuries Americans built the pretty Garden District after their own fashion. The plantation houses along the Mississippi for many miles to the north speak clearest of American – and slave – achievement. Their neo-classical grandeur in those days would of course have been quite deflated by the slave hovels, now gone, that once clustered around the master's house.

State facts

Date of statehood	30 April 1812	Total area	51,843 sq miles
Capital	Baton Rouge	Highest point ft	Driskill Mountain
Other cities	New Orleans,		535
	Shreveport, Lafayette	Main rivers	Mississippi, Red,
			Pearl, Sabine

Climate Sub-tropical, affected by continental weather patterns.
Geography Lowlands of marshes on Mississippi river flood plain; Red river valley lowlands; upland hills in the Florida Parishes; average elevation, 100 ft.
Time zone Central

People

			%
Population m	4.28	Under 18	28.9
% av. ann. growth 1980–92	0.2	Over 65	11.2
Pop. per sq mile	98.4	Urban	68.1
Birth rate per 1,000 pop.	17.1	Male	48.1
Death rate per 1,000 pop.	9.0	White	67.3
Pop. below poverty line %	23.6	Hispanic	2.2
Doctors per 100,000 pop.	188	Black	30.8
Hospital beds per 100,000 pop.	556	School spending per head	$4,378

The economy

GSP $m	79,138	Av. income per head $	15,712
No. of new corporations '000	9.0	% of national average	79

Structure of GSP	%		%
Construction	4.8	Manufacturing	15.7
Transportation, public utilities	11.3	Wholesale/retail trade	13.9
Services	15.4	Finance, insurance, real estate	15.2
Government	8.7	Other	15.0

Principal industries Wholesale and retail trade, government, manufacturing, construction, transportation, mining
Main crops Soybeans, sugar cane, rice, corn, cotton, sweet potatoes, pecans, sorghum

Politics

Senate J. Bennett Johnston (D; term expires 1997); John Breaux (D; term expires 1999)
House William Jefferson, Billy Tauzin, Cleo Fields, James A. Hayes (all D); R.L. Livingston Jr, Jim McCrery, Richard H. Baker (all R)

State government
Governor Edwin Edwards (D; term expires 1996)[a]
State Legislature Senate 34D, 5R; House 88D, 16R, 1 Ind
Total expenditure (1992) $12,741m

a March.

MAINE

Maine is the first place in the United States to see the dawn. The state is the most north-easterly and it borders more Canadian provinces than it does other American states; it has a sense of being at the edge of the United States.

Indeed, the laconic Mainers like to think of themselves as apart from their fellow Americans, a rugged, taciturn and self-reliant people, fit for a state, which as the local joke has it, has only two seasons: July and winter. They are indeed a rare breed. Though their state, at 33,200 square miles, is larger than the other New England states combined, it is less populous than any of them. Six-sevenths of Maine remains virtual wilderness. Its vast white pine forests, wild rivers and lakes and pink-granite mountains are more pristine than any east of the Mississippi.

Lobsters and lighthouses

Successive tribes of Indians hunted and fished along Maine's coast for at least 10,000 years. The English laid claim to the area by dint of John Cabot's visit in 1497 but both English and French subsequently founded settlements. The territorial dispute was not resolved until the French lost most of their North American holdings after 1763 following the French and Indian wars. Maine became part of colonial Massachusetts, only gaining its own statehood in 1820.

Though the early European explorers thought little of it, Maine's coast is today the state's social and economic mainspring. From the sandy and touristy beaches of York county in the south to the Canadian border is only 330 miles as a crow flies but the mostly rocky shoreline measures 3,500 miles. These are treacherous waters; there are 64 lighthouses to warn of shoals and reefs and to guide sailors to the sheltered harbours such as Bar Harbor. However, they provide much fishing, particularly of cod and Maine lobster, and they attract the millions of visitors that make tourism the state's second largest industry after manufacturing.

What goes up ...

Maine thrived on New England's property-cum-high tech boom in the 1980s. The economy doubled in size. The state enjoyed the third fastest per head growth in income in the nation. It rose from being the seventh poorest state to twenty-fifth richest. When the boom turned sour, Maine's economy went into its longest and severest recession in more than two decades. The state lost one job in sixteen. Employment was hardest hit in construction, manufacturing and the building-related retail trades. Federal defence cuts added a further 12% to the unemployment rolls.

Though the property overhang will last well into the 1990s and defence-related employment seems likely to keep shrinking, the common complaints of all New England states, Maine began to pull slowly out of recession in 1992. Canadians shopped more frequently in Maine to escape new goods and services taxes imposed in Canada in 1991. Tourism picked up as recession waned nationally and elsewhere in New England. Aquaculture, both off-shore fishing and salmon farms, thrived. Manufacturing, though employing fewer, had become more productive, especially the state's huge pulp and paper industry.

A beneficial legacy of the 1980s boom was that Maine's previously languid and low-wage commodity economy had become a more diversified and capital intensive middle-income one. This helped form new manufacturing industries and revitalise traditional ones such as metals, machinery and electronics. It also helped expand service industries, especially in communications, finance and professional and legal services. Ties to the international economy also increased, creating export markets for Maine's leather, electronics, forest products and machinery.

Productivity imperative

These changes have, though, heightened the challenge to Maine's restructured economy to be competitive. Though improving fast, absolute productivity levels in Maine remain well below the national average. Worryingly, much of manufacturing's productivity growth of the early 1990s came from one-off shrinking of businesses. Investment in new plant and equipment remains at below the national average, and is not closing the gap. Without more investment in capital equipment to produce technologically-driven productivity gains, Maine's manufacturers will be hard pressed to sustain competitive productivity gains into the future. The outlook is even more bleak in the service sector, where productivity is actually declining.

Maine must also get its public and social infrastructure to catch up with the new shape of its economy. The fiscal squeeze caused by the recession has hurt public reinvestment in communications and transport. The state has been slow to reform primary and secondary schooling and its universities to prepare students for an information-based economy, despite increasing its spending on education dramatically in recent years. But its budget remains a mess.

State facts

Date of statehood	15 March 1820	Total area	35,387 sq miles
Capital	Augusta	Highest point ft	Mt Katahdin 5,267
Other cities	Portland, Lewiston, Bangor	Main rivers	Androscoggin, Saco, Kennebee, Penobscot

Climate Southern interior and coastal, influenced by air masses from the south and west; northern clime harsher, average 100+ in snow in winter.
Geography Appalachian Mountains extend through state; western borders have rugged terrain; long sand beaches on southern coast; northern coast mainly rocky promontories, peninsulas, fjords.
Time zone Eastern Standard

People

			%
Population m	1.24	Under 18	24.8
% av. ann. growth 1980–92	0.8	Over 65	13.6
Pop. per sq mile	40.0	Urban	44.6
Birth rate per 1,000 pop.	14.1	Male	49.0
Death rate per 1,000 pop.	8.9	White	98.4
Pop. below poverty line %	10.8	Hispanic	0.6
Doctors per 100,000 pop.	178	Black	0.4
Hospital beds per 100,000 pop.	484	School spending per head	$5,969

The economy

GSP $m	23,474	Av. income per head $	18,226
No. of new corporations '000	2.3	% of national average	92

Structure of GSP	%		%
Construction	7.4	Manufacturing	19.3
Transportation, public utilities	8.1	Wholesale/retail trade	16.7
Services	16.5	Finance, insurance, real estate	17.0
Government	12.1	Other	2.9

Principal industries Manufacturing, services, trade, government, finance, insurance, real estate, construction
Main crops Potatoes, apples, hay, blueberries

Politics

Senate William Cohen (R; term expires 1997), George Mitchell (D; term expires 1995)
House Thomas Andrews (D); Olympia J. Snowe (R)

State government
Governor John R. McKernan Jr (R; term expires 1995)
State Legislature Senate 20D, 15R; House 90D, 61R
Total expenditure (1992) $3,152m

MARYLAND

Maryland's reputation for religious tolerance was not fortuitous: the colony's owner at its founding in 1634 was Lord Baltimore, a Catholic whose heirs depended upon Protestant kings for their title. By the end of the century, however, Protestants easily outnumbered Catholics. Even so, a tradition of tolerance means that Maryland today differs from the New England states to the north with their streak of puritanism, and from the states to the south (which Maryland uneasily joined in the war between the states) with their racial segregation and more rigid social castes. Maryland, with abundant natural produce such as oysters, crabs, corn and fruit, is more at ease with itself than many other nearby states.

An easy tolerance also has its raucous side. During Prohibition, drink ran freely in Baltimore (pronounced "Bawlmer" by the blue-collar Catholics in this still-great port city on the Chesapeake Bay). To this day, local politics in the state has a colourfully raw feel to it. In taking bribes as Richard Nixon's vice president, Spiro Agnew was merely extending best practice when Maryland's governor.

There she grows

Political colour, though, disguises what has really happened in Maryland over the past decade, which is a tale of extraordinary economic growth. That growth came not from downtown Baltimore, whose prominence has ebbed this past half-century: fewer than a fifth of Marylanders live in Baltimore compared with one-half before the second world war. Nor has has it come from federal-induced employment out of Washington, DC. In fact, between 1980 and 1987, the number of government jobs in the Washington and Baltimore area fell by over 20,000, a decline of 12%. Meanwhile, the number of service-sector jobs leapt by nearly 300,000, a 38% rise. The state's population – four-fifths of whom live around Washington and Baltimore – leapt by 12.5% between 1980 and 1990.

Clever links with Washington

There are a number of reasons for this growth. Though federal government has been trying to shrink, it still acts as a magnet for talent, particularly in the research fields. There are, for instance, more than 120 federal laboratories in the region. As a result, what is increasingly coming to be known by the ugly title of the Washington-Baltimore Metropolis boasts the highest concentration of college graduates, scientists and engineers in the country. Moreover, the revolving door between government and private enterprise keeps turning. New biotech firms and high-tech companies in electronics and aviation, among other fields, have sprouted in the so-called edge cities around Baltimore and Washington. Median household spendable income, at $39,400, is way above national levels.

On the road again

It is not just in the services and high-tech fields that Maryland has thrived. Baltimore, the epitome of an industrial, seabord port of the 19th and early 20th centuries, is once again reinventing itself as a manufacturing centre. The General Motors plant that produces minivans just outside the city is reckoned to be one of the country's most productive auto plants. And if America regains some pre-eminence as a car manufacturer (which seems now seems possible thanks to a decade of Japanese investment and competition), Baltimore is well-placed to benefit. As it is, the port is the largest importer and exporter of cars and light trucks.

The changed and the changeless

Growth has not been without a downside. The spread of hideous "exurbs" has defaced what a few decades ago was attractive (and productive) farmland. The Rockville Pike, an eight-lane highway that leads northwards out of Washington, has few rivals in its unbridled and uninspired commercial and residential development. Commuters have pushed up to the Pennsylvania border in the north and into Maryland's hilly and still wild panhandle to the west. And there now is little left of the country between Washington and Baltimore. These two urban areas have, to all intents, merged (in turn, forming a near-seamless "corridor" north all the way beyond New York). It is just a matter of time before their administrative units of government merge too.

For all that, much remains in the state that has changed little. The view from the sea of Annapolis, the state capital and the only one also to have served as the national capital before Washington was built, would still be recognisable to an 18th-century sailor. And many of the towns on the Eastern Shore, that fertile peninsula between the gunkholes and creeks of the Chesapeake Bay and the dunes of the Atlantic, have fewer links with the outside world than they did in the days of maritime trade with England and the West Indies.

State facts

Date of statehood	28 April 1788	Total area	12,407 sq miles
Capital	Annapolis	Highest point ft	Backbone
Other cities	Baltimore, Rockville,		Mountain 3,360
	Frederick	Main rivers	Potomac,
			Susquehanna

Climate Continental in the west; humid sub-tropical in the east.
Geography Eastern Shore of coastal plain and Maryland Main of coastal plain.
Time zone Eastern Standard

People

			%
Population m	4.91	Under 18	25.0
% av. ann. growth 1980–92	1.3	Over 65	11.0
Pop. per sq mile	502.1	Urban	81.3
Birth rate per 1,000 pop.	16.8	Male	48.5
Death rate per 1,000 pop.	7.8	White	71.0
Pop. below poverty line %	8.3	Hispanic	2.6
Doctors per 100,000 pop.	334	Black	24.9
Hospital beds per 100,000 pop.	405	School spending per head	$6,273

The economy

GSP $m	99,074	Av. income per head $	22,974
No. of new corporations '000	16.5	% of national average	116

Structure of GSP	%		%
Construction	6.3	Manufacturing	10.6
Transportation, public utilities	8.6	Wholesale/retail trade	17.6
Services	21.9	Finance, insurance, real estate	17.0
Government	16.7	Other	1.3

Principal industries Manufacturing, tourism
Main crops Corn, soybeans, greenhouse and nursery products

Politics

Senate Paul Sarbanes (D; term expires 1995), Barbara Mikulski (D; term expires 1999)
House Wayne Gilchrest, Helen Delich Bentley, Roscoe Bartlett, Connie Morella (all R); Benjamin L. Cardin, Albert Wynn, Steny H. Hoyer, Kweisi Mfume (all D)

State government
Governor William Schaefer (D; term expires 1995)
State Legislature Senate 38D, 9R; House 116D, 25R
Total expenditure (1992) $12,133m

MASSACHUSETTS

Massachusetts is old New England. No other state packs so much American history into such a small area. Ten years after the Pilgrim Fathers had disembarked at Plymouth Rock in 1620, John Winthrop and his fellow Puritans founded Boston a few miles up the Atlantic coast at the mouth of the Charles river. Though themselves fleeing persecution in Europe, the New World Puritans were intolerant of other religions. Many of New England's leading towns were founded by free-thinkers escaping the increasing fanaticism and persecution of the growing Massachusetts Bay colony.

It was not until the next century that Massachusetts shed its rigid Puritanism to emerge as the region's mercantile centre. Boston ships carried New England's lumber and fish to the world. British taxation of this thriving trade led ultimately to the American colonies' fight for independence, triggered by the Boston Tea Party protest against taxation without representation in 1773.

Oliver Wendell Holmes said of his native Boston that it was "the thinking centre of the Continent". Massachusetts is proud of its intellectual tradition nurtured at its great universities such as Harvard, founded as early as 1636. The state has shaped America's ideas of democracy, from the revolutionary ideals of liberty of Samuel Adams and John Hancock through the 19th-century advocates of individual expression such as Emerson and Thoreau and the leaders of the social reform movements of the late 1800s to the black civil rights leaders of the 1960s. "Massachusetts Liberal" and "Kennedy Democrat" have become Republican terms of abuse.

The state packs a lot of geography as well as history into its 8,284 square miles. Towards the New York border to the west, dairy farms nestle between the wooded Berkshire hills and the Taconic and Hoosac mountains. The broad Connecticut river flows north-south through the centre of the state, providing rich tobacco-growing soil. The rocky Atlantic coastline sweeps in to shelter Cape Cod Bay, then out again to form the sandy hook of Cape Cod. Further south are the islands of Martha's Vineyard and Nantucket.

Prosperous beginnings

Massachusetts's early prosperity came from the sea: fishing, whaling, and trading with Africa, China and the Indies. A "codfish aristocracy" was gradually supplanted by the Boston Brahmin, elite families such as the Lowells, the Cabots and the Lodges, who made their fortunes in the first half of the 19th century from banking, textiles, shipping and railways as an industrial market economy took hold.

Yankee industrialisation and ingenuity had brought factories and new products, but textiles and shoe-making became Massachusetts's leading industries. America's first successful textile mill was built at Lowell. This spawned a succession of drab industrial company towns, which provided jobs for the waves of mostly unskilled Irish, Italian and East European immigrants pouring in to the state from the middle of the 19th century.

Long decline, short miracle

Yet that marked the economy's high-water mark for almost 100 years. By the beginning of the 20th century, the textile mills and shoe factories had gone south for cheaper wages and lower taxes, Boston had been surpassed by New York as a port and by Chicago as an industrial centre. The decline continued until the 1960s.

It was reversed by the advent of the information age. The universities, which had always been an asset, now became an industrial advantage as well. Graduates of institutions such as Harvard and the Massachusetts Institute of Technology started high-tech computer, bio-medical and electronics companies in droves. Many were along State Highway 128, which skirts Boston. Route 128 became Silicon Valley East (though not as successful as Silicon Valley itself), and headquarters to such minicomputer-makers as Digital Equipment, Wang Laboratories and Prime Computer.

The 1980s saw a dramatic boom in the Massachusetts economy. At first blush it looked as if high-tech had transformed the state's dying industrial base, which again accounted for one in five jobs. Defence contractors thrived on the growth in federal defence contracts. Along with a boom in financial services (Boston has always been a centre of money management), this was all part of the "Massachusetts miracle" on which the state's governor, Michael Dukakis, launched his 1988 bid for the White House.

Like the Dukakis campaign, the Massachusetts miracle evaporated. In the economy's case, it was because the transformation of Massachusetts industry had not been as complete as it seemed. The heart of the boom had been construction, not high-tech. New homes and offices were being built at way beyond the rate population growth could support. When the over-heated property and banking markets went bust in the late 1980s, Massachusetts's economy took a nosedive.

The state went from the leading edge of the national economy to the bleeding edge. As one job in nine disappeared, the unemployment rate soared from well below average to well above.

Massachusetts was left in a fiscal mess, and with the second worst bond rating of any state (since dramatically upgraded). The other half of the miracle had been the rapid expansion of state spending on social programmes such as day-care, worker-training and the now infamous clean-up of Boston harbour. There was money for all this because of the soaring tax revenue that the boom was generating. Sales-tax revenue alone doubled between 1983 and 1988. When the slump came, revenue dried up but spending could not be turned off as rapidly. When cuts did come, they were painfully deep.

Down but not out

The challenge to Massachusetts is to ride out its recession. The overbuilding of the 1980s has to be absorbed and surviving banks have to start lending again. That takes time. Parts of the high-tech business base have to complete their restructuring, particularly the minicomputer-makers, who missed the switch in computing to desktop machines. Like textiles before it, making computer hardware is a business which has gone to the southern states and East Asia for good. Massachusetts's future in computing lies in software.

The high costs of doing business in the state must also be reduced. The property bust has deflated rents and house prices, just as rising unemployment has checked a rise in personal incomes which took Massachusetts residents from earning the national average to 20% above it in the 1980s. But the state remains well above the national average for taxes, utility rates and health-care costs. State finances, slowly being shepherded into order, have to be kept there.

Once recession is past, Massachusetts's future looks bright again. It possess the raw materials for the 21st century. It has a well-educated workforce: more than one in four workers have a degree. And the state is of world quality in graduate education and medical research. Boston has the venture capital firms to put bricks and mortar round the marketable ideas generated. The state is already home to more than 100 leading bio-tech and health-care companies. Massachusetts should be the economic leader of the new New England, too.

State facts

Date of statehood	6 February 1788	Total area	10,555 sq miles
Capital	Boston	Highest point ft	Mt Greylock 3,487
Other cities	Worcester,	Main rivers	Connecticut,
	Springfield, Lowell		Merrimack, Taunton

Climate Temperate with cold winters; colder and drier climate in west.
Geography Jagged indented coast from Rhode Island around Cape Cod; flat land yields to stony upland pastures near central region and gentle hilly country in west; except in west, land is rocky, sandy and not fertile.
Time zone Eastern Standard

People

			%
Population m	6.00	Under 18	23.1
% av. ann. growth 1980–92	0.4	Over 65	13.9
Pop. per sq mile	765.3	Urban	84.3
Birth rate per 1,000 pop.	15.4	Male	48.0
Death rate per 1,000 pop.	8.6	White	89.8
Pop. below poverty line %	8.9	Hispanic	4.8
Doctors per 100,000 pop.	337	Black	5.0
Hospital beds per 100,000 pop.	532	School spending per head	$6,323

The economy

GSP $m	144,791	Av. income per head $	24,059
No. of new corporations '000	11.7	% of national average	121

Structure of GSP	%		%
Construction	5.2	Manufacturing	18.7
Transportation, public utilities	7.0	Wholesale/retail trade	17.0
Services	25.1	Finance, insurance, real estate	16.8
Government	9.3	Other	0.9

Principal industries Services, trade, manufacturing
Main crops Cranberries, greenhouse, nursery, vegetables

Politics

Senate Edward Kennedy (D; term expires 1995), John Kerry (D; term expires 1997)
House John Olver, Richard E. Neal, Barney Frank, Martin Meehan, Edward J. Markey, Joseph P. Kennedy II, Joe Moakley, Gerry E. Studds (all D); Peter Blute, Peter Torkildsen (both R)

State government
Governor William F. Weld (R; term expires 1995)
State Legislature Senate 31D, 9R; House 124D, 35R, 1 Ind
Total expenditure (1992) $20,380m

MICHIGAN

Michigan's residents build more vehicles and own more boats than any other Americans. Detroit may be the ugly side of American industry but Michigan has some of the most beautiful boating in the country. From hydroplanes on the Detroit river to sailboats on one of the four Great Lakes that wash the state's shoreline (the longest of any state except Alaska), Michigan is the recreational-boating and fishing capital of America as well as home of its motor industry.

The Wolverine state comprises some 58,500 square miles spread over two peninsulas separated by the Straits of Mackinac. The straits link Lake Huron and Lake Michigan. Since 1958 they have been spanned by one of the world's longest suspension bridges. The scantily populated and unspoilt Upper Peninsula rises westward to the rugged ore-bearing Gogebic mountains near the Wisconsin border from the Sault Sainte Marie Canals which connect Lake Huron and Lake Superior.

The Lower Peninsula, with Lake Michigan to the west and Lake Huron to the east, is hilly tableland in the north giving way to rolling hills in the south towards Lake Erie and the Ohio and Indiana borders. The Lower Peninsula is rich in summer resorts but also contains the main cities: Detroit and neighbouring Warren, Livonia, Westland and Dearborn (home of Ford), the state capital Lansing, Grand Rapids, Flint and Ann Arbor.

A French settlement was established at Saulte Sainte Marie by 1668. Antoine Cadillac founded Detroit in 1701. The area passed to Britain after the French and Indian war in 1763, and thence to the United States 20 years later after the Revolutionary war. Michigan saw constant skirmishing between American and British forces and their Indian allies up to the war of 1812 during which the British retook Detroit. They were driven out the following year when William Harrison led his American troops into Canada following the American naval victory at the Battle of Lake Erie. Michigan gained statehood in 1837. Lansing was made state capital ten years later.

Auto dependence

The shape of the Michigan economy was set in 1899 when Ranson Olds set up the first car plant in Detroit. Nine years later Henry Ford started to produce the Model T there. General Motors was founded the same year. The fortunes of Michigan's economy have risen with those of Detroit and in the 1980s fell with them too. The state is not only the headquarters of the Big Three motor manufacturers, GM, Ford and Chrysler, but also has an extensive network of suppliers, sub-assemblers and R&D facilities owned by Japanese and European car makers as well as the American ones.

Like other mid-western states, Michigan was severely hit by the recession of the early 1980s, which exposed the car industry's lack of competitiveness, especially in comparison with its Japanese rival. The state lost 360,000 jobs – almost one in ten – between 1979 and 1982, when the unemployment rate hit 15%, a level not seen since the Great Depression. Despite creating new jobs more slowly than the nation as a whole, Michigan has since recovered those jobs and more – but not in manufacturing.

Diversifying

Over the past decade, all the net employment growth was in retailing and wholesaling and in services, particularly business services, health services and finance. Manufacturing, services, and the wholesale and retail trades now account equally for 24% of employment. Ten years ago almost one job in three was in manufacturing, fewer than one in five in trade and one in seven in services.

This diversification of the economy, though, masks the change in manufacturing, which still drives the state, accounting for just over one-quarter of output. The thrust of the state's economic revitalisation programme in the 1980s was to regenerate better basic manufacturing jobs rather than to establish new high-tech industries as did Massachusetts. Michigan's Route 128 was Automation Alley.

The loss of more than 100,000 high-paying motor industry jobs since the end of the 1970s means that the state is 35% less dependent on the Big Three motor manufacturers for employment than it was then. However, Michigan is still the leading state in motor industry output and the industry accounts for approaching 300,000 manufacturing jobs, almost one in three. Most of the employment is in small and medium sized parts suppliers..

So closely are Michigan and the motor industry linked that it is easy to imagine that the state makes nothing else. Yet it is in the top ten in the country for production of machinery, textiles, furniture, and rubber and plastics. There are also large food processing, pharmaceuticals and chemicals industries. Michigan is the second largest producer of iron ore and is a significant copper mining state. Its crops (cereals and fruit and vegetables) are worth as much as the output of its electronics firms. Tourism revenue has also been increasing steadily.

In better shape

The restructuring of the Michigan economy has undoubtedly and necessarily pushed down firms' cost base, particularly outside the highly-unionised Big Three car makers. Allied to the third largest investment in new plant and equipment in the 1980s after Texas and California, this has made Michigan companies, including even the car makers, more productive. Real income in the state grew only two-thirds as fast in the 1980s as did that for all Americans. Earnings per worker have fallen from 20% above the national average in 1979 to just 9% above it by last year, about average for an industrial state.

This has helped the broadening of Michigan's manufacturing base as has the state's research facilities for advanced industrial production, arguably the most extensive in America. Michigan consistently ranks in the top three for industrial R&D spending. Michigan's state university system, based on the University of Michigan in Ann Arbor and Michigan State University in East Lansing is reckoned to be second only to California's.

Detroit and other challenges

The challenges for Michigan remains to increase the state's manufacturing productivity by lowering relative costs and increasing investment in technology. It also has to decrease its dependence on motor industry employment even further. Michigan needs to retrain the younger part of its workforce with new manufacturing skills and to sustain the creation of labour-absorbing service jobs.

Michigan faces two social problems. One is renewing Detroit, whose centre has been decimated by white and black middle-class flight to the suburbs, and which has not seen the sort of regeneration that, say, Cleveland has achieved. When Detroit's recorded population fell below 1m, as it did in the 1990 census, it risked losing all sorts of federal aid.

The other issue is the state's budget. Keeping a lid on business taxes during recession in a state which has traditionally been able to afford a big-spending government has created a budget crisis for Michigan. Unlike most other states, Michigan is attempting to solve that by spending cuts alone. The pioneering cutting of social services by Michigan's Republican governor, John Engler, is being closely watched by other cash-short state governors.

State facts

Date of statehood	26 January 1837	Total area	96,705 sq miles
Capital	Lansing	Highest point ft	Mt Avron 1,979
Other cities	Detroit, Grand Rapids, Warren	Main rivers	Grand

Climate Well-defined seasons tempered by the Great Lakes.
Geography Low rolling hills give way to northern tableland of hilly belts in Lower Peninsula; Upper Peninsula is level in the east, with swampy areas; western region is higher and more rugged.
Time zone Eastern Standard

People

			%
Population m	9.44	Under 18	26.6
% av. ann. growth 1980–92	4.2	Over 65	12.2
Pop. per sq mile	166.1	Urban	70.5
Birth rate per 1,000 pop.	16.5	Male	48.5
Death rate per 1,000 pop.	8.5	White	83.4
Pop. below poverty line %	13.1	Hispanic	2.2
Doctors per 100,000 pop.	185	Black	13.9
Hospital beds per 100,000 pop.	418	School spending per head	$5,630

The economy

GSP $m	181,827	Av. income per head $	19,508
No. of new corporations '000	20.1	% of national average	98

Structure of GSP	%		%
Construction	3.8	Manufacturing	27.4
Transportation, public utilities	7.3	Wholesale/retail trade	15.6
Services	17.2	Finance, insurance, real estate	16.8
Government	10.0	Other	1.9

Principal industries Manufacturing, services, tourism, agriculture, mining
Main crops Corn, winter wheat, soybeans, dry beans, oats, hay, sugar beets, honey, asparagus, sweetcorn, apples, cherries, grapes, peaches, blueberries, flowers

Politics

Senate Donald Riegle Jr (D; term expires 1995), Carl Levin (D; term expires 1997)
House Bart Stupak, James Barcia, Dale Kildee, David Bonior, Sander Levin, William Ford, John Conyers Jr, Barbara-Rose Collins, John Dingell, Bob Carr (all D); Peter Hoekstra, Paul Henry, Dave Camp, Fred Upton, Nick Smith, Joseph Knollenberg (all R)

State government
Governor John Engler (R; term expires 1995)
State Legislature Senate 20R, 18D; House 55R, 55D
Total expenditure (1992) $19,914m

MINNESOTA

Minnesota is the trade and cultural heart of the central Snow Belt and home to a political liberalism that in American terms verges on the socialistic. It draws deeply on the social democratic traditions of Germany and Scandinavia, with which many of its inhabitants have family ties, and is best exemplified by the state's favourite political son, the Democratic politician, the late Hubert Humphrey. Minnesota's capital St Paul and its twin city of Minneapolis are among the nicest cities of America to live in, despite the long winters, in large part because of their excellent social services.

The North Star state is an assembled state. The part east of the Mississippi, whose source is Lake Itasca in northern Minnesota, was acquired by the United States from Britain after the Revolutionary war. The part west of the Mississippi was bought from France as part of the Louisiana Purchase of 1803. The northern strip bordering Canada was ceded by Britain in 1818. Statehood was achieved in 1858, shortly before a bloody uprising by the Sioux, who were subsequently driven from the state.

Minnesota is a Dakota Indian word meaning sky-tinted water, and not for nothing does the state also call itself the Land of 10,000 Lakes, though that undercounts them by one-third. Almost 5% of the state's 84,000 square miles is water, and its hilly central lakes region covers half the state. Minnesota's eastern border is Lake Superior and Wisconsin. To the north is Canada, to the west the Dakotas. To the south are the fertile plains of Iowa.

Rich and varied

Minnesota is rich in natural resources, farmland and *Fortune 500* companies, and has the further good fortune to be the economic centre of the upper Mid-West, which has been the healthiest part of the American economy in recent years. A well educated and hard working labour force makes the most of this.

The state produces 75% of America's iron ore, which is extracted from the Vermillion and Mesabi mountains in the north-east. Its farmers lead the nation in sugar beet production and rank highly in yields of wheat, corn, barley soybean, peas, potatoes and sunflower seeds. Minnesota is a leading hog state and also a big dairy one, being one of the largest producers of eggs, butter, milk and cheese.

Food processing is the largest sector of manufacturing, which accounts for one-fifth of the economy's output. With 17,000 acres of red pine, maple, oak and aspen forest, the state also has a large forest products industry, too. It is a leader in printing and paper products. St Paul produces more law books and calendars than anywhere else in North America.

The rest of Minnesota's manufacturing base is well diversified: machinery, chemicals, electric and electronic equipment, instrument-making and fabricated metal products. Health care is one of the state's largest employers. Cray Computer, the world's leading supercomputer maker, is based in the state as is General Mills, America's largest grain distributor, and the 3M company (one of the Ms stands for Minnesota). In the early 1990s nearly 20 *Fortune 500* companies were based in Minnesota.

Distribution and other attractions

Minnesota's location has made Minneapolis-St Paul America's third biggest haulage centre and Duluth, on Lake Superior, which was connected to the Atlantic with the opening of the St Lawrence seaway in 1959, America's busiest inland harbour. America's biggest shopping mall is at Bloomington, just south of the twin cities. Minnesota hopes that the 78-acre mall, which opened in 1992, will be an addition to its list of tourist attractions. Fifty Japanese tour groups were scheduled to come in its first year.

Tourism is already a leading dollar-earner for the state. Visitors come to the Twin Cities for the arts, then travel upstate for the fishing, hunting, water or winter sports, depending on the season. Summer visitors who stay in Minneapolis may catch the Minnesota Twins baseball team, which won the World Series in 1987 and 1991.

Holding on to the high life

The challenge for Minnesota is to hold on to the businesses that have brought it its prosperity. The neighbouring states of Wisconsin, Iowa and the Dakotas are wooing firms with the promises of lower costs. Minnesota is a good place to start a business, providing access to venture capital and a supportive state; but established businesses find that corporate income and business property taxes and workers' compensation insurance are among the highest in America. Minnesota believes in big government and needs revenue to spend on environmentalism and broad-based health insurance. However it has been the good public services and the quality of life which have attracted or retained the talent that has created the state's high value-added employment.

State facts

Date of statehood	11 May 1858	Total area	86,943 sq miles
Capital	St Paul	Highest point ft	Eagle Mountain
Other cities	Minneapolis,		2,301
	Bloomington, Duluth	Main rivers	Mississippi, St Croix,
			Red, Minnesota

Climate Northern part of the state lies in the moist Great Lakes storm belt; the western border lies at the edge of the semi-arid Great Plains.

Geography Central hills and lakes over half area; to the north-east, rocky ridges and lakes; to the north-west, flat plain; rolling plains and river valleys to the south.

Time zone Central

People

			%
Population m	4.48	Under 18	26.9
% av. ann. growth 1980–92	0.8	Over 65	12.5
Pop. per sq mile	56.3	Urban	69.9
Birth rate per 1,000 pop.	15.5	Male	49.0
Death rate per 1,000 pop.	8.0	White	94.4
Pop. below poverty line %	10.2	Hispanic	1.2
Doctors per 100,000 pop.	220	Black	2.2
Hospital beds per 100,000 pop.	533	School spending per head	$5,510

The economy

GSP $m	93,559	Av. income per head $	20,049
No. of new corporations '000	9.6	% of national average	101

Structure of GSP	%		%
Construction	8.7	Manufacturing	21.1
Transportation, public utilities	8.8	Wholesale/retail trade	16.6
Services	15.4	Finance, insurance, real estate	18.4
Government	9.7	Other	1.3

Principal industries Agri-business, forest products, mining, manufacturing, tourism

Main crops Corn, soybeans, wheat, sugar beets, sunflowers, barley

Politics

Senate David Durenberger (R; term expires 1995), Paul David Wellstone (D; term expires 1997)

House Tim Penny, Bruce Vento, Martin Sabo, James Oberstar, Colin Peterson, David Minge (all D); Jim Ramstad, Rod Grams (both R)

State government
Governor Arne Carlson (R; term expires 1995)
State Legislature Senate 45D, 22R; House 87D, 47R
Total expenditure (1992) $12,178m

MISSISSIPPI

Poor Mississippi ranks last of all the American states in health, literacy and income per head. This is not for want of trying. Gone are the days of sharecropping, a condition scarcely better than the slavery which preceded it. Gone, too, is the violently enforced racial segregation of 30 years ago at work, in social relations and at the ballot box. Today, Mississippi's politics is hearteningly bi-racial: many whites are increasingly willing to vote for black politicians.

Despite this, income per head is a mere 70% of the national average (an improvement, admittedly, on the 36% in 1940). One-third of Mississippi's adults cannot read. And more than half of those students who enter higher education then drop out. Most of these problems are concentrated among the 36% of the state's population that is black. Yet only a small proportion of whites would consider themselves comfortably off.

King Cotton

The irony about the state's most intense poverty is that it sits upon some of America's most fertile land. Mississippi is ribboned by rivers that water lush soils and green forests on their way to the Gulf coast. The antebellum houses, many now in ruins, stand as testimony to the land's productive powers. When cotton was king, between 1830 and 1860, Mississippi must have been a truly extraordinary realm. Natchez on the bluffs of the Mississippi is still an astounding place, home to the country's biggest collection of Greek Revival houses. Before the Civil War, Natchez boasted hundreds of freed slaves, and was confident enough to oppose secession.

After slavery, sharecropping

After the Civil War, rigid social and racial castes mired Mississippians in poverty and nostalgia. The huge enterprise of draining the flooded crescent of the Mississippi Delta might conceivably have provided a better life for the state's rural poor. Yet the hard-nosed landowners who planted cotton on this wide plain with topsoil 50 feet deep enforced the cheap system of sharecropping that in its brutality was not much different from slavery.

Sharecropping was rendered redundant after the first mechanical cotton picker was demonstrated in 1944 in a field just outside the Delta town of Clarksdale. The number of sharecroppers has since fallen by 98%, and this more than anything drove the great black migration into the northern cities of St Louis, Chicago and Detroit. The proportion of blacks in Mississippi has fallen from one-half in the 1940s to just over one-third today, where it has steadied.

No boom here

During the 1980s, though, Mississippi failed to create the kinds of new jobs that other states enjoyed. The state is far removed from the south's two great boom areas of Atlanta and Dallas-Fort Worth. Even growth in Memphis barely spread into Mississippi. Between 1980 and 1987 Mississippi created just 44,000 trade, finance and services jobs; it lost 8,000 manufacturing and construction jobs. Part of the problem is that over half of the state's employment depends upon agribusiness. And not enough value is added by jobs in Mississippi to the state's abundant produce before it is shipped out of state. Catfish farming once seemed to point to the way of the future: this new industry employed 3,000 people breeding, filleting and package the fish. Yet now the industry is troubled by the strains of hasty overproduction.

Bright spots and blues

Not everything about Mississippi's economy is glum news. Jackson, the state capital, has grown into a town of 200,000. It boasts prosperous suburbs, even if the southern side of town is still poor and black. Clarksdale is a mecca for lovers of America's greatest folk music, the blues (it was here that both Muddy Waters and Howlin' Wolf lived before they headed like so many for Chicago). And Tupelo, in the state's north-east, has become a magnet for furniture factories, partly because of the diligence of the town's civic leaders in providing space and workers who are better educated than in most of the state.

Race brake

In Tupelo it took a tornado that flattened the town several decades ago to convince the region's leaders, both black and white, on a common purpose. Some cyclonic equivalent may be needed for the same to happen in much of the rest of the state. For caste, in the form of race, is still the predominant brake upon prosperity. Nowhere has the issue become more polarised than in the matter of taxation. Two-thirds of the state budget goes towards public education, yet almost all whites send their children to private schools. Mississippians may now wish for a better future, but many are damned if they are going to pay even more for it.

State facts

Date of statehood	10 December 1817	Total area	48,434 sq miles
Capital	Jackson	Highest point ft	Woodall Mountain
Other cities	Biloxi, Greenville,		806
	Hattiesburg	Main rivers	Mississippi, Pearl,
			Big Black, Yazoo

Climate Semi-tropical, with abundant rainfall and long growing season.
Geography Low fertile delta between the Yazoo and Mississippi rivers; loess bluffs stretching around delta border; sandy Gulf coastal terraces followed by piney woods and prairie; rugged, high sandy hills in extreme north-east followed by black prairie belt. Pontotoc Ridge, and flatwoods into the north central highlands.
Time zone Central

People

			%
Population m	2.61	Under 18	28.6
% av. ann. growth 1980–92	0.3	Over 65	12.5
Pop. per sq mile	55.7	Urban	47.1
Birth rate per 1,000 pop.	16.9	Male	47.8
Death rate per 1,000 pop.	9.9	White	63.5
Pop. below poverty line %	25.2	Hispanic	0.6
Doctors per 100,000 pop.	133	Black	35.6
Hospital beds per 100,000 pop.	659	School spending per head	$3,344

The economy

GSP $m	38,135	Av. income per head $	14,088
No. of new corporations '000	3.6	% of national average	71

Structure of GSP	%		%
Construction	4.0	Manufacturing	27.6
Transportation, public utilities	9.3	Wholesale/retail trade	14.6
Services	12.3	Finance, insurance, real estate	14.0
Government	13.2	Other	5.0

Principal industries Manufacturing, food processing, seafood, government, wholesale and retail trade, agriculture
Main crops Cotton, soybeans, catfish, rice

Politics

Senate Thad Cochran (R; term expires 1997), Trent Lott (R; term expires 1995)
House Jamie Whitten, Mike Espy, Sonny Montgomery, Mike Parker, Gene Taylor (all D)

State government
Governor Kirk Fordice (R; term expires 1996)
State Legislature Senate 39D, 13R; House 93D, 27R, 2 Ind
Total expenditure (1991) $5,171m

MISSOURI

The great spread of America's population has for its geographical centre a point south-west of St Louis, Missouri. Truly mid-America, Missouri has, in its different regions, something of the social and geographical flavour of America's North, South, East and West. It can therefore lay claim to being the quintessential American state.

Missouri was not always at the heart of things. St Louis was long a frontier town: the "gateway to the West" to which the city's giant modern arch today bears testimony. It was settled in 1764 by French Creoles up from the South. It was the starting point for the Lewis and Clark expedition of 1804. The 900-mile Santa Fe trail was first blazed in 1822; the Pony Express followed. St Louis stands at the confluence of America's two greatest rivers, the Mississippi and the Missouri. Steamboats plied their trade with New Orleans, or brought fresh loads of German and other settlers down from Pittsburgh and points east. Later, the railroad brought blacks up from the Deep South to work in the new manufacturing industries that grew up around St Louis.

Crossroads' importance

Missouri was the northernmost slave state, and a contentious one. In what were known as the Border Wars, Missouri sent skirmishers over into what was then called Kansas Territory to frighten off abolitionists who were settling there in great numbers. Then a nasty guerrilla war was waged during the Civil War itself. But by the turn of the century, most Missourians had put that behind them. At the crossroads of America, St Louis thrived as a depot and a manufacturing centre. In 1904 Missouri was the country's fifth most populous state, and St Louis, host to the World's Fair of that year, its fourth biggest city.

Flat variety

Missouri has a surprisingly varied topography. The Missouri river itself runs diagonally across to St Louis from the state's north-western corner. North of the river lies the kind of glaciated plain for which the cornbelts of Nebraska and Iowa are best known. To Missouri's south-west run the wooded Ozark Plateau and Boston Mountains that provided iron ore and lead aplenty. Though these hills are not that high (no more than 1,700 feet above sea level), they have an appealing ruggedness.

Missouri's south-eastern corner, by contrast, boasts the rich, alluvial floodplains which count as the northernmost reach of the Mississippi Delta. Plenty of Missourians are unaware that this spongy area, known as the Botheel, was in 1811 home to what was thought to be America's most powerful ever earthquake. It destroyed the town of Madrid and was felt in Washington, DC. The quake altered the Mississippi's course as river banks caved in, and some 300 square miles of land sunk by up to 15 feet. The risk of another huge quake is real: today, signs say "Visit New Madrid while it's still here."

Diminished but not belittled

If Missouri has now slipped from its eminent position at the turn of the century (it is today merely the 15th most populous state), it is still very much alive. St Louis may be overshadowed by Chicago, an hour's quick flight to the north, and its city centre population may have halved over the past four decades as whites fled for the suburbs. But greater St Louis is still one of the country's 20 biggest metropolitan areas. It is home to some basic industries, such as the Anheuser-Busch brewing company and Monsanto chemicals. It is home to General Dynamics, a big defence contractor, and by the Lambert Field airport sits McDonnell Douglas, the state's largest employer. McDonnell Douglas has long played a key part in the region's economy, and since 1990 it has shed nearly a quarter of its jobs, to 32,500. With the big, long-established employers hardly expanding, job creation in St Louis has fallen to the service and trade jobs that sprang up during the 1980s.

Kansas City, the state's other big metro area, lies on Missouri's western border, its Art Deco skyscrapers rising from the central plains. Wheat pours off those plains into Kansas City, home to agri-businesses such as Ralston-Purina; cattle are sent by the thousand to its stockyards. Kansas City has long had wealth that is unexpected in a city so far from nowhere; one of America's first shopping centres, Country Club Plaza, was built 70 years ago by J.C. Nichols on the site of a pig farm.

Escape route

Yet the fastest growing bit of Missouri during the 1980s was neither St Louis nor Kansas City, but the Ozarks area around Springfield in the south-west of the state. This land of leafy hills and manmade lakes grew by nearly a fifth in the past decade as it filled with new developments for retirees and families who breezily explain they come to escape the crime of cities like St Louis and Chicago.

State facts

Date of statehood	10 August 1821	Total area	69,709 sq miles
Capital	Jefferson City	Highest point ft	Taum Sauk
Other cities	Kansas City, St Louis,		Mountain 1,772
	Springfield	Main rivers	Missouri, Mississippi,
			White, Osage

Climate Continental, susceptible to cold Canadian air, moist, warm Gulf air and drier south-west air.

Geography Rolling hills, open, fertile plains, and well-watered prairie north of the Missouri river; south of the river land is rough and hilly with deep narrow valleys; alluvial plain in the south-east; low elevation in the west.

Time zone Central

People

			%
Population m	5.19	Under 18	26.0
% av. ann. growth 1980–92	0.5	Over 65	14.1
Pop. per sq mile	75.4	Urban	68.7
Birth rate per 1,000 pop.	15.5	Male	48.2
Death rate per 1,000 pop.	10.4	White	87.7
Pop. below poverty line %	13.3	Hispanic	1.2
Doctors per 100,000 pop.	196	Black	10.7
Hospital beds per 100,000 pop.	559	School spending per head	$4,534

The economy

GSP $m	100,081	Av. income per head $	18,835
No. of new corporations '000	9.5	% of national average	95

Structure of GSP	%		%
Construction	3.9	Manufacturing	22.7
Transportation, public utilities	11.0	Wholesale/retail trade	16.7
Services	17.9	Finance, insurance, real estate	16.2
Government	10.0	Other	1.6

Principal industries Agriculture, manufacturing, aerospace, tourism
Main crops Wheat, barley, soybeans, hay, corn

Politics

Senate John Danforth (R; term expires 1995), Kit Bond (R; term expires 1999)

House William Clay Sr, Richard Gephardt, Ike Skelton, Alan Wheat, Pat Danner, Harold Volkmer (all D); James Talent, Mel Hancock, Bill Emerson (all R)

State government
Governor Mel Carnahan (D; term expires 1997)
State Legislature Senate 20D, 13R, 1 vac; House 100D, 63R
Total expenditure (1992) $9,018m

MONTANA

Its name is suggestive of the immense mountain ranges that form the Continental Divide at Helena, the capital city, but Montana is also a Great Plains state, where high grasses once nourished wild buffalo herds. Brutal winters make the broad plains in the east even more sparsely populated than the mountainous western provinces. Montana is "Big Sky" country, its western boundary marked by the jagged Bitterroot Range of the Rockies. Less than 25% of the state's population live in metropolitan areas, such as they are. This is small town America where the biggest city, Billings, boasts fewer than 115,000 residents.

Relying on its rich mineral deposits and its rugged cattle ranchers, Montana's economy has changed little in the 100 years since statehood. It also has the peculiar distinction of being the best place on earth to find dinosaur remains; Ekalaka is home to a complete skeleton of the duck-billed anatosaur.

Fur, meat and mining

French-Canadian traders were the first white men to arrive in Montana, but the region remained little known until after America acquired it through the Louisiana Purchase in 1803. Subsequent outsiders followed in predictable procession: explorers, fur trappers, missionaries, miners, cattle ranchers, farmers and sodbusters.

Lewis and Clark spent much of their expedition in Montana, but it was the "Mountain Men" who really opened the territory through the fur trade. Montana saw few of the transients that made their way to Oregon country between 1840 and 1860. The first onrush of settlers arrived only after the discovery of gold in 1852, when mining camps mushroomed at Bannack and Virginia City. Little more than crude shanty towns, the ephemeral first settlements were as colourful as they were lawless.

The grasslands in the east attracted ranchers after the Civil War; in 1866 the first cattle were driven over the Bozeman Trail from Texas. Sioux and Nez Perce Indians fiercely resisted encroachment on their land, most famously at Little Bighorn, where George Custer and his forces met their Last Stand in 1876. The victory would be short-lived, however. Rampant slaughter of the buffalo in the 1870s further subjugated the Indians by starving them into dependence on the federal government. By the end of the century, most tribes in Montana had been shuttled on to reservations.

As the railroad reached west, ranches spread across the plains, and cow towns such as Billings and Missoula sprouted into cities. Fierce rivalries erupted between cattle and sheep-ranchers over grazing rights, but the era of the open range ended with statehood in 1889. With the discovery of silver and copper, mining continued to dominate the "treasure state". A scramble for copper claims shaped Montana's political life as companies struggled for control of the mines. The state's extractive economy led to class warfare politics; the Anaconda Mining Company enjoyed a virtual lock on the state for 40 years and Montana, remote from the political jetlanes, remains the most marginally Republican and most pro-union state in the Rockies.

Range on the Rim

Prospects for sodbusters who came to Montana at the turn of the century ended badly with the drought of 1919 and the dust storms that followed. Farmers began to vanish as quickly as they had appeared; by 1929 Montana – the only state in the union that lost population in the 1920s – was already well accustomed to depression. The government stepped in with federal dam and irrigation projects to aid agriculture and to open grazing lands to cultivation. Demand for copper during and after the second world war buoyed the state's economy through the 1950s. It got another boost from the energy crisis of the 1970s when Montana's coal came more into demand.

Mining has decreased in importance and both mining towns and ranching counties have lost population in recent years as the economies of small cities have grown. Mike Mansfield, Montana's senator for 24 years and ambassador to Japan for 12, brokered special trade ties with east Asia. Montana now swaps beer, dogsleds and dandelion extract in return for Japanese investment and tourism. Government provides about 25% of the state's non-farm jobs, but tourism is the second ranking industry in Montana. Two entrances to Yellowstone National Park lie in the state's south-east corner, while Montana's mountain streams draw fly-fishermen and abundant wildlife attracts hunters.

State facts

Date of statehood	8 November 1889	Total area	147,046 sq miles
Capital	Helena	Highest point ft	Granite Peak
Other cities	Billings, Great Falls,		12,799
	Missoula	Main rivers	Missouri, Yellowstone

Climate   Colder, continental climate with low humidity.
Geography   Rocky Mountains in western third of the state; eastern two-thirds gently rolling northern Great Plains.
Time zone   Mountain

People

			%
Population m	0.82	Under 18	27.4
% av. ann. growth 1980–92	0.4	Over 65	13.4
Pop. per sq mile	5.7	Urban	52.5
Birth rate per 1,000 pop.	14.5	Male	49.5
Death rate per 1,000 pop.	8.7	White	92.7
Pop. below poverty line %	16.1	Hispanic	1.5
Doctors per 100,000 pop.	158	Black	0.3
Hospital beds per 100,000 pop.	573	School spending per head	$5,127

The economy

GSP $m	13,104	Av. income per head $	16,062
No. of new corporations '000	1.6	% of national average	81

Structure of GSP	%		%
Construction	6.8	Manufacturing	7.7
Transportation, public utilities	11.2	Wholesale/retail trade	14.0
Services	16.0	Finance, insurance, real estate	16.5
Government	13.9	Other	13.9

Principal industries   Agriculture, timber, mining, tourism, oil and gas
Main crops   Wheat, barley, sugar beets, hay, oats

Politics

Senate   Max Baucus (D; term expires 1997), Conrad Burns (R; term expires 1995)
House   Pat Williams (D)

State government
Governor   Marc Racicot (R; term expires 1997)
State Legislature   Senate 30D, 20R; House 53R, 47D
Total expenditure (1992) $2,398m

NEBRASKA

Nebraska is like a billiard table propped up at one end. In the west arid plains in the rain shadow of the Rocky Mountains roll eastward and imperceptibly downward. Only between the 98th parallel and the Missouri river in the easternmost quarter of the state is the rainfall reliable enough for the ordered farmlands and neat small towns where two-thirds of the state's people live.

Early white Nebraskans record their awe at the endless ocean of prairie that they called the "sea of Nebraska". Most came in one great wave of settlement during the 1880s, when the rains were promisingly abundant, and when Omaha was growing into a raucous stockyard city, the eastern terminus of the Union Pacific.

From one farm crisis to another

In that decade Nebraska's population leapt from 450,000 to 1m. Then in the 1890s came the first of many long droughts, and the state's population growth slowed. The farm bust produced Nebraska's liveliest politics, which included the populist movement led by William Jennings Bryan, the Democrats' three-time presidential nominee. Bryan denounced the gold standard and advocated government-induced inflation to bail farmers out.

Today, Nebraska's population is just 1.6m. Its numbers barely grew during the 1980s, which saw another "farm crisis". This one was brought about more by speculation and overborrowing, but the cries for a bail-out were not much quieter than a century earlier.

Yet plenty of Nebraska's westernmost counties have been losing people since the 1920s and the dustbowl years, to which hundreds of abandoned farmhouses now bear testimony. In the future, Nebraska is consigned to a sort of rolling rural crisis. The state still has too many farms given the paucity of rainfall, and even more farms will become redundant once the Ogalalla aquifer runs dry in the next century. Well before then, however, a different problem will confront the state: almost half of its farmers will reach retirement age in the next ten years, and there is not enough young talent to take over.

The story is the same with Nebraska's other businesses, many of which are farm-related. A class of veterans from the second world war returned to Nebraska and thrived as an entrepreneurial class. A billionaire from Omaha, Warren Buffett, is only the best-known of this generation. Their offspring, sadly, have long since headed for the west coast and for the big cities of the Mid-West.

State facts

Date of statehood	1 March 1867	Total area	77,358 sq miles
Capital	Lincoln	Highest point ft	Johnson Township
Other cities	Omaha, Grand Island,		5,426
	Bellevue	Main rivers	Missouri, Platte, Niobrara

Climate Continental semi-arid.
Geography Plains of the central lowland in the eastern third, rising to the Great Plains and hill country of the north central and north-west.
Time zone Central

People

			%
Population m	1.61	Under 18	27.3
% av. ann. growth 1980–92	0.2	Over 65	14.1
Pop. per sq mile	20.9	Urban	66.1
Birth rate per 1,000 pop.	15.4	Male	48.7
Death rate per 1,000 pop.	9.2	White	93.8
Pop. below poverty line %	11.1	Hispanic	2.3
Doctors per 100,000 pop.	172	Black	3.6
Hospital beds per 100,000 pop.	640	School spending per head	$4,676

The economy

GSP $m	31,115	Av. income per head $	19,084
No. of new corporations '000	3.1	% of national average	96

Structure of GSP	%		%
Construction	3.4	Manufacturing	13.5
Transportation, public utilities	9.8	Wholesale/retail trade	15.6
Services	15.4	Finance, insurance, real estate	16.0
Government	13.3	Other	13.0

Principal industries Agriculture, food processing, manufacturing
Main crops Corn, sorghum, soybeans, hay, wheat, beans, oats, potatoes, sugar beets

Politics

Senate J. James Exon (D; term expires 1997), J. Robert Kerrey (D; term expires 1995)
House Doug Bereuter, Bill Barrett (both R); Peter Hoagland (D)

State government
Governor Ben Nelson (D; term expires 1995)
State Legislature Unicameral body; all classed as senators; elected as nonpartisans.
Total expenditure (1992) $3,471m

NEVADA

This desert full of miners and gamblers has often been America's fastest growing state in the union. Known as the "second-chance state", Nevada has the lowest percentage of born-in-state residents; about a third of new arrivals come from neighbouring California. Nearly two-thirds of the state's population live in Las Vegas Valley. The city itself, "Armageddon in neon", has consistently rated among the top ten fastest growing metropolitan areas in the country.

The balance of the state's residents live mostly in the 50-mile corridor along the eastern slope of the Sierras. Built on a reputation as the country's divorce capital, Reno, "the biggest little city in the world", is the northern complement to Las Vegas.

Sober beginnings

Nevada, which means "snow-covered" in Spanish, was claimed by Spain in 1776. By the time newly independent Mexico owned the region in 1843 only Indians had lived on the desert's vast perimeter. After President William Henry Harrison commissioned John Fremont to find safe passage through the rugged West to the Pacific, prospectors rushing to California passed through Nevada. But it was religious freedom, not wealth, which was sought by Nevada's first settlers.

Brigham Young ordered his Mormon legions to expand west from Salt Lake City into present-day Nevada. In 1851 they established the state's first permanent settlement as a service station in the heart of Carson Valley, at present-day Genoa. Mormon farms soon dotted the landscape. But two years later the discovery of gold and silver near Dayton signalled Nevada's future. Frustrated miners had been tossing away the gummy, black Gold Canyon sand until one had some of the bluish muck assayed. Word spread quickly that the sandy clay was almost pure silver.

During the next 20 years, the Comstock lode produced immense wealth; mines such as the Ophir, the Belcher and the Crown Point became household words across America. Then with the 1873 Coinage Act, known locally as the "Crime of '73", Congress demonetised silver and stopped coining silver dollars; 20 years of statewide depression followed. The Silver Party, which was formed to repeal the act, came to dominate state politics, but the search for another bonanza continued.

Gambling and divorce

American naturalist John Muir had called Nevada's mines

"sins against science", but the state was about to build its economy quite literally on the business of sin. In 1931, with the country in depression and the state about to go bankrupt, Nevada legalised gambling and reduced the residency requirement for divorce to six weeks. Both industries boomed after the second world war. Lax controls led to scandal and corruption; in 1951 the Kefauver Crime Commission hearings in Las Vegas revealed that the underworld called the shots. Most of the casinos were owned by mobsters until Howard Hughes, Nevada's reclusive "first citizen", bought them out in 1967, ushering in an era of corporate control.

Six thousand new residents moved to Nevada each week in the 1980s, transforming Reno and Las Vegas from divorce capital and remote desert gambling den to metropolitan areas of 750,000. The influx has eroded the historic dominance of the Democratic party; although both of Nevada's senators are Democrats, the state produces clear Republican majorities in presidential races. This is not the conservatism of family values (Nevada is home to the highest percentage of non-family households), but rather that of new migrants to the free-wheeling West who arrive convinced that they can beat the odds.

The state is still mining, but for less glamorous goods: today Nevadans dig for diatomaceous earth, the stuff of swimming pool filters and kitty litter. The state has become a regional distribution and credit card operations centre, but fully half of Nevada's jobs are in services, double the national average. Gaming and tourism, the economic mainstays, generate sufficient income for the state to make income, corporate and inheritance taxes unnecessary, and the cost of living is low.

Recent events show that Nevada's economy can dip when California's takes a dive. In 1990 Hilton laid off workers, Bally defaulted on its debt, Aladdin filed for bankruptcy and Landmark closed. New emphasis on making Las Vegas and Reno "destination resorts", has successfully drawn trade from less racy clientele such as the American Booksellers Association and the Southern Baptist Convention. Gross gaming revenues in 1991 were in excess of $5.5 billion.

Unemployment, though below the national average, is still uncomfortable at 6.6%; the largest single industry decline has been in construction, down by 5,000 jobs in 1991. Nevada's long-term problem is growth: Las Vegas is guzzling water to maintain lawns, golf greens and waterfalls in the bleakest desert in North America.

State facts

Date of statehood	31 October 1864	Total area	110,567 sq miles
Capital	Carson City	Highest point ft	Boundary Peak
Other cities	Las Vegas,		13,140
	Reno, Henderson	Main rivers	Humboldt, Colorado

Climate Semi-arid and arid.
Geography Rugged north–south mountain ranges; southern area is within the Mojave Desert; lowest elevation Colorado River Canyon, 470 ft.
Time zone Pacific

People

			%
Population m	1.33	Under 18	25.5
% av. ann. growth 1980–92	4.3	Over 65	11.0
Pop. per sq mile	12.1	Urban	88.3
Birth rate per 1,000 pop.	18.0	Male	50.9
Death rate per 1,000 pop.	7.2	White	84.3
Pop. below poverty line %	10.2	Hispanic	10.4
Doctors per 100,000 pop.	159	Black	6.6
Hospital beds per 100,000 pop.	308	School spending per head	$4,910

The economy

GSP $m	27,960	Av. income per head $	20,266
No. of new corporations '000	11.0	% of national average	102

Structure of GSP	%		%
Construction	10.3	Manufacturing	4.0
Transportation, public utilities	8.6	Wholesale/retail trade	13.4
Services	34.3	Finance, insurance, real estate	13.6
Government	10.0	Other	5.8

Principal industries Gaming, tourism, mining, manufacturing, government, agriculture, warehousing, trucking
Main crops Alfalfa seed, potatoes, hay, barley, wheat

Politics

Senate Harry M. Reid (D; term expires 1999), Richard Bryan (D; term expires 1995)
House James H. Bilbray (D); Barbara F. Vucanovich (R).

State government
Governor Bob Miller (D; term expires 1995)
State Legislature Senate 10D, 10R, 1 undecided; House 29D, 13R
Total expenditure (1991) $3,436m

NEW HAMPSHIRE

"Live free, or die." No state has a more apt motto than New Hampshire. In politics, commerce and taxation, New Hampshiremen believe in hands-off government. No state taxes its citizens less: New Hampshire has neither income tax nor a general sales tax. The famously crusty and right-wing state is also alone in having a last-resort right to revolution enshrined in its constitution. Every fourth year New Hampshire takes centre stage in national politics, holding the earliest presidential primaries. The only modern president who has won the White House without winning New Hampshire first is Bill Clinton.

The state's 18-mile coast was settled by French and English traders in the 17th century. But it was not until the following century that the inland was colonised. Freethinkers fleeing from Massachusetts slowly pushed north up the Connecticut river and inland from the deep-water port of Portsmouth. New Hampshire's geography is varied for a 9,000 square mile wedge. Sandwiched between the coast and the forbidding White Mountains in the north, is a lush central lakes region. To the south, are the rolling Monadnock hills and the unglamorous industrial towns of the Merrimack Valley: Manchester, Concord and Nashua.

Grit and granite

New Hampshire realised early that its land was ill-suited to farming. Despite its small size, it is the eleventh largest industrial economy in the nation. Manchester was once the centre of the American textile industry. Now it is high-tech industries which are the backbone of its economy, employing more than 10% of the workforce. A big wood and paper products industry is based in Berlin in the north.

The harsh terrain of the "Granite State" does support two industries: quarrying and tourism. The latter thrived as early as the mid-19th century when lavish resort hotels were built. It remains a key year-round industry, attracting hunters, fishermen, hikers, skiers, and scenery and solitude seekers.

New Hampshire's industrial renaissance and fast growth in the 1980s has been affected by the recession of the early 1990s. The silver lining is that the slowdown has eased threatening labour shortages and fast rising property prices. The state has been as unencumbering fiscally on business as on its citizens. But as the New Hampshire economy becomes more integrated with the world's (exports more than doubled to $1.2 billion over the 1980s), the state will have to spend more on infrastructure, which will tax its citizens' reluctance to be taxed.

State facts

Date of statehood	21 June 1788	Total area	9,351 sq miles
Capital	Concord	Highest point ft	Mt Washington
Other cities	Manchester,		6,288
	Nashua, Rochester	Main rivers	Merrimack, Salmon
			Falls, Androscoggin, Connecticut

Climate Highly varied, due to its nearness to high mountains and ocean.
Geography Low, rolling coast followed by countless hills and mountains rising out of a central plateau.
Time zone Eastern Standard

People

			%
Population m	1.11	Under 18	25.2
% av. ann. growth 1980–92	1.6	Over 65	11.8
Pop. per sq mile	123.8	Urban	51.0
Birth rate per 1,000 pop.	15.8	Male	49.0
Death rate per 1,000 pop.	7.7	White	98.0
Pop. below poverty line %	6.4	Hispanic	1.0
Doctors per 100,000 pop.	200	Black	0.6
Hospital beds per 100,000 pop.	432	School spending per head	$5,500

The economy

GSP $m	24,504	Av. income per head $	22,934
No. of new corporations '000	2.4	% of national average	116

Structure of GSP	%		%
Construction	5.6	Manufacturing	23.5
Transportation, public utilities	6.1	Wholesale/retail trade	15.8
Services	18.5	Finance, insurance, real estate	20.8
Government	8.5	Other	1.2

Principal industries Tourism, manufacturing, agriculture, trade, mining
Main crops Dairy products, nursery and greenhouse products, hay, vegetables, fruit, maple syrup and sugar products

Politics

Senate Robert Smith (R; term expires 1997), Judd Gregg (R; term expires 1999)
House Bill Zeliff (R); Dick Swett (D)

State government
Governor Steve Merrill (R; term expires 1995)
State Legislature Senate 13R, 11D; House 254R, 138D, 5 others, 3 vac
Total expenditure (1992) $2,013m

NEW JERSEY

There is not much garden left in the garden state. New Jersey is the fifth smallest state at less than 8,000 square miles, but has the ninth largest population, almost 8m, and is the most densely populated. New Jersey had a booming 1980s.

New Jersey is bounded to the north and east by New York and the Atlantic ocean. To the west across the Delaware river is Pennsylvania and to the south Delaware Bay. Southern New Jersey has always been less industrialised. Cape May, at the south-eastern tip, was one of the earliest seaside resorts and still has Victorian villas. Atlantic City, another resort on the sandy Jersey shore, built America's first boardwalk in 1870. After casino gambling was legalised in 1977, it became the Las Vegas of the east.

The often swampy southern coastal plain covers two-thirds of the state, rising northwards through intensely urban northern New Jersey to the Appalachian mountains which brush the north-west of the state. North-eastern New Jersey is part of the Piedmont Plateau, low plains broken by high ridges such as the Palisades that line the Hudson river separating the state from New York city. New Jersey's main deep-water ports – Newark, Elizabeth and Hoboken – are in the north-east.

In the early days of European colonisation, the area was part of the New Netherlands. A year after the British took it from the Dutch in 1664, the land between the Hudson and Delaware rivers was granted to Lord John Berkeley and Sir George Carteret. They later sold it to Quakers. It returned to the British crown in 1702. Until 1738, New York's governor also served as New Jersey's.

Located between Philadelphia and New York City, the state saw much fighting in the Revolutionary war. Among the some 100 battles on its soil were Trenton, which followed Washington's crossing of the Delaware, and Princeton. These English defeats were turning points in the war. New Jersey was the third state to ratify the constitution, in 1787. Trenton became state capital three years later. It is the second oldest state capital in America.

Industrialising the garden

There is still forest and farmland in the garden state, but the number of farms is dwindling. There are now barely 8,000, but New Jersey is a leading grower of cranberries, blueberries, spinach, green peppers, asparagus and tomatoes. It is also the fourth leading peach-growing state. New Jersey has been industrialising for almost as long as it has been a state.

Newark, Paterson, Camden and Trenton were leading industrial towns by the first half of the 19th century. Today, despite its small size, New Jersey ranks as the eighth largest state economy. Its residents have the second highest income per person in the nation, moving up from fifth-highest in the mid-1980s.

The state is America's leading producer of pharmaceuticals and ranks second in chemicals, which is the largest manufacturing industry in the state by both employment and value of output. Merck, Schering-Plough and Johnson & Johnson are among world-class companies headquartered in the state. New Jersey has one of the most preeminent concentrations of chemical and pharmaceutical R&D facilities in the world.

The state also ranks in the national top ten for production of office and business machines, rubber and plastics, commercial printing, instruments, petrochemicals, food and paper products, electrical and electronic equipment, electrical machinery, fabricated metal and film and television production. The past decade has seen New Jersey diversify its traditional economic base into one less dependent on blue-collar industrial employment and more on high-value added manufacturing and knowledge-based white-collar industries. Manufacturing, services and finance both now account roughly equally for around one-fifth of state domestic product.

Building on knowledge ...

One sign of the changing mix of the economy is the increasing concentration of R&D facilities in the state. Every eleventh dollar spent by government and industry on R&D in America is spent in New Jersey. This builds on a tradition of scientific research and industrial inventiveness which dates back to the days of Albert Einstein at Princeton in the 1930s and before that to Thomas Edison in the 19th century. For the size of its population, the state has more boffins and engineers than any other. It ranks fourth in patents awarded. Scientists from the state have won 11 Nobel prizes, seven of them coming from Bell Labs.

... and location

Another sign of the diversification of the economy is the number of corporate head offices and of back-offices of international banks and Wall Street firms that the state has attracted, particularly from higher-taxing New York. New Jersey ranks third in the number of corporate and divisional head offices within its borders. It is home to more than 20 *Fortune 500* companies, including Allied-Signal and Campbell Soup. Prudential, the world's largest insurance company, has its head office in Newark.

The state has attracted more than 1,100 foreign companies. New Jersey ranks seventh in foreign direct investment and has the fourth highest employment by foreign-owned firms. Swiss-owned Hoffmann-LaRoche is the state's biggest foreign employer. Foreign investment is concentrated in pharmaceuticals, electronics and telecommunications.

Among traditional service industries, tourism and distribution remain important. The container port at Newark-Elizabeth is one of the world's busiest. Newark is one of America's fastest growing cargo airports. The state's location within overnight delivery of more than 60m Americans between Washington, DC and Boston and the development of its highways in the 1950s earns the state the nickname of the Crossroads of the East.

High-tech future?

The challenges to the state turn on its ability to continue the diversification of its economy into high-tech manufacturing and research-based industry and senior-level white collar jobs. Though the state ranks fourth in the number of high-tech jobs it has, these account for only one job in eight, well above the national average but less than would be expected in a state touting itself as being on technology's cutting edge, especially in fields such as bio-medicine, fibre-optics, genetic engineering and laser technology.

The state's politically-sensitive budget problems also raise questions about the extent to which New Jersey will be able to afford to pay for two of the things that contributed so much to its growth in the 1980s: incentives for businesses to move to and to expand in the state, and the vast system of education and vocational training geared towards servicing a high-tech economy.

A third challenge is remaining cost-competitive with surrounding states. New Jersey's budget deficit has already forced tax rises. Businesses are complaining about the cost of complying with the environmental protection laws – necessarily some of the strictest in the country given its chemicals plants and oil refineries – and about health costs. Yet if New Jersey is to sustain its growth it will need to lower the cost of doing business. It will also have to sustain its level of public services, especially education and health, to attract and retain the high-quality workforce it will need.

State facts

Date of statehood 18 December 1787 Total area 8,722 sq miles
Capital Trenton Highest point ft High Point 1,803
Other cities Newark, Jersey City, Main rivers Hudson, Passak,
Patterson Raritan, Delaware

Climate Moderate, with marked difference between NW and SE extremities.
Geography Appalachian valley in the NW also has highest point;
Appalachian highlands, flat-topped NE–SW mountain ranges; Piedmont
plateau, low plains broken by high ridges (Palisades) rising 400–500 ft;
coastal plain, covering three-fifths of state in SE, gradually rises from sea
level to gentle slopes.
Time zone Eastern Standard

People

		%
Population m	7.79	Under 18	23.9
% av. ann. growth 1980–92	0.5	Over 65	13.6
Pop. per sq mile	1,049.9	Urban	89.4
Birth rate per 1,000 pop.	15.8	Male	48.3
Death rate per 1,000 pop.	9.0	White	79.3
Pop. below poverty line %	7.6	Hispanic	9.6
Doctors per 100,000 pop.	246	Black	13.4
Hospital beds per 100,000 pop.	485	School spending per head	$10,219

The economy

GSP $m	203,375	Av. income per head $	26,457
No. of new corporations '000	28.0	% of national average	133

Structure of GSP	%		%
Construction	5.4	Manufacturing	18.4
Transportation, public utilities	9.2	Wholesale/retail trade	16.6
Services	19.6	Finance, insurance, real estate	20.7
Government	9.4	Other	0.7

Principal industries Services, trade, manufacturing
Main crops Hay, corn, soybeans, tomatoes, blueberries, cranberries, peaches

Politics

Senate Bill Bradley (D; term expires 1997), Frank Lautenberg (D; term expires 1995)
House Robert Andrews, William J. Hughes, Frank Pallone Jr, Herbert
Klein, Robert G. Torricelli, Donald M. Payne, Robert Menendez (all D); Jim
Saxton, Christopher H. Smith, Marge Roukema, Bob Franks, Dean A. Gallo,
Richard A. Zimmer (all R)

State government
Governor James Florio (D; term expires 1994)
State Legislature Senate 27R, 13D; House 58R, 22D
Total expenditure (1992) $21,330m

NEW MEXICO

The ancient is alive and well in New Mexico. America's oldest continuously inhabited village sits atop a 365-foot mesa at Acoma. Overlooking the Rio Grande which runs the length of the state, perched above broad semi-arid plains, "Sky City" was built by Anasazi Indians at least 1,000 years ago. New Mexico is the northernmost outpost of the Indian-Spanish civilisations of the Cordillera, and that influence dominates the state. It has the highest percentage of Hispanics in the country (some of whose roots reach back 500 years to the Spanish Inquisition); only Hawaii and Alaska rival New Mexico for its primacy of native cultures.

Successive waves of American settlement have peculiarly shaped New Mexico. The eastern part of the state, settled mostly by Anglos in the last 50 years, owes its growth to mining and nuclear research, but cattle ranches and desolate military bases give the region the feel of Texas. A small town in the south, Truth or Consequences, takes its name from a popular game show. Santa Fe, with its signature adobe architecture and more than 300 restaurants, has become the second-largest art centre in the country and a mecca for the well-to-do.

This is the countryside canopied by ever-changing skies that inspired Georgia O'Keefe's broad-brushed landscapes. But for all its stunning scenery, New Mexico is no environmentalist's haven. Grey Ranch, a 500 square-mile spread of southwestern wonder, was preserved not by the government but by a private conservation group; Carlsbad is pegged to host a nuclear waste dump.

Atomic growth

Spanish explorers in 1540, expecting to discover a land as rich as gold-endowed Aztec Mexico, optimistically named the northern territory New Mexico. Instead they found Pueblo Indians living in adobe dwellings dug into cliffsides and tending modest crops. Disappointed but undeterred, Spanish conquistadors and missionaries built their first settlement in Santa Fe in 1609. They imposed their language and religion in a hurry; forced conversions led to bloody Indian revolts against the colonisers, but the town grew rapidly in the 1700s nonetheless.

After the Louisiana Purchase in 1803, Americans began daring to cross into New Mexico territory. By 1821 its borders were thrown wide open by Mexican independence, and wagonloads of goods arrived the next year from Missouri. The Treaty of Guadalupe Hidalgo made most of New Mexico officially American in 1848, but the Civil War tested its political affinities. When Confederate forces lost supplies, they retreated south, leaving the bulk of the region in Union hands. More than six decades passed, however, before New Mexico was admitted in 1912 as the 47th state.

The second world war dramatically changed New Mexico when an isolated boys' school tucked into the mountains northwest of Santa Fe became the chosen site of the Manhattan Project, the government's top secret plan to develop an atomic bomb. The test bomb was detonated – "flashing with the brightness of several suns at midday" – in the remote desert outside Alamogordo in July 1945. Los Alamos remains a major centre of nuclear research and, with 7,000 jobs, a major employer.

Albuquerque, New Mexico's biggest city, provides the link between past and future in the state. Since J. Robert Oppenheimer arrived in 1940, the town's population has exploded. Its economy has enjoyed some of the same growth and diversification from the arrival of white-collar industry, but Albuquerque is far more dependent on government than most Sunbelt cities. Income levels are lower here and, at 16%, the ten-year growth rate is well below those of Phoenix, Dallas or even El Paso.

Still asking what the country can do for it

As the country's leading producer of uranium, New Mexico derives much of its wealth from mining. "Little Texas" provides oil and some cotton from irrigated fields, and much of New Mexico's farmland is used for grazing. But government is New Mexico's economic mainstay, accounting for about 18% of the jobs in the state. Pete Domenici, New Mexico's most prominent politician, closely tends the research laboratories at Los Alamos and Sandia. He aims to shepherd the federal facilities into prosperous post-cold war enterprises. Qualms about the effects of military cutbacks have been quelled somewhat since the government in 1990 named Kirtland Air Base the site for one of four federal "superlabs".

State facts

Date of statehood	6 January 1912	Total area	121,598 sq miles
Capital	Santa Fe	Highest point ft	Wheeler Peak
Other cities	Albuquerque,		13,161
	Las Cruces, Roswell	Main rivers	Rio Grande, San Juan,
			Pelos, Canadian

Climate Dry, with temperatures rising or falling 5°F with every 1,000 ft elevation.

Geography Eastern third, Great Plains; central third Rocky Mountains (85% of the state is over 4,000 ft elevation); western third high plateau.

Time zone Mountain

People

			%
Population m	1.58	Under 18	29.7
% av. ann. growth 1980–92	1.6	Over 65	10.9
Pop. per sq mile	13.0	Urban	73.0
Birth rate per 1,000 pop.	18.1	Male	49.2
Death rate per 1,000 pop.	7.2	White	75.6
Pop. below poverty line %	20.6	Hispanic	38.2
Doctors per 100,000 pop.	183	Black	2.0
Hospital beds per 100,000 pop.	411	School spending per head	$4,692

The economy

GSP $m	25,414	Av. income per head $	15,353
No. of new corporations '000	2.7	% of national average	77

Structure of GSP	%		%
Construction	5.7	Manufacturing	6.6
Transportation, public utilities	10.0	Wholesale/retail trade	13.8
Services	18.0	Finance, insurance, real estate	15.6
Government	17.7	Other	12.6

Principal industries Government, services, trade

Main crops Hay, onions, wheat, pecans, corn, cotton, sorghum

Politics

Senate Pete Domenici (R; term expires 1997), Jeff Bingaman (D; term expires 1995)

House Steven Schiff, Joe Skeen (both R); Bill Richardson (D)

State government

Governor Bruce King (D; term expires 1995)

State Legislature Senate 27D, 15R; House 52D, 18R

Total expenditure (1992) $4,169m

NEW YORK

Were New York a country, it would be the ninth largest economy in the world. Only California among the states has a larger population or economy. The Empire state is a pugnacious, cosmopolitan, making-good, making-money sort of place. If any state has energy, ambition and attitude, it is New York. It may also be the last state in America with wit.

For all its problems, New York City remains one of the world's great cities. It is not only the city that never sleeps; it is the city that never lets you sleep. Yet to overlook the rest of the state is to do a great disservice to a beautiful swathe of America stretching from the ocean dunes of Long Island to the Great Lakes and Canada.

In the surprisingly poor north are the raw peaks of the high Adirondacks. Lake Champlain and the steep Taconic mountains separate New York from the length of New England to the east. To the west, beyond the glacial Finger Lakes, are Niagara Falls and the Lakes Ontario and Erie. Downstate New York narrows like a funnel south of the Catskill mountains, following the broad Hudson valley till it hits the Atlantic at Manhattan. Long Island trails out at a right angle parallel to the Connecticut shore.

The area was Iroquois territory before Verrazano, Hudson and Champlain sailed the waters that today bear their names in the 16th and early 17th centuries. The Dutch were the earliest European settlers. Peter Minuit, the first governor of the New Netherlands, famously bought Manhattan from the Iroquois for 60 guilders.

The English seized the increasingly prosperous colony in 1664. It remained the centre of British colonial power until the end of the Revolutionary war. George Washington, was inaugurated as first president of the United States in New York city in 1789. New York was usurped as the political capital, but its commercial ascendancy was largely unchecked through the Gilded Age at the end of the 19th century and even past the Great Depression which followed the 1929 crash of the New York Stock Exchange.

Melting pot

In the 19th and early 20th centuries, New York was point of entry for most immigrants into America, first Irish and Germans, later eastern European Jews and Italians. Between 1855 and 1924, more than 20m immigrants came to New York. If any state was America's melting pot, it was New York. New York City had the sweatshops, slums and smells, but also the fortunes to show for it.

As a result, New York politics is built on money and ethnic coalitions which have mostly found a home in the Democratic party. An uneasy coalition of blacks, Latinos and Jews currently holds sway. Since the days of Boss Tweed's Tammany Hall, New York has alternated between political corruption and reformism, without ever deciding firmly in favour of one or the other. Today New York is going through one of its cleaner phases, with organised crime and corruption at a relatively low ebb.

After the second world war New York City became home to both the United Nations and its third great wave of immigrants, blacks from the south and Hispanics from the Caribbean. The white middle class fled to the suburbs, and the city's manufacturing industries to the Sunbelt. That cut the city's tax base and started the creeping urban decay that would lead to the city's fiscal crisis in the 1970s.

But New Yorkers know no other way than to live on the edge of chaos. The 1980s brought financial boom times and then a property bust. The 1990s are bringing an economy heading for the 21st century and another regenerative wave of immigration, from Asia and the former Soviet Union and its European satellites.

A view of tomorrow

"A microcosm of America to be" is how New York was once described. The state's economy has always led America's, its pre-eminence assured by the opening of the Erie canal connecting the Hudson and the Great Lakes in 1825. The canal opened the Mid-West to settlement and promoted the internal trade which let America's interior change from a subsistence economy into a market-based one. New York city was this trade's entrepot and financier, in many senses the crucible of America's market capitalism.

Today, New York is leading the nation in restructuring its knowledge-intensive industries which increasingly drive its economy so they can compete in emerging global markets for services. New York long ago made the transformation from an economy based on manufacturing to one more equally based on information-technology, services and trade. Financial services alone generate more than one-fifth of gross state product. So do other white-collar businesses, including business, legal and medical services and the media. Even though New York is still a leading manufacturing centre, manufacturing accounts for only one-seventh of the state's output.

This is also reflected in employment, which differs considerably from that of the nation as a whole. The share of jobs accounted for by services and finance in New York, at more than 40%, is more than one-third again higher than for the national economy. The state's financial services jobs contribute as much to total personal income as do manufacturing jobs. In the national economy manufacturing generates three times the earnings that financial services do.

The preponderance of finance and other service jobs helped New York thrive in the 1980s, but it hurt the state when the debt deflation of the early 1990s hit. Following the slump in overheated property and banking markets, the recession was most severe downstate. New York's finance and associated service jobs are concentrated in New York city. The city leads the nation in the finance, accounting, insurance and communications industries – one reason is that New York city has more *Fortune 500* companies headquartered in it than any other city in America. Half of the financial services jobs lost in America during the 12 months to June 1991 were New York jobs.

Old and new industry

With New York city also accounting for nearly half the jobs in the state, its economic trends have a powerful effect for good and ill on the state. In all, New York lost some 250,000 jobs, almost all of those created since the mid-1980s. But like Rustbowl states that lost thousands of jobs in the recession of the early 1980s but then made great manufacturing productivity gains, New York will have the most efficient and profitable information-intensive industries in the 1990s. It has already become globally competitive in important services such as finance, telecommunications and tourism.

While manufacturing employment has fallen to barely 13% of total employment, New York still ranks in the top ten states as a leading producer of aerospace equipment, chemicals, electronics, food and beverages, machinery, paper products, rubber and plastics, and textiles and clothing. New York manufacturing workers rank among the most productive in the country. Industrial production is concentrated in the south of the state, in and around New York City and on Long Island, where the state's electrical and electronics, transport equipment (including aerospace) and printing and publishing industries are based.

New York is no longer America's breadbasket, but it remains a significant grower of fruit and vegetables. It has the second heaviest crop of apples and is a leading dairy state. It also has a burgeoning wine industry both around the Finger Lakes and on the eastern end of Long Island.

Foreign attractions

Recently upstate New York, particularly the Buffalo-Niagara Falls conurbation, has reversed its long-term industrial decline (its main industry was steel-making) thanks to an influx of Canadian investment following the free trade agreement between the United States and Canada, and because Canadian companies have moved south to escape Ontario's taxes, red tape and rising labour costs, and Quebec's nascent separatism.

As well as Canadian investment, New York has attracted inward investment most notably recently from Germany, Japan and Britain, particularly in property and financial services but also in manufacturing. The state has the third highest stock of foreign direct investment after Texas and California and the second highest number of people working for foreign-owned firms.

Trading and tourist importance

With the port it now shares with New Jersey still one of the busiest in the world, and the John F Kennedy airport one of the busiest in the country, New York remains central to America's foreign trade. As well as being an entrepot, the state has the second highest number of export-related manufacturing jobs. In the services exports are growing rapidly; tourism is now the state's second largest industry.

Challenges for today

Three big policy challenges face New York for the 1990s. The first is to appreciate how much employment in the state has switched from manufacturing to services, and that increasingly services' contribution to state domestic product will come from efficient but high-value-adding professional, technical and managerial jobs. This makes education crucial to develop a competitive workforce. The state has more universities than any other, but the concerns are most acute in New York city's schools and over remedial education for New Yorkers failed by the schools over the past 20 years.

The restructuring of the economy also means that New York city will no longer be able to play its traditional role of absorbing waves of unskilled immigrant labour. The sweatshops that traditionally gave large numbers of new New Yorkers the first step on the economic ladder are just not going to be there. What low-paid non-skilled service jobs there will be will offer little scope for advancement. The political and welfare system will have to adjust to that, too.

The second big challenge facing the state is to apply the principal of service-sector restructuring to one of its largest service industries: government. New York has more bits of government than any other state. New Yorkers have the highest tax burden per head in the country. Too many tax dollars are tied up in producing red tape. That must be cut if New York is to provide an economic environment that is competitive with other states. It will also have to get to grips with the largest state debt in the country.

The third policy challenge is to improve the productivity and competitiveness of the state's manufacturing and knowledge industries by applying new technology to products and processes. Many of New York's universities are leaders in their fields such as information systems (Columbia), biotechnology and supercomputing (Cornell), telecommunications (Polytechnic Institute of New York), healthcare (State University of New York), computer software (Syracuse) and optical technologies (Rochester). But much of the research work done in the state is basic research. There is a need for more applied R&D so that discoveries can become products and services quickly.

Who loves New York?

New York city has additional problems of its own. Its infrastructure is crumbling. So are its schools. Fiscal crisis never seems far away, especially because of the demands on its welfare services caused by homelessness, AIDS, drugs, unemployment among youths and minorities, and the reluctance of the Federal government to spend on cities, including America's biggest. Yet crime is falling, people are moving back to the city and entrepreneurial immigrants from Eastern Europe, Asia and Latin America arrive daily. The future looks bright if chaotic, but New Yorkers wouldn't want it any other way.

House Gary L. Ackerman, Floyd H. Flake, Thomas J. Manton, Jerrold Nadler, Charles E. Schumer, Edolphus Towns, Major R. Owens, Nydia Velazquez, Carolyn Maloney, Charles B. Rangel, Jose Serrano, Eliot L. Engel, Nita M. Lowey, Michael R. McNulty, Maurice Hinchey, Louise M. Slaughter, John J. LaFalce, G. Hochbrickner (all D); Rick Lazio, David Levy, Susan Molinari, Hamilton Fish Jr, Benjamin A. Gilman, Gerald Solomon, Sherwood L. Boehlert, John McHugh, James T. Walsh, Bill Paxon, Jack Quinn, Amo Houghton Jr, Peter King (all R)

State facts

Date of statehood	26 July 1788	Total area	54,556 sq miles
Capital	Albany	Highest point ft	Mt Marcy 5,344
Other cities	New York, Buffalo, Rochester	Main rivers	Hudson, Mohawk, Susquehanna, St Lawrence

Climate Variable; the south-east region moderated by the ocean.
Geography Highest mountains in Adirondacks; St Lawrence-Champlain lowlands from Lake Ontario NE; Hudson-Mohawk lowland follows rivers N and W, 10–30 miles wide; Atlantic coastal plain in SE; Appalachian Highlands, half the state west of Hudson, include Catskills, Finger Lakes; plateau of Erie-Ontario lowlands.
Time zone Eastern Standard

People

			%
Population m	18.12	Under 18	24.4
% av. ann. growth 1980–92	0.3	Over 65	13.1
Pop. per sq mile	383.7	Urban	84.3
Birth rate per 1,000 pop.	16.5	Male	47.9
Death rate per 1,000 pop.	9.2	White	74.4
Pop. below poverty line %	13.0	Hispanic	12.3
Doctors per 100,000 pop.	315	Black	15.9
Hospital beds per 100,000 pop.	563	School spending per head	$8,658

The economy

GSP $m	441,068	Av. income per head $	23,534
No. of new corporations '000	63.8	% of national average	119

Structure of GSP	%		%
Construction	4.6	Manufacturing	14.1
Transportation, public utilities	8.4	Wholesale/retail trade	15.5
Services	22.5	Finance, insurance, real estate	23.1
Government	11.0	Other	0.8

Principal industries Manufacturing, finance, communications, tourism, transportation, services
Main crops Apples, cabbage, cauliflower, celery, cherries, grapes, corn, peas, snap beans, sweetcorn

Politics

Senate Daniel Patrick Moynihan (D; term expires 1995), Alfonse D'Amato (R; term expires 1999)
House See list on page 153.

State government
Governor Mario M. Cuomo (D; term expires 1995)
State Legislature Senate 34R, 27D; House 101D, 49R
Total expenditure (1992) $53,329m

NORTH CAROLINA

Early explorers of America's east coast were wild boosters of the lands they had discovered. In 1585 two such Englishmen described North Carolina as "the most plentiful, fruitful, and wholesome of all the world". To this day, many would still agree. During the 1980s the state's population grew by 13%; yet it still has one of the highest percentages of native-born population in the country. And if many North Carolinians have now moved to new, leafy developments around the Charlotte and Raleigh-Durham growth areas, they remain close to North Carolina traditions of a strong and sometimes fierce Baptist faith, and a loyal sense of community.

If it is the Piedmont region in central North Carolina which is now the state's economic heart, it was the Coastal Plains which were first settled – if the ships bringing immigrants did not first flounder upon the treacherous Outer Banks. The plains were home to the famous Lost Colony and Virginia Dare, the first English child born in America, though why the whole settlement disappeared is a mystery.

By the mid-18th century Dutch Moravians and others from Pennsylvania had put down roots in the fertile rolling land of the Piedmont. Bang in the state's centre is the University of North Carolina at Chapel Hill, the state's oldest university, founded in 1795. Others have followed, endowing North Carolina with a strong progressive bent; today they provide the underpinning to the state's high-tech boom.

Textiles and tobacco

The Piedmont has long been home to a large industrial base which grew up around tobacco and textiles. Nowadays no respectable congressman from the state fails to call for more tobacco subsidies and more textile protection from foreign competition. Low-paying jobs in one of the country's least unionised states are one reason why North Carolina used to have a reputation as backward. Yet North Carolina's future lies not in protection but in vigorous enterprise. During the 1980s feeble unions worked to the state's advantage. Businesses, including many high-tech ones, have flocked to North Carolina. Over the past decade, Charlotte and Raleigh-Durham have become big airport hubs. Thanks to these new businesses, the number of jobs in the state has grown by one-fifth, though North Carolina's below-average schools still struggle to ready its students for these new high-skill jobs. Even so, North Carolina's success is as good a model as any for America's future.

State facts

Date of statehood	21 November 1789	Total area	53,800 sq miles
Capital	Raleigh	Highest point ft	Mt Mitchell 6,684
Other cities	Charlotte, Greensboro, Winston-Salem	Main rivers	New River, Watauga, French Broad, Chowan, Roanoke

Climate Sub-tropical in south-east, medium-continental in mountain region; tempered by the Gulf Stream and the mountains in west.

Geography Coastal plain and tidewater, two-fifths of state, extend to fall line of rivers; Piedmont plateau, also two-fifths, hills 200 miles wide; southern Appalachian mountains contain Blue Ridge and Great Smokey mountains.

Time zone Eastern Standard

People

			%
Population m	6.84	Under 18	24.3
% av. ann. growth 1980–92	1.3	Over 65	12.4
Pop. per sq mile	140.5	Urban	50.4
Birth rate per 1,000 pop.	15.8	Male	48.5
Death rate per 1,000 pop.	8.7	White	75.6
Pop. below poverty line %	13.0	Hispanic	1.2
Doctors per 100,000 pop.	190	Black	22.0
Hospital beds per 100,000 pop.	439	School spending per head	$4,857

The economy

GSP $m	130,085	Av. income per head $	17,667
No. of new corporations '000	11.9	% of national average	89

Structure of GSP	%		%
Construction	3.9	Manufacturing	30.0
Transportation, public utilities	8.5	Wholesale/retail trade	15.8
Services	13.2	Finance, insurance, real estate	13.8
Government	12.1	Other	2.7

Principal industries Manufacturing, agriculture, tobacco, tourism

Main crops Tobacco, soybeans, corn, peanuts, small sweet potatoes, feed grains, vegetables, fruits

Politics

Senate Jesse Helms (R; term expires 1997), Lauch Faircloth (R; term expires 1999).

House Eva Clayton, Tim Valentine, Martin Lancaster, David E. Price, Steve Neal, Charles Rose III, Bill Hefner, Melvin Watt (all D); Howard Coble, Alex McMillan, Cass Ballenger, Charles Taylor (all R)

State government
Governor Jim Hunt Jr (D; term expires 1997)
State Legislature Senate 39D, 11R; House 78D, 42R
Total expenditure (1992) $13,625m

NORTH DAKOTA

This is the American heartland, appropriately situated at the heart of the North American continent and bordered on the east by the Missouri river. Sod barns, wood-frame houses and lonesome windmills still stand stoically across this slice of the vast, treeless expanse of the Great Plains. Settled in a rush of migration around the turn of the century, North Dakota's population has little fluctuated and life here little changed since it achieved statehood in 1889. Today the state has the lowest crime rate in the country and boasts both the highest productivity rate and the highest life expectancy.

Steamboat travel on the Red river in the north opened channels for the furious and short-lived fur trade. Its demise gave way to farming, which remains the state's economic mainstay. The railway arrived in 1870 in fits and starts (accounting for the placement of boom-and-bust towns that dot the southern state), bringing new settlers, and forts were built throughout the territory to protect homesteaders from Indians.

Farm fixated

The drier Missouri Plateau in the west was settled later, as frontiersmen (Teddy Roosevelt among them) looked to the craggy Badlands as cattle country. Overgrazing and the severity of winter wiped out the industry; frugal German immigrants eventually came to carve out farms.

A raging dissatisfaction with farm policy steers North Dakota politics, making the state temperamentally inclined to vote against all incumbent administrations. Lonely marginal farmers formed the Non-Partisan League (NPL) in 1915 to put grain elevators and railroads in public hands. Their frankly socialist agenda tempered as the NPL merged with the Democrats, but the state's "prairie populist" politicians betray the early NPL heritage with their fierce opposition to GATT and free trade with Canada.

A breakthrough in processing of hard spring wheat revolutionised production in 1870 and farmers set to planting the "amber waves of grain" – red fife, bluestem and durum wheats – for which the state is now famous. Hardy potatoes and sugar beets also grow here. Ranching in the arid western plains, plus strip mining and some oil production provide the state with some diversification. But three years of drought, failing commodity prices and volatile farm policy have made for tough economic times. Only 39% of the state's manufacturing jobs are in rural areas where just 25% of the population now lives; out-migration has been rife.

State facts

Date of statehood	2 November 1889	Total area	70,704 sq miles
Capital	Bismarck	Highest point ft	White Butte 3,506
Other cities	Fargo, Grand Forks, Minot	Main rivers	Missouri, Red

Climate Continental, with a wide range of temperature and moderate rainfall.
Geography Central lowland in the east comprises the flat Red River Valley and the Rolling Drift Prairie; Missouri Plateau of the Great Plains on the west.
Time zone Central

People

			%
Population m	0.64	Under 18	27.0
% av. ann. growth 1980–92	-0.2	Over 65	14.6
Pop. per sq mile	9.2	Urban	53.3
Birth rate per 1,000 pop.	14.5	Male	49.8
Death rate per 1,000 pop.	8.9	White	94.6
Pop. below poverty line %	14.4	Hispanic	0.7
Doctors per 100,000 pop.	170	Black	0.6
Hospital beds per 100,000 pop.	813	School spending per head	$4,119

The economy

GSP $m	11,231	Av. income per head $	16,854
No. of new corporations '000	0.8	% of national average	85

Structure of GSP	%		%
Construction	4.6	Manufacturing	6.0
Transportation, public utilities	11.4	Wholesale/retail trade	17.1
Services	15.0	Finance, insurance, real estate	18.7
Government	12.8	Other	14.4

Principal industries Agriculture, mining, tourism, manufacturing
Main crops Spring wheat, durum, barley, rye, flaxseed, oats, potatoes, dried edible beans, honey, soybeans, sugar beets, sunflowers, hay

Politics

Senate Byron Dorgan (D; term expires 1999), Kent Conrad (D; term expires 1999)
House Earl Pomeroy (D)

State government
Governor Edward Schafer (R; term expires 1997)
State Legislature Senate 25D, 24R; House 65R, 33D
Total expenditure (1992) $1,513m

OHIO

Ohio is the workshop of America. Only California and New York churn out a greater value of manufactures. A list of Ohio's ten biggest cities – the state capital, Columbus, Cleveland, Cincinnati, Toledo, Akron, Dayton, Youngstown, Parma, Canton and Lorain – reads like a gazetteer of Rust-Bowl America, but Ohio is the prime example of how industrial America has refound its international competitiveness.

The Buckeye state is a succession of plains rolling southward from Lake Erie, which forms Ohio's northern border, to Kentucky and West Virginia the other side of the Ohio river, which marks Ohio's southern border. Pennsylvania is to the east beyond the Allegheny plateau and Indiana to the west.

French explorers and Virginian fur traders were the first Europeans in the area before the United States acquired the Northwest Territory after the Revolutionary war. The first settlement was established by war veterans at Marietta in 1788. An Indian war did not end until General "Mad Anthony" Wayne won the Battle of Fallen Timbers in 1794. In the war of 1812 against the British, Commodore Oliver Perry's naval victory at the Battle of Lake Erie and William Harrison's subsequent drive into Canada stopped further British incursions.

Today, with a population of just over 11m, Ohio is the seventh most populous state, though at 41,000 square miles it is only the 35th largest. Nine out of ten Ohioans live in or around the ten biggest cities, which are mostly near Lake Erie or on tributaries of the Ohio river. Ohio is blue-collar America, albeit in modern form. The state ranks below the national average in heads of households holding a university degree, though the improvement in tertiary education has been one of the cornerstones of the state's economic renaissance.

Ohio has given America eight presidents: William Henry Harrison, Grant, Hayes, Garfield, Benjamin Harrison, McKinley, Taft and Harding. All were Republicans except for the Whig William Henry Harrison, and all were born before the end of the Civil War. Among more recent politicians of note is the former astronaut, John Glenn, a Democratic senator. With the seventh most electoral college votes, Ohio plays a weighty, if not pivotal, role in presidential elections.

Rustbelt reshined

Manufacturing dominates the Ohio economy, much of it still related to its traditional mainstay, the motor industry. It accounts for nearly one-third of state domestic product, although its share of employment has fallen to less than one quarter, reflecting the painful restructuring of the 1980s.

Ohio is the largest producer of trucks in America, and ranks second after Michigan in overall motor industry output. It is the leading state in the nation for rubber and plastics production. It ranks in the top five for aircraft, chemicals, electronics and machinery. It ranks in the top ten for food processing, missiles and space vehicles, paper products and oil refining. Its extractive industries lead in lime quarrying, and are significant in coal, clay, sand, salt and gravel.

Although the motor plants are spread around the state, most of Ohio's main cities are associated with particular industries. Cleveland is known for vehicle parts, refining and steel-making; Cincinnati for machine tools and jet engines; Toledo for glass and vehicles parts; Akron for polymers (no longer tyres); Dayton for office machines and heating and cooling equipment; Youngstown for steel-making; Canton for ball bearings.

These cities went through hard times in the 1980s when the recession of the early part of the decade wreaked havoc on manufacturing employment in the state and exposed how uncompetitive much of the industrial Mid-West had become. Jobs were being lost to the lower-wage, lower-tax Sunbelt states, and markets to foreign rivals, particularly those from Asia. In a Darwinian struggle for industrial survival, Ohioan companies were not proving the fittest.

Post-recession strategy

The response of Ohio's public-policy makers was in many ways a model for all of industrial America facing the twin challenges of greater external competition and the switch from a manufacturing- to an information-based economy. The state's competitiveness strategy was based on the twin assumptions that a low-wage service economy could not be a substitute for high-wage manufacturing one; and that Ohio manufacturers could not compete with Sunbelt and Asian factories on labour cost, and so would have to compete on labour quality. That meant raising worker productivity and changing a decades-old culture of adversarial relations between labour and management, and of distance between the public and private sectors.

The strategy had four thrusts: first, public money for firms to modernise the industrial infrastructure, particularly by getting productivity-boosting new technologies into factories and especially the medium and small firms that employ half the workforce; second, industrial training to modernise the skills of the workforce to maximise the investment in new technology; third, investment in universities to increase the number of graduate engineers and to expand advanced R&D facilities that could be used by business and spin-off high-tech start-ups; fourth, aggressive pursuit of inward foreign direct investment to bring in new jobs, production technologies and labour-relations models, and of new export markets for Ohioan firms.

Now to maintain momentum

The strategy turned round Ohioan industry to such an extent that it was relatively unscathed by the recession of the early 1990s. Productivity gains were especially achieved in motor, chemicals and fabricated metals industries. The state has established in its universities leading R&D centres for clean-coal technology, aeronautics, liquid crystal technology, space-related advance materials and mapping technology, transport and medicine. It has attracted more than 300 new foreign firms, including 100 Japanese ones. Ohio has more Japanese motor and motor-parts makers than any other state. Honda established the first Japanese car transplant factory at Marysville. Nissan has a huge mini-van joint venture with Ford.

One in eight jobs in Ohio is now related in some way to international trade. Ohio is second in the nation in export related jobs. It is the sixth ranked exporting state. Its exports include Hondas to Japan. The state has its own export credit guarantee scheme and trade offices in Tokyo and Brussels.

The challenges facing Ohio arc to maintain the momentum of improving the skills of its technical and professional workforce and its technical infrastructure now other states are doing the same. For all its undoubted progress in tertiary education it starts from a low base. It needs to step up the conversion of academic research into commercial products. It also needs to ensure that the incentives it offers foreign investors for job creation are creating high-value added jobs. It must continue to develop its export markets, especially for the new industries it is creating. It must also continue to diversify its economy. In the 1980s, its service-sector employment was the sixth fastest growing in America. Retailing, wholesaling and tourism, from which it has the ninth highest revenue in America, thanks to the development of conference business, are fast growing service sectors.

State facts

Date of statehood	1 March 1803	Total area	44,828 sq miles
Capital	Columbus	Highest point ft	Campbell Hill 1,549
Other cities	Cleveland, Cincinnati, Toledo	Main rivers	Maumee, Portage, Ohio, Miami

Climate Temperate but variable; weather subject to much precipitation.
Geography Generally rolling plain; Allegheny plateau in east; Lake Erie plains extend southward; central plains in the west.
Time zone Eastern Standard

People

			%
Population m	11.02	Under 18	25.6
% av. ann. growth 1980–92	0.2	Over 65	13.2
Pop. per sq mile	269.0	Urban	74.1
Birth rate per 1,000 pop.	15.4	Male	48.2
Death rate per 1,000 pop.	9.1	White	87.8
Pop. below poverty line %	12.5	Hispanic	1.3
Doctors per 100,000 pop.	196	Black	10.6
Hospital beds per 100,000 pop.	466	School spending per head	$5,451

The economy

GSP $m	211,545	Av. income per head $	18,624
No. of new corporations '000	17.9	% of national average	94

Structure of GSP	%		%
Construction	3.7	Manufacturing	27.5
Transportation, public utilities	8.0	Wholesale/retail trade	15.5
Services	17.0	Finance, insurance, real estate	16.1
Government	9.5	Other	2.7

Principal industries Manufacturing, trade, services
Main crops Corn, hay, winter wheat, oats, soybeans

Politics

Senate John Glenn (D; term expires 1999), Howard Metzenbaum (D; term expires 1995)
House David Mann, Tony Hall, Ted Strickland, Marcy Kaptur, Louis Stokes, Sherrod Brown, Thomas Sawyer, James A. Traficant Jr, Douglas Applegate, Eric Fingerhut (all D); Willis D. Gradison, Michael G. Oxley, Paul Gillmor, David Hobson, John Boehner, Martin Hoke, John Kasich, Deborah Pryce, Ralph Regula (all R)

State government
Governor George Voinovich (R; term expires 1995)
State Legislature Senate 20R, 13D; House 53R, 46D
Total expenditure (1992) $24,770m

OKLAHOMA

The "Sooner" state took its nickname from the over-anxious homesteaders who jumped the gun on an April morning in 1889 when the government invited white settlers to race across the line into former "Indian Territory" and stake their claims in the great rush for range that has been memorialised in Hollywood musicals. The high prairies in the west of the state are part of the Great Plains, frozen by winter winds and scorched by summer sun. Elevations decline toward the east, except in the highlands of the Ozark plateau and the Ouachita Mountains.

Religion and a rough edge

Most residents live in metropolitan areas, principally in the eponymous capital city and in Tulsa. The latter, built on the state's vast oil reserves, has fancied itself "the oil capital of the world". If it falls somewhat shy of its boast, Tulsa has at least a tradition of pretentiousness; even in the early years, before Pentecostal faith healer Oral Roberts built his headquarters, university and 60-floor City of Faith hospital here, Tulsa residents looked down upon the muddy-booted "Okies" from Oklahoma City. It was then and is now one of America's most conservative cities.

There is a rougher-hewn feel to the capital; residents are said to prefer chicken-fried steak to stir-fried chicken, and the capitol building, surrounded by oil rigs which were still pumping as late as 1989, still lacks its dome. Muskogee was the patriotic subject of a 1969 song, "Okie from Muskogee", but the town has a corrupt and crime-ridden past. The state's southern roots are recognisable in the south-east corner. Little Dixie is still mostly poor and rural, but government-built highways connect people to jobs in more vibrant areas and retirement communities have sprung up along the lakes.

Unsettled by wars and winds

Oklahoma was the home of the Plains Indian tribes, including the Comanche and Apache, when it came under American control with the Louisiana Purchase in 1803. Before white settlers arrived it had been settled in a hurry in the 1830s by the "Five Civilised Tribes" marshalled there from Georgia and Alabama over the Trail of Tears by Andrew Jackson's troops. County names recall the Cherokee, Chickasaw, Choctaw, Creek and Seminole the federal government forced to move there. Today only California has more Native American residents than does Oklahoma, not just on reservations, but assimilated throughout the state.

After the Civil War, the government began assigning some of the tribes' lands to other, more recently displaced Indians, but with the opening of cattle paths like the Chisholm trail, white settlers pressed for the right to move there. A strip was opened in 1889 which precipitated the great land grab. Territory that remained was made available to homesteaders in 1906.

By the 1890s Oklahoma had already become a major oil producer. Successful farming made the state's economy grow rapidly in the new century's early decades, until erosion and drought carried away soil in tremendous dust storms. In *Grapes of Wrath* John Steinbeck dramatised what became the greatest internal migration of the 1930s, as Okies fled the Dust Bowl and traced Route 66 to the greener grasses of California. Not until the 1970s sent oil prices soaring would the state population return to pre-Depression levels.

The cycles of Oklahoma's precarious economies have made for an unstable state politics as well. Most early settlers were southerners and historically Democratic. The south and east of the state still lean left, but the northwestern wheat counties and big cities have tended to vote Republican since the 1950s.

Surviving on pork and barrels

Oklahoma's economy was revitalised during the second world war and for a while since then the energy-related industries made Oklahoma one of the fastest-growing states in the Sunbelt. But the boom was short-lived and burst in 1982 just as the state's farm economy collapsed. The auction of drill rigs, derrick trailers and tractors became the 1980s emblem of Oklahoma's modern dustbowl.

Energy and agriculture are still Oklahoma's leading industries, but both have taken a pounding since the 1980s. The state's efforts to diversify since then have allowed it to weather this decade's economic ills rather admirably; manufacturing now accounts for almost 15% of output. American Airlines bases its maintenance and engineering facility as well as its SABRE reservation system in Tulsa, providing 10,000 jobs. The Federal Aviation Administration expanded operations in Oklahoma City in 1991, as did Hertz's reservation system in the capital. Small business growth throughout the state has helped push Oklahoma's unemployment rate down from 6.7% to 5.7% since 1991. Local government incentives have attracted food processing factories; a penny tax in the Panhandle attracted 2,000 jobs with Seaboard Pork.

State facts

Date of statehood 16 November 1907 Total area 69,903 sq miles
Capital Oklahoma City Highest point ft Black Mesa 4,973
Other cities Tulsa, Norman, Lawton Main rivers Arkansas, Red, Canadian, Cimarron

Climate Temperate; southern humid belt merging with colder northern continental; humid eastern and dry western zones.
Geography High plains predominate the west, hills and small mountains in the east; the east central region is dominated by the Arkansas River Basin and Red River Plains, in the south.
Time zone Central

People

			%
Population m	3.21	Under 18	26.7
% av. ann. growth 1980–92	0.2	Over 65	13.5
Pop. per sq mile	46.8	Urban	67.7
Birth rate per 1,000 pop.	15.1	Male	48.7
Death rate per 1,000 pop.	9.6	White	82.1
Pop. below poverty line %	16.7	Hispanic	2.7
Doctors per 100,000 pop.	147	Black	7.4
Hospital beds per 100,000 pop.	467	School spending per head	$3,939

The economy

			%
GSP $m	52,342	Av. income per head $	16,198
No. of new corporations '000	7.1	% of national average	82

Structure of GSP	%		%
Construction	3.5	Manufacturing	14.2
Transportation, public utilities	11.1	Wholesale/retail trade	15.8
Services	16.0	Finance, insurance, real estate	13.8
Government	14.6	Other	11.0

Principal industries Manufacturing, mineral and energy exploration and production, agriculture, printing and publishing
Main crops Wheat, hay, peanuts, grain sorghum, soybeans, corn, pecans, oats, barley, rye

Politics

Senate David Boren (D; term expires 1997), Don Nickles (R; term expires 1999)
House Mike Synar, Bill Brewster, Dave McCurdy, Glenn English (all D); James M. Inhofe, Ernest Jim Istook (both R)

State government
Governor David Walters (D; term expires 1995)
State Legislature Senate 37D, 11R; House 69D, 32R
Total expenditure (1992) $7,371m

OREGON

The Cascade Mountains split the state into lush coast on the west and sagebrush plains and high deserts to the east. Oregon's first city, Astoria, perched at the mouth of the Columbia, maintains the rugged feel of a western outpost, but the state's New England heritage is unmistakable in orderly Portland. Its slow, cautious growth has kept it second to Seattle as the north-west's major metropolis, but a modern light-rail system now shuttles commuters across the winding Willamette river into Portland's dynamic downtown.

White-collar jobs have come to the state with businesses such as Nike, which is headquartered here. The influx of computer companies such as Tektronics and Intel have made Portland's outskirts Oregon's "Silicon Forest". But one need only look as far as the old lumber barons' mansions on "The Heights" overlooking the city to be reminded of timber's enduring dominance in the state.

Trail-blazers

Oregon's terrain is similar to that of Washington, with which it shares a lot of history, as well as a border. The search for a shortcut between the oceans drew Oregon's first explorers. Fur traders, in furious and profitable pursuit of pelts, soon followed. But it was Thomas Jefferson's determination to strengthen American claims to the Columbia watershed that blazed the 2,000-mile North-west Trail from Missouri across the Continental Divide.

The expedition of Lewis and Clark paved the way for the "Oregon fever" which spread through America, bringing thousands of settlers to the territory in the Great Migration of 1840 to 1860. Railway speeded growth of the lumber industry, Oregon's economic mainstay, after its arrival in 1880. The state's development since has been closely connected to the construction of massive hydroelectric plants along the Columbia river.

Oregon still tends to chart its own course. It was the first state in the country to pass a bottle bill, first to decriminalise marijuana and first to allow abortions. In 1991 it radically redesigned its educational system, forcing students in high school to choose between pursuing college or learning a trade. It also proposed plans to ration government-financed healthcare for the poor; this was struck down by the federal government, which feared it violated the Americans with Disabilities Act.

With innovation has often come a willingness – to a fault – to entertain new ideas. Oregon's tolerance was made famous by the cult leader Bhagwan Shree Rajneesh, who took over a small town in eastern Oregon until his commune was shut down by federal prosecutors.

Politically the state is fidgety. Portland leans reliably left, but towns to the south (including the capital of Salem) have a Yankee conservatism about them. People in the semi-arid interior vote like Idaho Republicans, far removed from the logger-liberal coast.

In 1990 Oregon voters sent their legislature a confounding (if characteristic) mixed message. They elected the state's first female governor, a Democrat who promised change and new social programmes, meanwhile limiting the state's funds by passing an initiative that slashed property taxes and forced the state to cut its budget by 15%. Ever-experimental Oregon – still true to its thrifty New England roots – seems determined to prove that new ideas can subsist on a severe financial diet.

Trendiness tempered by timber

Logging is Oregon's economic equivalent of Washington's Boeing: the industry supplies nearly a third of the state's factory jobs. The dependence is uncomfortable. Employment fell by more than 11% in 1990/91. But most Oregonians remain surprisingly sanguine about job prospects; they assume high-tech industries will absorb those laid off in other sectors.

State facts

Date of statehood	14 February 1859	Total area	98,386 sq miles
Capital	Salem	Highest point ft	Mt Hood 11,239
Other cities	Portland, Eugene, Gresham	Main rivers	Columbia, Willamette, Snake

Climate Coastal mild and humid climate; continental dryness and extreme temperatures in the interior.
Geography Coast Range of rugged mountains; fertile Willamette River Valley to east and south; Cascade Mountain Range of volcanic peaks east of the valley; plateau east of Cascades, remaining two-thirds of state.
Time zone Pacific

People

			%
Population m	2.98	Under 18	25.7
% av. ann. growth 1980–92	1.0	Over 65	13.8
Pop. per sq mile	31.0	Urban	70.5
Birth rate per 1,000 pop.	15.1	Male	49.2
Death rate per 1,000 pop.	8.6	White	92.8
Pop. below poverty line %	12.4	Hispanic	4.0
Doctors per 100,000 pop.	205	Black	1.6
Hospital beds per 100,000 pop.	339	School spending per head	$5,972

The economy

GSP $m	52,118	Av. income per head $	18,202
No. of new corporations '000	8.4	% of national average	92

Structure of GSP	%		%
Construction	4.0	Manufacturing	19.6
Transportation, public utilities	9.6	Wholesale/retail trade	16.4
Services	17.3	Finance, insurance, real estate	16.9
Government	11.8	Other	4.4

Principal industries Forestry, agriculture, tourism, high technology, manufacturing
Main crops Hay, grass seed, farm forest products, wheat, potatoes

Politics

Senate Mark Hatfield (R; term expires 1997), Bob Packwood (R; term expires 1999)
House Elizabeth Furse, Ron Wyden, Peter DeFazio, Mike Kopetski (all D); Bob Smith (R)

State government
Governor Barbara Roberts (D; term expires 1995)
State Legislature Senate 16D, 14R; House 32R, 28D
Total expenditure (1992) $8,229m

PENNSYLVANIA

Pennsylvania led America into revolution and heavy industry. It led the decline of great industries such as steel and coal. After hard times, the Keystone state, which is the fifth biggest state economy, is now trying to lead itself into a post-industrial future.

The area's first European settlers were Swedes, who lost a 12-year-old settlement on Tinicum island to the Dutch in 1653. Control passed to England with the capture of New Netherlands in 1664. What is now Pennsylvania was granted to William Penn, a Quaker, in 1681. Penn's city of "brotherly love", Philadelphia, was capital of the United States for most of the time between 1776, when the Declaration of Independence was signed in the city, to 1800. The constitution was also drawn up there, in 1787. The Liberty Bell is opposite Independence Hall, where the two documents were drafted.

Gettysburg, site of one of the pivotal battles of the Civil War, is in the richly historic state, whose southern border, with Maryland, formed part of the Mason-Dixon Line. The Delaware river, with Philadelphia and its deep-water port on its western bank, separates Pennsylvania from New Jersey. The south-east of the state sits on the Piedmont plateau. Most of the old steel towns such as Allentown, Scranton, Reading and Bethlehem, are there, between the Delaware and Susquehanna rivers.

The coal-bearing Allegheny mountains run diagonally across the state from south-west to north-east, reaching 3,000 feet at points. To the west on the Allegheny plateau are the West Virginia and Ohio borders. The Allegheny, Ohio and Monongahela rivers meet at Pittsburgh, the state's second largest city. Pennsylvania has a short north-eastern shoreline on Lake Erie and a long northern border with New York.

The first trade union in America was formed by Philadelphia shoemakers in 1792. The state has long had a reputation, which it has taken the death of heavy industry to kill, for confrontation between labour and management. Pennsylvania is also home to the Amish, one of the groups of Pennsylvania Dutch (a corruption of Deutsch), descendants of German families that have farmed in south-eastern Pennsylvania for more than two centuries.

Steel, coal, oil and the railroad

Pennsylvania's economy was built on railways, steel, coal and oil, which was discovered in the state in the mid-1800s. It was the state of Carnegie and Mellon. As recently as the 1960s, Pennsylvania was one of the most heavily industrialised areas in the world. Steel, chemicals, electrical and industrial equipment poured forth from the mills and factories around Pittsburgh and Philadelphia.

Today manufacturing accounts for only one-fifth of employment and state domestic product. The state ranks in the top ten in aerospace, chemicals, electronics and machinery production, but Pennsylvania's steel and coal industries had started to die in the 1970s, unable to compete with mills and mines from Japan to Brazil and slow to change increasingly obsolescent high-cost methods. After two painful decades of restructuring, the much shrunken steel industry is re-emerging as a supplier of specialty steels.

After two decades of decline Pennsylvania is rebuilding its economy on a quartet of industries that its policy-makers believe can both exploit the state's natural resources and provide a diversified high-value-added manufacturing base: food processing, hardwoods, pharmaceuticals, and printing and publishing

Agri-business is now the largest industry. Pennsylvania has a larger rural population than any other state and the most fertile soil east of the Mississippi. It is a leading producer of vegetables, mushrooms, fruit, poultry, eggs and dairy products, and is the largest fruit-importing state in America. There are now more than 2,000 food processing firms in Pennsylvania. Pennsylvania State University is a national leader of food technology and agricultural research. The state capital, Harrisburg, holds the world's largest annual indoor farm show.

Three-fifths of Pennsylvania is forested with oak, cherry, ash and other hardwoods. Pennsylvania has larger commercial reserves of hardwood, at 16m acres, than any other state, and one-eighth of the hardwood reserves in America.

Pennsylvania has long been a main landing point for imported paper, and the state is a leading producer of paper products. A future role as a centre of printing and publishing is premised on cheap access to water and energy, and a good location for distribution.

Drugs and high-tech

Pharmaceuticals is the most high-tech of Pennsylvania's four industries for the future. Every 11th pharmaceuticals worker in America is already employed in Pennsylvania. The industry is being built around Philadelphia and the south-eastern counties, where there is a growing concentration of R&D facilities. Pharmaceuticals are the main reason that the state has the fourth-highest number of high-tech firms in the nation. Pittsburgh, which lost 100,000 manufacturing jobs in the 1980s, has become a centre of software research. Johnstown is being turned into a centre for powdered-metals research.

Pennsylvania spends more taxpayers' dollars to support technology development and to attract new technology businesses than any other. It concentrates on connecting university research with business and on getting advanced technology into small and medium-sized manufacturing companies. A state-financed data network connects the seven leading universities. This lets businesses have access to the research being carried out at those universities and to the Pittsburgh Supercomputing Centre.

Training up and cleaning up

The main challenge for Pennsylvania is to continue the diversification of its economy, and to find ways of revitalising old steel and mining areas, that have been bypassed by the move into more high-tech-based manufacturing and services. There are still considerable pockets of unemployment in the state. The state's fastest growing service industries – healthcare, education, finance and tourism – are based in Pittsburgh and Philadelphia.

Pennsylvania also needs to ensure its workforce is ready for the new industries. Customised retraining has been a key part of the state's economic redevelopment policy, but too many high-school children do not go on to college for an economy basing its future on high-tech.

A third challenge is to clean up the state after a century of heavy industry. Tough environmental protection laws only started to be passed in the late 1980s. These concentrate on recycling and toxic waste disposal. Only now are they being expanded to return contaminated industrial sites in depressed areas to productive use, and to protect now-needed farmland from development. Pennsylvania also needs to provide the "clean and green" environment that will attract high-tech businesses and tourists. The state also needs to maintain its budgetary conservatism so that it can continue investment in basic infrastructure and technology development.

House Thomas Foglietta, Lucien Blackwell, Robert Borski, Ron Klink, Tim Holden, Paul E. Kanjorski, John Murtha, Marjorie Mezvinsky, William Coyne, Paul McHale, Austin Murphy (all D); Bill Clinger Jr, Curt Weldon, Jim Greenwood, Bud Shuster, Joseph McDade, Robert S. Walker, George Gekas, Rick Santorum, William Goodling, Thomas Ridge (all R)

State facts

Date of statehood	12 December 1787	Total area	46,058 sq miles
Capital	Harrisburg	Highest point ft	Mt Davis 3,213
Other cities	Philadelphia,	Main rivers	Susquehanna,
	Pittsburgh, Erie		Allegheny, Delaware

Climate Continental with wide fluctuations in seasonal temperatures.
Geography Allegheny mountains run south-west–north-east, with Piedmont and Coast Plain the SE triangle; Allegheny Front a diagonal spine across the state's centre, north and west rugged plateau falls to Lake Erie Lowland.
Time zone Eastern Standard

People

			%
Population m	12.01	Under 18	23.7
% av. ann. growth 1980–92	0.1	Over 65	15.7
Pop. per sq mile	267.9	Urban	68.9
Birth rate per 1,000 pop.	14.5	Male	47.9
Death rate per 1,000 pop.	10.3	White	88.5
Pop. below poverty line %	11.1	Hispanic	2.0
Doctors per 100,000 pop.	235	Black	9.2
Hospital beds per 100,000 pop.	552	School spending per head	$6,980

The economy

GSP $m	227,898	Av. income per head $	20,253
No. of new corporations '000	17.3	% of national average	102

Structure of GSP	%		%
Construction	4.6	Manufacturing	21.6
Transportation, public utilities	9.9	Wholesale/retail trade	15.4
Services	20.5	Finance, insurance, real estate	16.2
Government	9.8	Other	2.0

Principal industries Steel, travel, health, apparel, machinery, food & agriculture
Main crops Corn, hay, mushrooms, apples, potatoes, winter wheat, oats, vegetables, tobacco, grapes

Politics

Senate Arlen Specter (R; term expires 1999), Harris Wofford (D; term expires 1995)
House See list on page 171.

State government
Governor Robert P. Casey (D; term expires Jan 1995)
State Legislature Senate 25D, 25R; House 105D, 98R
Total expenditure (1992) $28,109m

RHODE ISLAND

Barely 1,200 square miles, the smallest state in the union makes up by having the longest formal name: the State of Rhode Island and Providence Plantations. Wedged between Connecticut and Massachusetts, "Little Rhody" is mainly mainland, not an island, though the state contains 35 of them.

A million people, a quarter of whom claim Irish descent, live in Rhode Island, making it the third most densely populated state. Three out of five Rhode Islanders live in or around picturesque Providence, the state capital and yet another New England town founded in the 17th century as a haven from the autocratic Puritanism of the Massachusetts colony. The state has long maintained a tradition of religious and intellectual freedom. Quakers and New Dealers were to find a home among Providence's seven hills. The city's synagogue was the first in America. In 1764 wealthy Baptists founded Brown University, a member of the Ivy League. Now secular, Brown remains the centre of the state's intellectual life.

In the 19th century Providence was a centre for textiles and light manufacturing. Both industries are mostly long gone, though today jewellery and electronics have brought a modest industrial revival to the state's manufacturing, which accounts for 21% of the economy.

Boats on the bay

Rhode Island is dominated by Narragansett Bay. This gives a 400-mile coastline to a state that can be driven across in less than two hours. Providence and Newport were leading ports from the earliest days. Over the years, Rhode Island became a centre first for pirates raiding shipping in the North Atlantic and then for the West Africa–West Indies–New England slave trade. Subsequently it became a home to the US Navy. The active sailors left in 1974 but the Naval War College remains.

Newport thinks of itself as the world's yachting capital. The America's Cup, yachting's premier race, was held off Newport from 1851 until 1983, when the cup was lost to Australia. The biennial Bermuda race starts there; the single-handed transatlantic race ends there.

Newport is also the centre of the state's burgeoning tourist industry. It was where the millionaires of the Gilded Age built their seaside "cottages" to escape the summer heat of New York and Baltimore. Today it is tourists by the million who troop round Newport's grand houses and its restored colonial buildings, as well as more modern attractions such as the Tennis Hall of Fame.

State facts

Date of statehood	29 May 1790	Total area	1,545 sq miles
Capital	Providence	Highest point ft	Jerimoth Hill 812
Other cities	Warwick, Cranston, Pawtucket	Main rivers	Blackstone, Pawtucket

Climate Invigorating and changeable.
Geography Eastern lowlands of Narragansett Basin; western uplands of flat and rolling hills.
Time zone Eastern Standard

People

			%
Population m	1.00	Under 18	23.2
% av. ann. growth 1980–92	0.5	Over 65	15.2
Pop. per sq mile	961.8	Urban	86.0
Birth rate per 1,000 pop.	15.1	Male	47.7
Death rate per 1,000 pop.	9.2	White	91.4
Pop. below poverty line %	9.6	Hispanic	4.6
Doctors per 100,000 pop.	254	Black	3.9
Hospital beds per 100,000 pop.	430	School spending per head	$6,834

The economy

GSP $m	18,807	Av. income per head $	20,299
No. of new corporations '000	2.5	% of national average	102

Structure of GSP	%		%
Construction	3.4	Manufacturing	21.3
Transportation, public utilities	6.3	Wholesale/retail trade	16.9
Services	21.4	Finance, insurance, real estate	17.8
Government	11.5	Other	1.4

Principal industries Manufacturing, services
Main crops Nursery products, turf, potatoes, apples

Politics

Senate John Chafee (R; term expires 1995), Claiborne Pell (D; term expires 1997)
House Jack Reed (D); Ronald K. Machtley (R)

State government
Governor Bruce Sundlun (D; term expires 1995)
State Legislature Senate 39D, 11R; House 85D, 15R
Total expenditure (1992) $3,181m

SOUTH CAROLINA

Few states have matched South Carolina's performance over the past two decades in shaking off the stigma of a backward, southern past to embrace a bright, high-tech future. Half a century ago the state was poor and illiterate. For the two-fifths of the state that was black, life was still nasty, brutish and short. Today, manufacturing companies, both American and foreign, are coming to South Carolina for its competitive wages and lack of labour unions. Retirees from the north and the Mid-West, lured by the sub-tropical climate, have snapped up beachside property. Development along the thriving seaboard – hurricanes notwithstanding – is far from hitting its limits.

Plantation roots

South Carolina's enduring poverty until a little more than a generation ago was the vestige of a former plantation economy. The earliest planters came in the 18th century to grow indigo, rice and cotton along the swampy lowlands of the coast. The town of Charleston stands today as testimony to their wealth. Along with wealth, though, went the pride of independence that at crucial times has cost the state dear. During the Revolutionary war 137 engagements were fought on South Carolinian soil. In December 1860 the state was the first to vote on secession from the Union. On April 12th 1861 the Confederate attack on Fort Sumter, off Charleston, marked the start of the Civil War. Charleston itself suffered a debilitating siege until the Confederates abandoned it in February 1865. After the war stubborn segregationalism ensured the state's backwardness until the 1950s.

From textiles to BMW

Manufacturing came to South Carolina in the 1920s with textile mills, but it was in the 1970s that the state went out to woo business. Success was rapid. The companies that came to set up have in turn given the state reason to forge a consensus on improving education, roads and the like. South Carolina's success has been not merely creating jobs, but of raising their quality. One in four of the state's jobs – a high proportion – still lie in manufacturing, which often pays low wages. But while the number employed in manufacturing, at 375,000, has stayed fairly constant since the early 1970s, the number of total jobs has risen from 900,000 to 1.5m. The fact that Germany's BMW opened its first ever North American plant in South Carolina is a mark of just how far the state has come.

State facts

Date of statehood	23 May 1788	Total area	32,008 sq miles
Capital	Columbia	Highest point ft	Sassafras
Other cities	Charleston,		Mountain 3,560
	North Charleston, Greenville	Main rivers	Pee Dee, Santee,
			Savannah

Climate Humid sub-tropical.
Geography Blue Ridge province in north-west has highest peaks; Piedmont lies between the mountains and the fall line; coastal plain covers two-thirds of the state.
Time zone Eastern Standard

People

			%
Population m	3.60	Under 18	26.2
% av. ann. growth 1980–92	1.2	Over 65	11.6
Pop. per sq mile	119.7	Urban	54.6
Birth rate per 1,000 pop.	16.8	Male	48.4
Death rate per 1,000 pop.	8.4	White	69.0
Pop. below poverty line %	15.4	Hispanic	0.9
Doctors per 100,000 pop.	161	Black	29.8
Hospital beds per 100,000 pop.	406	School spending per head	$4,537

The economy

GSP $m	60,150	Av. income per head $	15,989
No. of new corporations '000	5.7	% of national average	81

Structure of GSP	%		%
Construction	3.9	Manufacturing	25.7
Transportation, public utilities	8.2	Wholesale/retail trade	15.4
Services	13.6	Finance, insurance, real estate	15.9
Government	15.5	Other	1.8

Principal industries Tourism, agriculture, manufacturing
Main crops Tobacco, soybeans, corn, cotton, peaches, hay

Politics
Senate Strom Thurmond (R; term expires 1997), Ernest F. Hollings (D; term expires 1999).
House Arthur Ravenel Jr, Floyd Spence, Bob Inglis (all R); Butler Derrick Jr, John M. Spratt Jr, James Clyburn (all D)

State government
Governor Carroll A. Campbell Jr (R; term expires 1995)
State Legislature Senate 30D, 16R; House 73D, 50R, 1 Ind
Total expenditure (1992) $8,946m

SOUTH DAKOTA

The Missouri river which snakes through the centre of South Dakota has shaped the state's history. Indian villages thrived along the river's banks, and its waters carried European settlers to the territory. Cattle replaced the bison that used to roam the plains here, and the prairie grasses have long been ploughed into wheat crops. But the western half of the state remains a timeless moonscape of soft sediment and volcanic ash. Mount Rushmore is in South Dakota.

Treaties signed throughout the mid-1800s formally established the Black Hills as Indian land, but George Custer's discovery of gold there in 1874 touched off a rush of prospectors to the region. Indian refusal to sell the land to the federal government upon demand precipitated the Great Plains Indian Wars. Their leaders became legends – Red Cloud, Big Foot, Crazy Horse, Sitting Bull – but defeat was inevitable and settlement continued apace.

Gold lured some of the West's most colourful characters to South Dakota, Wild Bill Hickock, Calamity Jane and Texas Jack among them. But it was the stoical Scandinavian and German immigrants who streamed in as farming boomed late in the century that created a lasting foundation for the state's economy. When South Dakota was admitted to the Union in 1889 the Census Bureau declared the American frontier officially closed.

Parched earth and poker

America's largest gold mine is in the mineral-rich Black Hills. Most of South Dakota's arid west though is great, empty expanse interrupted by the odd ranch; the irrigated east yields grain crops. Agriculture remains key to the state's economy, but low taxes have drawn white-collar business. Citicorp brought new economic prospects to the state when it moved its credit card operations to Sioux Falls in 1981. Other banks followed and the move spawned the building of shopping and medical centres. Rapid City enjoyed similar growth, as did other mid-sized towns along the freeways; almost every other county in South Dakota lost population.

The state is wracked by bitter disputes over water policy; reservoir levels are low, hurting both fishing and boating businesses. Tumbleweeds as big as cars rolled into Mobridge in 1989, the same year casinos were made legal in South Dakota. Government experiments in gambling have brought millions in new tourist revenue. Still, South Dakota's Corn Palace in Mitchell and Wall Drug, a 46,000-square foot emporium that snares 75% of the freeway traffic, remain mainstays of the state's thriving tourism industry.

State facts

Date of statehood	2 November 1889	Total area	77,121 sq miles
Capital	Pierre	Highest point ft	Harney Peak 7,242
Other cities	Sioux Falls, Rapid City, Aberdeen	Main rivers	Missouri, Grand, Moreau, James, Vermilion

Climate Characterised by extremes of temperature, persistent winds, low precipitation and humidity.
Geography Prairie Plains in the east; rolling hills of the Great Plains in the west; the Black Hills rise to 3,500 ft in the south-west corner.
Time zone Central

People

			%
Population m	0.71	Under 18	28.7
% av. ann. growth 1980–92	0.2	Over 65	14.7
Pop. per sq mile	9.4	Urban	50.0
Birth rate per 1,000 pop.	15.8	Male	49.2
Death rate per 1,000 pop.	9.4	White	91.6
Pop. below poverty line %	15.9	Hispanic	0.8
Doctors per 100,000 pop.	140	Black	0.5
Hospital beds per 100,000 pop.	775	School spending per head	$4,255

The economy

GSP $m	11,135	Av. income per head $	16,558
No. of new corporations '000	1.0	% of national average	83

Structure of GSP	%		%
Construction	4.2	Manufacturing	9.8
Transportation, public utilities	9.2	Wholesale/retail trade	16.8
Services	15.6	Finance, insurance, real estate	16.7
Government	13.2	Other	14.5

Principal industries Agriculture, services, manufacturing
Main crops Corn, oats, wheat, sunflowers, soybeans, sorghum

Politics
Senate Larry Pressler (R; term expires 1997), Tom Daschle (D; term expires 1999).
House Tim Johnson (D)

State government
Governor George Mickelson (R; term expires 1995)
State Legislature Senate 20D, 15R; House 41R, 29D
Total expenditure (1992) $1,418m

TENNESSEE

Tennessee – the name was taken from Tanasi, the Indians' name for the fat brown river that winds its way through the state – could easily be three states, so different to this day are the western, central and eastern regions. The first whites, known as Overmountain men, began to push through the Appalachians of eastern Tennessee in the 1760s. The frontiersmen in this remote but beautiful region had a fierce doggedness about them. Their most famous case of independence was an attempt to found a 14th state of the union in the Appalachians – called Franklin – before Tennessee proper was granted statehood in 1796.

Those settlers who hacked their way to the other side of the mountains found rolling, bluegrass land in what is now central Tennessee. By contrast, the Mississippi's flat flood-plains in western Tennessee, which supported slaves and plantations, have more in common with the Mississippi Delta to the south than with the rest of Tennessee.

Regional differences

Three regions, and three stars to the state flag. All Tennesseans were (and still are) proud of Old Hickory: Andrew Jackson, a travelling Nashville lawyer and hero of the battle against the English at New Orleans became, in 1830, the first (Democratic) president from Tennessee. Andrew Johnson became the ineffectual (Republican) second after Abraham Lincoln was assassinated. But with the Civil War, the state's sensibilities diverged again for good. Throughout the war, the hill regions of eastern Tennessee remained a Unionist hotbed while the state as a whole joined the Confederacy. To this day Tennessee votes in presidential elections along those age-old lines, with loyal Republicans in the east, yellow-dog Democrats in central Tennessee and the west.

Yet if party lines are drawn more rigidly in Tennessee than in most states, there has been plenty of room for political flair. It may have been an old-fashioned Democratic party machine from Memphis which delivered most of the state's Democratic votes for much of this century, but that was nevertheless a strong enough base for two liberal senators, Estes Kefauver and Albert Gore Senior, to buck the southern habit during the 1950s and early 1960s and vote for civil rights. They were greatly helped by the backdrop of the New Deal Tennessee Valley Authority, which tamed an unpredictable flood-river, furnished a source of cheap electricity and created thousands of needed jobs. When Republicans held the balance of power in the state in the

1970s, they were moderate by southern standards – interested, above all in improving the state's education and attracting investment. With the latter well under way, the Democrats are firmly back in power as old party lines reestablished themselves during the 1980s.

Foreign-fuelled growth

During the 1980s the population of most of the states along the Mississippi barely grew or even shrank. But Tennessee grew by 6.2%. The Nashville metropolitan area grew by nearly three times that. The main impetus was foreign direct investment. Tennessee has been seeking foreign investment as long as the Rustbelt states of the Great Lakes have been decrying it. The first Japanese company set up shop in 1977, when Nissan opened a forklift truck distribution centre. The company followed with a pick-up truck manufacturing plant at Smyrna.

Today, over 300 foreign operations are based in Tennessee. There are more than 50 Japanese factories and over 30 Japanese distribution centres, making Tennessee second only to California in terms of Japanese direct investment. Nor is it just foreigners attracted to Tennessee's weak unions but good labour relations and an absence of state corporate income tax. General Motors chose to build its ground-breaking Saturn plant at Spring Hill, not far from Nashville. Nor is it just manufacturing at which Tennessee excels. A number of entrepreneurs have made the state their base. Notable among them is Chris Whittle, who has built up a media and education empire in Knoxville.

Cotton, music and services

Two great cities, Nashville and Memphis, have always accentuated Tennessee's extremes: overwhelmingly white Nashville is the home to country music and Memphis to predominantly black jazz and blues. And over the past decade it has been Nashville which has seen heady economic growth. That does not mean that Memphis, a cotton city built on the banks of the Mississippi for another era, should be written off. Not only is it still the world's biggest market for spot cotton, but it is carving out a position for itself as a services and distribution centre. This, for instance, is home to Federal Express's delivery hub. And, between St Louis and New Orleans, Nashville and Dallas-Fort Worth, there really is no city save Memphis.

State facts

Date of statehood	1 June 1796	Total area	42,146 sq miles
Capital	Nashville	Highest point ft	Clingmans Dome
Other cities	Memphis, Knoxville,		6,643
	Chattanooga	Main rivers	Mississippi,
			Tennessee, Cumberland

Climate Humid continental to the north; humid sub-tropical to the south.
Geography Rugged country in east; Great Smoky Mountains of Unakas; low ridges of Appalachian Valley; flat Cumberland Plateau; slightly rolling terrain of Interior Low Plateau, the largest region; Eastern Gulf Coastal Plain to west; Mississippi Alluvial Plain in extreme west.
Time zone Central

People

			%
Population m	5.02	Under 18	24.8
% av. ann. growth 1980–92	0.8	Over 65	12.7
Pop. per sq mile	121.9	Urban	60.9
Birth rate per 1,000 pop.	15.4	Male	48.2
Death rate per 1,000 pop.	9.2	White	83.0
Pop. below poverty line %	15.7	Hispanic	0.7
Doctors per 100,000 pop.	196	Black	16.0
Hospital beds per 100,000 pop.	582	School spending per head	$3,736

The economy

GSP $m	92,267	Av. income per head $	17,341
No. of new corporations '000	8.3	% of national average	87

Structure of GSP	%		%
Construction	4.3	Manufacturing	24.0
Transportation, public utilities	7.9	Wholesale/retail trade	17.5
Services	16.8	Finance, insurance, real estate	15.2
Government	11.9	Other	2.4

Principal industries Trade, services, construction, transportation, communications, public utilities, finance, insurance, real estate
Main crops Soybeans, greenhouse/nursery, cotton/lint

Politics

Senate Harlan Matthews (D; term expires 1997), James Sasser (D; term expires 1995)
House Marilyn Lloyd, Jim Cooper, Bob Clement, Bart Gordon, John S. Tanner, Harold E. Ford (all D); Jimmy Quillen, John J. Duncan Jr, Don Sundquist (all R)

State government
Governor Ned McWherter (D; term expires 1995)
State Legislature Senate 20D, 13R; House 63D, 36R
Total expenditure (1992) $9,568m

TEXAS

Texas has always insisted upon its special identity, which the state's last governor, Clayton Williams, well understood. His stetsons were (to the rest of America, at least) of outrageous proportions, and he was always booted – he owned no shoes. Many Texans now point to the white-collar economic revolution under way in the state and worry that this image of cattle drives and big oil is just what Texas should not be taking into the 21st century. Others say that were it not for an old-fashioned Texan spirit, the state's inhabitants would not now be transforming a poor, barren land that borders the third world into one of the world's economic powerhouses.

It was not many years after America's independence that Texas's vast tracts began to obsess a motley bunch of dreamers. Aaron Burr, later famous for killing Alexander Hamilton, was one of the first and biggest boosters of the land (Texas, Louisiana and Arkansas) that lay between the Mississippi and the Spanish dominions. After the battle of Waterloo a group of Bonapartist adventurers, their eye on Mexico's silver mines, revived Burr's dreams of a settlement, but their expeditionary force was a fiasco. It was not until 1821 that Stephen Austin led 300 families across the Sabine river to found the first Texan settlement.

The Mexican connection

Early Texan settlers got ample encouragement, in the form of grants, concessions and land, from a newly independent Mexico. Quickly, though, Mexicans became unnerved by the influx of Americans, who soon outnumbered them three-to-one. In 1830 Mexico sent troops into Texas to stem the tide. Two years later Austin went to Mexico City to convey the settlers' grievances against Mexico to the new Mexican dictator, Antonio Lopez de Santa Anna. Austin was arrested on his way home and imprisoned; on his release in 1835 he exhorted Texas to rebel. When Mexican troops were sent to Gonzales to confiscate a cannon, Texans hung a banner over it that read "Come and take it". Thus began the Texas revolution.

It is so very Texan that the historical event of the revolution that is Texas's best known cultural export, the siege of the Alamo, ended in defeat. The 188 Texans were wiped out in February and March 1836 by 5,000 Mexican soldiers under General Santa Ana's command. This event is better known to the state's schoolchildren than the victory over the Mexicans of Sam Houston's army at the Battle of San Jacinto two months later.

Even that victory was not final. In 1842 the Mexicans recaptured San Antonio (a town founded by Spanish missionaries in 1718), and fighting continued until the truce of 1844. In 1846, however, President Polk goaded the Mexicans into a war that was utterly disastrous for them. Only two years later they had been forced to sell to America for a paltry $15m, in one of history's most shameless land-grabs, not just Texas, but also Colorado, Wyoming, Nevada, Utah, Arizona, New Mexico and California.

Once more unto the breach

Less than two decades later, Texas once again found itself at war, this time as part of the losing Confederacy which it wholeheartedly joined. The war saw long blockades by Union forces of two Texan ports, Galveston (near Houston) and Indianola. And the last battle of the Civil War, Palmito Ranch, was even fought on Texas soil: ironically, it was won by the Confederates. Again, defeat did not mean disaster. For after the war both blockaded ports grew vigorously. Moreover, the thousands of pronghorn cattle which had roamed wide during the Civil War were rounded up and driven north to markets that paid ten times what beef had got before the war. This was the cowboy's life.

Black gold boom

The 20th century came to Texas with a boom. For in 1901 oil was discovered on the Gulf Coast at Spindletop. Oil was later discovered in the barren, western region around Midland-Odessa (where President George Bush made his fortune as an oilman). Texas swiftly became the world's biggest producer of oil.

But oil was a commodity just like the livestock on the rangelands and the cotton of the north-east that had been Texas's staple hitherto. Further, an economy that depends for its health upon primary resources is a volatile one, and Texas (a naturally rowdy state) developed volatile politics to boot. Texans were distrustful of the state's Wall Street financiers, whom they felt imposed a rentier economy upon them. The Democrats who ran the state for most of this century fought hard for what Texans call the "awl" business. A xenophobic patriotism began to express itself in a vigorous anti-communism and a stand for higher military spending. When this fused with a particularly virulent form of the Southern Baptist faith, a new and fervent breed of Republicans sprang up, starting in Dallas in the 1950s. By 1960 fur-clad Republicans were physically assaulting Lyndon and Lady Bird Johnson in the lobby of Dallas's grandest hotel. Soon after, these Republicans helped plunge Texas into national disrepute for being the state where John Kennedy was assassinated.

Still proud but not so isolationist

Those days of an angry and isolationist conservatism are now gone, even if many Americans saw their resurgence in 1992 in the presidential ambitions of Ross Perot, a Dallas billionaire. Yet the change between 1963 and the latter half of the 1980s should not be understated. The oil business is an example. Where once crude oil could be pumped from the ground at minimum cost, this is no longer so. When in the mid-1980s the rest of the country boomed on the back of cheap oil, the Texan economy slumped: its banks and thrifts went spectacularly bust, and the state was left littered with empty properties. In 1980 fully 28% of its state revenues came from energy. Today that figure is under 10%.

Resourcefulness beyond oil

But as so often in Texan affairs, this disaster is not the whole story. Because finding oil in Texas is no longer the cakewalk it once was, the state's energy sector has developed a great expertise – centred around muggy Houston, the oil-city of the world – in high-skill areas of drilling, extracting and refining oil. It is these skills that are a more valuable strength to the Texan energy sector than the oil beneath the ground.

Moreover, the need for high-technology in the oil business, plus the fabulous revenues that oil brought to the state for so long, have endowed Texas with a huge fund of technological prowess. It was during the 1960s that Texas Instruments sprang up in North Texas (today employing some 30,000), and that success story was repeated by Houston's Compaq during the 1980s. Recently, too, biotech and other medical technology firms have thrived around San Antonio, whilst Houston has its own growing rival to California's Silicon Valley.

Business ethics

It was also during the 1960s that Ross Perot set up his pioneering computer-systems firm, Electronic Data Systems (EDS). The firm became famous for its North Dallas conservatism: for its uniform of white shirts and dark suits and its quasi-militaristic corporate ethic. But this simple description is to underestimate the changes that Dallas, which started out life as a cotton town, has undergone. During the 1980s the Dallas-Fort Worth "metroplex" grew by nearly a third, and into the top ten metropolitan areas in America, as it established its pre-eminence as a financial, distribution and high-technology centre. True, those North Dallas suburbs are not only among America's most affluent, they are also among the most heavily Republican. At the same time, the area has filled up with educated young men and women, many of them Yankees. These are generally liberal on social issues (which the Republican part is not). After all, Dallas has one of the highest percentages of working women in the country. And it is in this context that the Ross Perot phenomenon must be placed: pro-business, anti-government and pro-women's rights.

National barometer

There are many reasons to think that what Texas stands for today, so America will stand for tomorrow. America's fourth largest state has finally diversified away from oil: service sectors today account for four-fifths of all non-farm jobs. It therefore weathered the 1990–91 recession better than most, with the highest job growth of the ten biggest states.

There are other pointers. Houston, with its free-market principles evident even in its zoning (ie, planning) rules (they are non-existent) has long been the centreless forerunner of the way many American cities are going. Most of all, Texas, more than any other state bar California, has learnt to look outwards. No state will benefit more from a free-trade agreement with Mexico, whose border region is already fast merging here with America's. Texas already exports over $12 billion-worth a year to Mexico, a third of all its exports.

House Jim Chapman, Charles Wilson, Ralph Hall, John Bryant, Jack Brooks, Jake Pickle, Chet Edwards, Pete Geren, Bill Sarpalius, Greg Laughlin, Kika de la Garza, Ron Coleman, Charles Stenholm, Craig Washington, Henry B. Gonzalez, Martin Frost, Mike A. Andrews, Solomon Ortiz, Frank Tejeda, Gene Green, Eddie Bernice Johnson (all D); Sam Johnson, Joe Barton, Bill Archer, Jack Fields Jr, Larry Combest, Lamar Smith, Tom DeLay, Henry Bonilla, Dick Armey (all R)

State facts

Date of statehood	29 December 1845	Total area	268,601 sq miles
Capital	Austin	Highest point ft	Guadalupe Peak
Other cities	Houston, Dallas,		8,749
	San Antonio	Main rivers	Rio Grande, Colorado,
			Red, Sabine

Climate Extremely varied; driest region is the Trans-Pecos; NE is wettest.
Geography Gulf Coast Plain in the south and SE; North Central Plains slope upward with some hills; the Great Plains extend over the Panhandle, broken by low mountains; Trans-Pecos is the southern extension of the Rockies.
Time zone Central

People

			%
Population m	17.66	Under 18	28.7
% av. ann. growth 1980–92	1.8	Over 65	10.2
Pop. per sq mile	67.4	Urban	80.3
Birth rate per 1,000 pop.	18.6	Male	49.2
Death rate per 1,000 pop.	7.4	White	75.2
Pop. below poverty line %	18.1	Hispanic	25.5
Doctors per 100,000 pop.	175	Black	11.9
Hospital beds per 100,000 pop.	441	School spending per head	$4,651

The economy

GSP $m	340,057	Av. income per head $	17,892
No. of new corporations '000	34.6	% of national average	90

Structure of GSP	%		%
Construction	4.1	Manufacturing	16.9
Transportation, public utilities	11.0	Wholesale/retail trade	15.6
Services	16.9	Finance, insurance, real estate	15.1
Government	11.4	Other	9.0

Principal industries Trade, services, manufacturing
Main crops Cotton, sorghum, grains, vegetables, citrus fruits, pecans, peanuts

Politics
Senate Lloyd Bentsen (D; term expires 1995), Phil Gramm (R; term expires 1997)
House See list on page 185

State government
Governor Ann Richards (D; term expires 1995)
State Legislature Senate 18D, 13R; House 92D, 58R
Total expenditure (1992) $29,749m

UTAH

"This is the place", Brigham Young declared in 1847 as he stood atop the western slope of the Wasatch Range and surveyed the desolate valley of the Great Salt Lake below. Hoping to find sanctuary in a land that "nobody else wanted", the Mormon leader chose to settle his flock of faithful in this region of Pleistocene-era lake beds, rugged peaks and vast salt flats. The early pioneers, members all of Joseph Smith's Church of Jesus Christ of Latter-day Saints, laid out towns with huge city blocks, built sturdy houses and planted thousands of trees.

Utah's hub and heart has from the start been in Salt Lake City, though the city today is, ironically, the least Mormon and most cosmopolitan part of Utah. The real heartland of the Mormon church lies to the south, in Provo, home of Brigham Young University.

Utah's Mormons, better educated, more affluent and healthier than the average American, insist that their values are those of the American mainstream. But Utah, the most Republican state in the union and the one with the highest fertility rate, is decidedly a "nation apart".

Pilgrims of prosperity

Ute, Paiute and Navajo Indians inhabited Utah when Spanish missionaries arrived in 1776. The territory still belonged to Mexico when the Mormons started settling in, but it passed to America the following year with the 1848 Treaty of Guadalupe Hidalgo. Population increased exponentially in the 1850s as hoards of believers flowed into the region. Unlike other settlers, Mormons lived in relative peace with the Indians. But as wagon trains en route to Oregon passed through, tensions with "Gentiles" mounted. Eastern politicians whipped up anti-Mormon sentiment by campaigning against the "twin relics of barbarism", slavery and polygamy; Utah's request for statehood was denied.

Hostilities escalated into the Utah war of 1857, which pitted settlers against American troops. After more than 1,000 Mormon men were imprisoned on polygamy charges, the church appealed to the Supreme Court to test the constitutionality of the anti-polygamy laws. A decision was still pending in 1877 when Brigham Young died, survived by 16 wives and 44 children. The petition for statehood was granted in 1896 when a new Mormon president announced he had received a revelation to repudiate polygamy.

The railroad spelled the end of the western frontier and, for Utah, the end of the nearly exclusive rule of the Mormons. While the church maintained that mining was a godless pursuit, prospectors poured into the state to make fortunes from its vast mineral resources.

Although the moral underpinnings have changed little since the state's founding, Utah's story in the 20th century is largely one of assimilation. Brigham Young had asserted that farming should be the primary Mormon occupation, but he also wanted the Desert Empire to be self-sufficient; his successors have been true to that wish. Mining accelerated, and the discovery of uranium in 1952 touched off a boom in the state. The aerospace industry has since provided both jobs and prestige for Utah.

Utah's political partisanship has changed with its self-image. As the target of religious persecution and colonial victim of ruthless east coast financiers, Utah backed Democrats, and in the 1940s provided staunch support to the New Dealers. The state's transformation to generator of wealth, with successful businesses and allegiance to "traditional American family values", has since pulled it to the right.

Thriving through thrift

With 65% of its residents teetotalling church members, Utah remains unmistakably Mormon, and the congregation is growing. "Zion" has drawn converts from the Mid-West, northern England and Scandinavia. The church owns two Salt Lake City newspapers, a TV station, major holdings in insurance and real estate, and the largest department store in the city, the Zion Cooperative Mercantile Institution (ZCMI).

Utah has consistently had one of the strongest economies in America. Much of the population is still indirectly involved in extractive industry. But extension of the Colorado river projects was a boon to Utah's irrigation-dependent crops, and the growth of defence-related industry provided the state with early diversification.

In 1991, as job growth declined nationally, Utah attracted 22,400 new jobs and for four years had sustained job growth rates of better than 3%. This solid economic performance statewide hides the "Two Utahs" dichotomy between metropolitan and rural areas. The transition to a service and trade-based economy has been harder on remote counties, and many have lost population. Layoffs also loom in military industry, but United Parcel Service, J.C. Penney and Novell are among the companies whose expansion in the state is expected to provide more than ample employment in services. The state's spectacular scenery, its dramatic canyonlands and world-class skiing, keep tourism Utah's most reliable economic mainstay.

State facts

Date of statehood	4 January 1896	Total area	84,904 sq miles
Capital	Salt Lake City	Highest point ft	Kings Peak 13,528
Other cities	West Valley City, Provo, Sandy	Main rivers	Colorado, Green, Sevier

Climate Arid; ranging from warm desert in south-west to alpine in north-east.

Geography High Colorado plateau is cut by brilliantly-coloured canyons of the south-east; broad, flat, desert-like Great Basin of the west; the Great Salt Lake and Bonneville Salt Flats to the north-west; Middle Rockies in the north-east run east–west; valleys and plateaus of Wasatch Front.

Time zone Mountain

People

			%
Population m	1.81	Under 18	36.1
% av. ann. growth 1980–92	1.8	Over 65	8.8
Pop. per sq mile	22.1	Urban	87.0
Birth rate per 1,000 pop.	21.1	Male	49.7
Death rate per 1,000 pop.	5.2	White	93.8
Pop. below poverty line %	11.4	Hispanic	4.9
Doctors per 100,000 pop.	185	Black	0.7
Hospital beds per 100,000 pop.	309	School spending per head	$3,092

The economy

GSP $m	28,135	Av. income per head $	15,325
No. of new corporations '000	5.0	% of national average	77

Structure of GSP	%		%
Construction	3.9	Manufacturing	16.5
Transportation, public utilities	12.4	Wholesale/retail trade	15.7
Services	17.5	Finance, insurance, real estate	14.6
Government	15.5	Other	3.9

Principal industries Services, trade, manufacturing, government, construction

Main crops Hay, wheat, apples, barley, alfalfa seed, corn, potatoes, cherries, onions

Politics

Senate Orrin Hatch (R; term expires 1995), Robert Bennett (R; term expires 1999)

House Karen Shepherd, William Orton (both D); James V. Hansen (R)

State government

Governor Mike Leavitt (R; term expires 1997)

State Legislature Senate 18R, 11D; House 49R, 26D

Total expenditure (1992) $3,767m

VERMONT

Vermont is where city-weary New Yorkers and 1960s refugees alike move to find the idyll of rural America. It is where millions of Americans go to hike in the cool and wooded mountains or fish quiet lakes in summer, to admire turning leaves in autumn, and to ski in winter.

The only New England state without a coast, landlocked Vermont is separated on its eastern boundary from New Hampshire by the upper Connecticut river. To its west, beyond Lake Champlain in the north and over the Taconic mountains in the south, is upstate New York, of which it was once part, at least in New York's eyes. Due north is Canada.

In the 16th century the area that is now Vermont was first claimed by Europeans as part of the French possessions in the New World. Englishmen from Massachusetts, and later Connecticut and New York, arrived in the 18th century, but the state capital, Montpelier, serves as a reminder of the French past. In the 19th century the state recorded two unlikely footnotes in history: the most northerly action in the Civil War was a Confederate raid on St Albans; and Rudyard Kipling, who married a Vermonter, wrote the first two *Jungle Books* in Brattleboro.

Green and clean

Until the 1960s, Vermont's population was ageing, shrinking and Republican. Since then it has become younger, larger and more confused in its politics. The state remains New England Republican but has become as green as its car-licence plates. In 1970 the state passed a law restricting development and promoting conservation of its wildernesses. The new if unlikely alliance of native-son farmers and immigrant backwoods artisans keeps things that way. Vermont today has the toughest anti-pollution laws in the country. It sends Washington the only Socialist in Congress.

The economy is built on tourism and the land: dairy and cattle farming, apple orchards and maple syrup. There is a big lumber industry: Vermont coined the word "logjam". Granite (in which it ranks second in the nation) and marble extraction have been important industries for more than a century. Most of America's tombstones come from Vermont.

The state has a long tradition of precision-tool making and recently has attracted electronic industries spilling over from Massachusetts. Because of its development controls, Vermont did not boom in the 1980s like other New England states, but neither did it suffer so much in the downturn.

State facts

Date of statehood	4 March 1791	Total area	9,615 sq miles
Capital	Montpelier	Highest point ft	Mt Mansfield 4,393
Other cities	Burlington, Rutland, South Burlington	Main rivers	Poultney, White, Winooski, Connecticut

Climate Temperate, with considerable temperature extremes; heavy snowfall in mountains.

Geography Green Mountains north–south backbone 20–36 miles wide; average altitude 1,000 ft.

Time zone Eastern Standard

People

			%
Population m	0.57	Under 18	25.3
% av. ann. growth 1980–92	0.9	Over 65	12.0
Pop. per sq mile	61.6	Urban	32.2
Birth rate per 1,000 pop.	14.7	Male	48.9
Death rate per 1,000 pop.	8.0	White	98.6
Pop. below poverty line %	9.9	Hispanic	0.7
Doctors per 100,000 pop.	253	Black	0.3
Hospital beds per 100,000 pop.	404	School spending per head	$6,992

The economy

GSP $m	11,502	Av. income per head $	18,834
No. of new corporations '000	1.5	% of national average	95

Structure of GSP	%		%
Construction	7.3	Manufacturing	19.7
Transportation, public utilities	7.4	Wholesale/retail trade	15.6
Services	17.5	Finance, insurance, real estate	19.7
Government	9.7	Other	3.1

Principal industries Manufacturing, tourism, agriculture, trade, finance, insurance, real estate, government

Main crops Dairy products, apples, maple syrup, silage, corn, hay

Politics

Senate Patrick Leahy (D; term expires 1999), James Jeffords (R; term expires 1995)

House Bernard Sanders (Ind)

State government

Governor Howard Dean (D; term expires 1995)

State Legislature Senate 16R, 14D; House 87D, 57R, 4 Ind, 2 others

Total expenditure (1992) $1,430m

VIRGINIA

No state, not even Massachusetts, has done more than Virginia to shape the course of American history. It was at Jamestown in Tidewater, Virginia that the first permanent English settlement was established, with great effort and also with poor leadership, in May 1607. Twelve years later, Jamestown introduced the first black slaves to North America. In 1675, Bacon's Rebellion (Jamestown again) was the first American revolt against the crown.

Eight of America's presidents have been Virginians, including George Washington, Thomas Jefferson and James Madison, and this is no coincidence. For among Virginia's landed elite there developed during the 1770s unparalleled notions of government and of liberty. The contradiction of philosopher slave-owners propounding equal rights is plain to see. But proof of their wisdom lies in the Constitution, a document by which America defines itself today.

Rich beginnings

At the time of the American Revolution, Virginia was the richest and most heavily populated of the 13 colonies. Yet it was not long before the state was overtaken in that claim by Pennsylvania and New York. Somehow, that first American generation failed to seed successive generations with its talents. (Robert E. Lee and Stonewall Jackson were the two exceptions, and these were reluctant heroes.) Planters worked the tobacco lands to exhaustion, and then became breeders of humans for export to the growing South. The landed gentry, impoverished before the Civil War, was devastated during it. It was to the great misfortune of Richmond, the state capital, that it was also chosen as the Confederate capital for its proximity to Washington, DC and for its ironworks and port. War swirled around Richmond and up and down the state. At the end of the Civil War the ruling class sank back into a consolable past. Industry and modernisation in the last half of the 19th century and the first half of the 20th passed much of Virginia by.

Strong recovery

The last throes of this uniquely Virginian pessimism came in the late 1950s with the "massive resistance" of governor Harry Byrd (his machine had run the state since 1925) to federal orders to integrate the schools. That resistance collapsed, and its failure opened the way to a 30-year period of extraordinary prosperity for Virginia that has slowed only recently along with the rest of America. During the 1980s

Virginia created 100,000 new, non-farming jobs a year.

That prosperity has spread far beyond the traditional manufacturing and tobacco heartland around Richmond. Norfolk is one of the east coast's finest natural harbours and official home to the American navy. With 125 warships and 100,000 sailors there, the navy spends $2 billion a year. The shipbuilding and repair yards of Newport News ring still to the sound of hammers. And the interstate corridor down the Shenandoah valley sees new businesses creeping further south from the Washington area each year, for better or for worse, given the beauty of the valley and the Blue Ridge mountains and the Appalachians that mark its edge.

Northern edge

But it is in the area near Washington itself that Virginia has seen its most spectacular growth. Northern Virginia has one-quarter of the state's population and jobs, yet during the 1980s it had two-fifths of all employment growth.

Arlington county in northern Virginia has long been a dormitory suburb for federal employees, and those have grown enormously in number over the past three decades. Even that growth does not compare to the "edge city" of Tyson's Corner in neighbouring Fairfax county. On what was gentle farmland 30 years ago stands the largest (and, many say, the ugliest) concentration of office space between downtown Washington and Atlanta, Georgia. This edge city has cut its ties with Washington's urban centre. It is home to many small businesses and to many Asian and Latino communities, as well as to prosperous whites. These residents often have little occasion to go to the nation's capital ten miles away. Fairfax is now also home to some of the country's largest companies, including General Dynamics and Mobil Oil. During the 1980s Arlington and Fairfax counties shot up to become the second and third richest counties in the country.

Good government

In 1989 the state elected its first black governor, Doug Wilder, a Democrat and a grandson of slaves. This led many to predict that the state's politics was undergoing the same kind of revolution as its economy. Only to a certain degree: Wilder believes in good government and low taxes, and this is as Virginian a tradition as any. It all looks set to work towards the state's continued well-being.

State facts

Date of statehood	25 June 1788	Total area	42,777 sq miles
Capital	Richmond	Highest point ft	Mt Rogers 5,729
Other cities	Virginia Beach,	Main rivers	James, York,
	Norfolk, Newport News		Potomac, Rappahanock

Climate Mild and equable.
Geography Mountain and valley region in west, including Blue Ridge mountains; rolling Piedmont plateau; tidewater, coastal plain, at eastern shore.
Time zone Eastern Standard

People

			%
Population m	6.38	Under 18	24.5
% av. ann. growth 1980–92	1.5	Over 65	10.9
Pop. per sq mile	161.0	Urban	69.4
Birth rate per 1,000 pop.	16.1	Male	49.0
Death rate per 1,000 pop.	7.8	White	77.4
Pop. below poverty line %	10.2	Hispanic	2.6
Doctors per 100,000 pop.	213	Black	18.8
Hospital beds per 100,000 pop.	456	School spending per head	$5,487

The economy

GSP $m	136,497	Av. income per head $	20,629
No. of new corporations '000	16.9	% of national average	104

Structure of GSP	%		%
Construction	6.6	Manufacturing	16.0
Transportation, public utilities	8.9	Wholesale/retail trade	14.3
Services	17.7	Finance, insurance, real estate	16.2
Government	18.1	Other	2.2

Principal industries Services, trade, government, manufacturing, tourism, agriculture
Main crops Tobacco, soybeans, peanuts, winter wheat, corn, far grain, tomatoes, apples, summer and sweet potatoes

Politics

Senate John Warner (R; term expires 1997), Charles Robb (D; term expires 1995)
House Owen B. Pickett, Robert Scott, Norman Sisisky, Lewis F. Payne Jr, James Moran, Rick Boucher, Leslie Byrne (all D); Herbert H. Bateman, Robert Goodlatte, Thomas J. Bliley Jr, Frank R. Wolf (all R)

State government
Governor L. Douglas Wilder (D; term expires 1994)
State Legislature Senate 22D, 18R; House 58D, 41R, 1 Ind
Total expenditure (1992) $13,063m

WASHINGTON

Famously wet Washington lies at the far north-west corner of the 48 continental states. Bisected by the Cascade mountains, the state actually has two distinct climates. The lush Olympic Peninsula is the rainiest region of mainland America, but to the east lie the drier ponderosa forests of the Okanoga Highlands, the semi-arid Columbia river basin, and the "Inland Empire" around Spokane, where rich volcanic topsoil of the Palouse ridges reaches 200 feet deep. Tucked between the two major mountain ranges, Seattle sits on one of Puget Sounds many inlets. The city's steep streets trace valleys carved out by glaciers from the last Ice Age, but even Seattle's flannel-shirted ease cannot conceal the prosperity of this thoroughly modern metropolis.

The rougher-hewn atmosphere of small lumber towns along the north coast and the 172 San Juan Islands are in stark contrast to Washington's gentle side. As if to remind residents of the divide that has shaped this state, Mount St Helens, dormant for 123 years, erupted in 1980 in a burst of pyrotechnics that stunned the West.

Arrowheads and aerospace

Washington was home to the Chinook, Nez Perce and Yakima tribes when Captain James Cook explored the area in 1778. Spanish and English expeditions came as early as the 16th century in search of a fabled Northwest Passage. By 1780 that quest was replaced by fierce competition in the fur trade. America held this territory jointly with England until "Fifty-four forty or fight" (referring to a proposed northern boundary along the 54th parallel) became the slogan of the 1844 presidential campaign; war was averted when America settled for a northern frontier along the 49th.

Railroads brought the first great influx of settlers to the state in 1880. Gold-seekers made their way to inland towns like Republic and Oroville to find their fortunes, while other entrepreneurs built towns and lumber empires along the sinuous channels of Puget Sound.

In 1900 Frederick Weyerhauser, whose timber company had logged the Great Lakes territory, bought 900,000 acres in Washington and Oregon. He introduced a more environment-friendly technique than the "cut-and-run" principle which had guided most logging in America, but the consolidation of the timber industry prompted the International Workers of the World to unionise. Labour relations remained difficult for decades.

The waters of the great Columbia river and its tributary, the Snake, inspired massive government interest in the state.

Franklin D. Roosevelt enthusiastically oversaw construction of the Grand Coulee and Bonneville dams which provided the cheapest electricity in the country. With the first world war, Washington became the logical location for the huge aluminium plants needed for building aircraft. The relationship stuck; aircraft manufacturing boomed during the second world war and has been the state's industrial base ever since.

Boeing has its headquarters in Everett, just north of Seattle, where it employs over 100,000 people. Washington's dependence on the company earned Henry "Scoop" Jackson, who represented the state for more than 40 years, his epithet as "the Senator from Boeing". But other, high-tech firms have sprouted here, too, most visibly in Bill Gates's Microsoft firm. Mimicking the pattern repeated in various pockets of the Pacific Rim, Washington's economy has been helped by the growth of small, white-collar enterprise that has made the state America's largest exporter.

Swimming upstream

Washington's Scandinavian and labour union heritage made it so reliably Democratic for so many years that Roosevelt's campaign manager used to refer to "the 47 states and the Soviet of Washington". The political pendulum has since swung away from the blue-collar base which lay beneath that political power. Today Washington is a commonwealth with close partisan competition and an affluent electorate whose liberal impulses are concentrated more on cultural than economic issues.

Washington weathers tough economic times whenever aerospace takes a nosedive. The state endured its own little recession in the 1970s when the government cancelled its order for supersonic transport and Boeing laid off a third of its workforce. Cutbacks in defence spending may not augur well for the industry in the longer-run, but by 1992 Boeing had four years of production in backlog totalling $100 billion. While General Motors and IBM issued layoff notices in 1991, Boeing was passing out year-end bonuses.

More worrisome for Washington's 5m residents is a built-in tension between proprietors of the state's greatest resources. Once exploited by all parties, Washington's forests and rivers are now battlegrounds for environmentalists. Preserving the spotted owl's habitat is said to come at the cost of 40,000 logging jobs; increasing the state's electric capacity will foul rivers that have long been the spawning ground for Pacific salmon. The state's economic formula is now tourism versus timber, fishing versus fission.

State facts

Date of statehood	11 November 1889	Total area	71,302 sq miles
Capital	Olympia	Highest point ft	Mt Rainier 14,410
Other cities	Seattle, Spokane, Tacoma	Main rivers	Columbia, Snake

Climate Mild, dominated by the Pacific Ocean and protected by the Rockies.
Geography Olympic Mountains, on north-west peninsula; open land along coast to Columbia river; flat terrain of Puget Sound Lowland; Cascade mountains region's high peaks to the east; Columbia Basin in central portion; highlands to the north-east; mountains to the south-east.
Time zone Pacific

People

			%
Population m	5.14	Under 18	26.4
% av. ann. growth 1980–92	1.8	Over 65	11.7
Pop. per sq mile	77.1	Urban	76.4
Birth rate per 1,000 pop.	16.3	Male	49.6
Death rate per 1,000 pop.	7.5	White	88.5
Pop. below poverty line %	10.9	Hispanic	4.4
Doctors per 100,000 pop.	213	Black	3.1
Hospital beds per 100,000 pop.	305	School spending per head	$5,331

The economy

GSP $m	96,233	Av. income per head $	20,398
No. of new corporations '000	11.5	% of national average	103

Structure of GSP	%		%
Construction	6.0	Manufacturing	16.7
Transportation, public utilities	8.2	Wholesale/retail trade	18.6
Services	16.7	Finance, insurance, real estate	14.7
Government	14.7	Other	4.4

Principal industries Aerospace, forest products, food products, primary metals, agriculture
Main crops Hops, spearmint oil, raspberries, apples, asparagus, pears, cherries

Politics

Senate Slade Gorton (R; term expires 1995), Patty Murray (D; term expires 1999)
House Maria Cantwell, Al Swift, Jolene Unsoeld, Jay Inslee, Thomas S. Foley, Norman D. Dicks, Jim McDermott, Mike Kreidler (all D); Jennifer Dunn (R)

State government
Governor Mike Lowry (D; term expires 1997)
State Legislature Senate 28D, 21R; House 66D, 32R
Total expenditure (1992) $15,627m

WEST VIRGINIA

The history of raw, rugged West Virginia has told of more busts than booms, and the past decade has been no exception. During the 1980s, the state's population fell by 8%, to 1.79m. The state's sulphurous coal, discovered during the 19th century, has long persuaded West Virginians to eke an often dangerous living in the mountain hollows rather than head for the industrial cities of Mid-West. Coal boomed during the first and second world wars. It boomed again during the energy crises of the 1970s. But low coal prices during the 1980s, coupled with the 1990 Clean Air Act's penalisation of dirty coal, has left West Virginia wondering what the next decade brings.

Mountain country

Part of the answer certainly lies with what impressed the earliest English, Welsh and Scots settlers: the beauty of its wild rivers and mountains. And while those mountains for the past century have been viewed as an unwelcome impediment to extracting coal and to building heavy industries, their future value lies in their ability, so close to the populous east coast, to draw visitors.

The same mountains were also responsible for the state's existence separate from Virginia, of which it was long part. The mountaineers' grudge was that Richmond, Virginia's capital, overly represented the "Tidewater" interests of the coastal plantations. Few slaves had been imported into the mountains, so once the Civil War had broken out, West Virginia announced its loyalty to the Union to become, in 1863, America's 35th state.

Mining heritage

If West Virginia today is one of the country's most Democratic states it is thanks to John Lewis and the United Mine Workers Union, which organised coal workers against the state's unscrupulous mining interests. During the New Deal and the war, Lewis was as crucial an ally to Franklin Roosevelt as he was a thorn in the president's side.

Today mining employs just 5% of the workforce. The steel towns of the northern panhandle have collapsed. The chemical plants along the Kanawha river around Charleston, the state's capital, are equally an environmental embarrassment and a source of jobs. Only the state's eastern panhandle has thrived over the past few years, mainly through tourism, and it is not lost on the rest of the state that this region boasted less heavy industry to start with.

State facts

Date of statehood	20 June 1863	Total area	24,231 sq miles
Capital	Charleston	Highest point ft	Spruce Knob 4,861
Other cities	Huntington, Wheeling, Parkersburg	Main rivers	Ohio, Potomac, Big Sandy, Guyandotte

Climate Humid continental climate except for marine modification in the lower panhandle.

Geography Ranging from hilly to mountainous; Allegheny Plateau in the west, covers two-thirds of the state; mountains here are the highest in the state, over 4,000 ft.

Time zone Eastern Standard

People

			%
Population m	1.81	Under 18	24.2
% av. ann. growth 1980–92	-0.6	Over 65	15.2
Pop. per sq mile	75.2	Urban	36.1
Birth rate per 1,000 pop.	12.6	Male	48.0
Death rate per 1,000 pop.	11.0	White	96.2
Pop. below poverty line %	19.7	Hispanic	0.5
Doctors per 100,000 pop.	166	Black	3.1
Hospital beds per 100,000 pop.	575	School spending per head	$5,415

The economy

GSP $m	27,922	Av. income per head $	15,065
No. of new corporations '000	2.2	% of national average	76

Structure of GSP	%		%
Construction	4.8	Manufacturing	15.6
Transportation, public utilities	13.0	Wholesale/retail trade	13.1
Services	13.6	Finance, insurance, real estate	16.2
Government	10.7	Other	13.0

Principal industries Manufacturing services, mining, tourism
Main crops Apples, peaches, hay, tobacco, corn, wheat, oats

Politics

Senate Robert Byrd (D; term expires 1995), John D. Rockefeller IV (D; term expires 1997)
House Alan B. Mollohan, Bob Wise Jr, Nick Joe Rahall II (all D)

State government
Governor Gaston Caperton (D; term expires 1997)
State Legislature Senate 32D, 2R; House 79D, 21R
Total expenditure (1992) $4,598m

WISCONSIN

West of the Great Lakes but just north of Chicago, Wisconsin is historically the first state of the north-west, territory that stretched to the Pacific coast. Distinguished by its profusion of lakes (there are more than 8,500), Wisconsin is mostly gently rolling uplands that give way to prairies in the southern state.

Northern Wisconsin was once America's largest virgin timberland. Towns along the river are still dotted with paper mills, but the Wausau insurance company is among the big enterprises that have grown up in the small cities built on timber industries.

Wisconsin is one of the states that gave birth to the Republican Party in 1854. The German-Americans who arrived en masse favoured it for decades until Robert LaFollette and his turn-of-the-century Progressive Movement took the state by storm. Nestled into the placid rural counties in the south is Madison, where *The Progressive* is still published. This long-time liberal bastion delivered a stunning political upset in 1990 when it voted Robert Kastenmeier, its Democratic veteran of 32 years' standing, out of office and sent a young Republican to Congress.

Dairy farmers have made western Wisconsin, where pioneers once tried to scratch out crops, America's premier dairy country. But it was beer, of course, that "made Milwaukee famous". The city started as a Yorker-Yankee village and today even Brewer's Hill, near the old Schlitz brewery, is gentrifying. But Milwaukee's Teutonic heritage is unmistakable; it is the most obese state in the union.

Built on foment and fermentation

When Frenchman Jean Nicolet arrived at the site of Green Bay in 1634 in search of furs and the Northwest Passage, it was home of the Winnebago and Kickapoo Indians. These tribes were replaced by the Ottawa and the Huron who were forced by white settlement further east. What would become Wisconsin belonged to Great Britain until it formally passed to America in 1763 as part of the Northwest Territory. It fell again to the British during the war of 1812.

Large-scale white settlement began in the 1820s, when pioneers crossed the Great Lakes and came via the Erie canal. Conflicts with Indians in Wisconsin culminated in the Great Hawk wars of 1832, clearing the way for the massive influx of German immigrants who arrived in the 1850s. Great pine forests supported the logging boom in the 1870s. Pioneers once tried to scratch out crops in the hills that had been clear-cut, but dairy cattle came at last to graze here.

In the early part of the century the steady habits and high skills of local farmers provided a good labour pool for factory work; Johnson Wax (with its Frank Lloyd Wright-designed tower) located in Racine, Parker Pens in Janesville, and the old Nash plant, later run by American Motors and Chrysler, took root in Kenosha. But this era was also one of political turbulence. LaFollette's Progressives used government to improve the lot of Wisconsin's ordinary citizens (an idea borrowed from German liberals and later adopted by American New Dealers). Other states followed their social reform legislation, but LaFollette's dream of forming a national party was never realised.

In 1915 William J. Simmons founded a new Ku Klux Klan whose primarily anti-Catholic agenda found a receptive populace in Wisconsin, and the KKK became a force of considerable political importance in the 1920s. The milk strikes burped on the political screen in 1933, but it was a protest born of familiar farm politics. Joseph McCarthy and his anti-Communist rampage after 1946 threatened to alter the political face of Wisconsin forever.

Trouble brewing

Milwaukee has always been a blue-collar town, its skyline one of smokestacks and church steeples. The city lost 60,000 manufacturing jobs between 1979 and 1982, but Milwaukee stuck to its manufacturing base, adding 44,000 jobs in the last two years of the 1980s. As a result it was much better poised to withstand the economic ills of the early 1990s. The city leads the nation in mining gear, cranes and independent foundries, and Rockwell International has doubled sales to $1.5 billion. Brewing now employs fewer than 4,000 Wisconsin workers, but Milwaukee is still a high-wage union town with sturdy houses and streets lined with bars.

With its mixed agricultural and industrial base, Wisconsin's economy continued to expand in the postwar period. But fewer farm families and less acreage reflected the trend away from small farms in the state. Dairying is still the single most important factor in the agricultural economy, while machinery, paper and electrical equipment set the pace in manufacturing. But the dairy industry is in trouble. Cows have become more productive just as demand has declined. Wisconsin factories have created thousands of jobs in recent years, largely because of exports. The trouble spot has been an increase in business failures, apparently the result of shrinkage among small-town merchants who had depended on farm customers.

State facts

Date of statehood	29 May 1836	Total area	65,499 sq miles
Capital	Madison	Highest point ft	Timms Hills 1,951
Other cities	Milwaukee, Green Bay, Racine	Main rivers	Mississippi, St Croix, Wisconsin

Climate Long cold winters and short warm summers tempered by the Great Lakes.
Geography Narrow Lake Superior Lowland plain met by Northern Highland which slopes gently to the sandy crescent Central Plain; Western Upland in the south-west; three broad parallel limestone ridges running north–south are separated by wide and shallow lowlands in the south-east.
Time zone Central

People

			%
Population m	5.01	Under 18	26.6
% av. ann. growth 1980–92	0.5	Over 65	13.3
Pop. per sq mile	92.2	Urban	65.7
Birth rate per 1,000 pop.	14.9	Male	48.9
Death rate per 1,000 pop.	8.8	White	92.2
Pop. below poverty line %	10.7	Hispanic	1.9
Doctors per 100,000 pop.	189	Black	5.0
Hospital beds per 100,000 pop.	469	School spending per head	$5,972

The economy

GSP $m	93,978	Av. income per head $	18,727
No. of new corporations '000	7.0	% of national average	94

Structure of GSP	%		%
Construction	3.4	Manufacturing	27.7
Transportation, public utilities	7.5	Wholesale/retail trade	14.8
Services	15.2	Finance, insurance, real estate	17.4
Government	9.5	Other	4.5

Principal industries Manufacturing, trade, services, government, transportation, communications, agriculture, tourism
Main crops Corn, beans, beets, peas, hay, oats, cabbage, cranberries

Politics

Senate Herbert Kohl (R; term expires 1995), Russell Feingold (R; term expires 1999)
House Scott Klug, Steve Gunderson, Thomas E. Petri, Toby Roth, Jim Sensenbrenner (all R); Les Aspin, Gerald D. Kleczka, Thomas Barrett, David R. Obey (all D)

State government
Governor Tommy Thompson (R; term expires 1995)
State Legislature Senate 18D, 15R; House 52D, 47R
Total expenditure (1992) $8,937m

WYOMING

Wyoming, dominated by short grass and sagebrush, is sliced through diagonally by the Rocky mountains. Still largely unsettled, this is the Cowboy state. There are three times as many cattle here as there are people; only Alaska has fewer residents per square mile than thinly-populated Wyoming. Government controls nearly half of the land, and the state has a rustic look to it.

The lonesome state

Fort Laramie, built in 1834, was Wyoming's first white settlement, and army posts remained the only stations for decades until Mormons founded an agricultural mission at Fort Supply to serve travellers on the church's route to Utah. The railroad brought homesteaders and in 1872 America established the first national park to preserve Yellowstone's geysers and thermal pools. But these symbols of encroaching order were exceptions to the general lawlessness that came with growth in Wyoming.

Primary dependence, basic instincts

Coal fired the state's economy in those days; Wyoming sits on the nation's largest deposit. Then oil boomed at the Salt Creek Field, turning Casper into a refinery town. But new industry brought little gentility to the state. The Teapot Dome scandal of the 1920s, when President Harding's secretary of state accepted a $400,000 bribe in exchange for lease of vast underground reserves, highlighted corruption in the state.

Primary production dominates the state's economy and mining remains its leading source of income. Wyoming is one of the country's leading producers of petroleum and natural gas, and the second largest uranium extractor. The recent oil boom brought in the big operators again: Amoco and other major oil companies planted drilling rigs in the Overthrust belt near Evanston while coal was mined in vast quantities up north. Sheep and cattle ranching top Wyoming's agricultural output, but the state raises dry grain crops and irrigated fields yield acres of sugar beet. Tourism is the third highest earner for the state.

There is general agreement that Wyoming should diversify its economy and that the government should have a hand in doing so. But state government is small and introspective, while the federal government is perceived as distant, and mistrusted.

State facts

Date of statehood	10 July 1890	Total area	97,818 sq miles
Capital	Cheyenne	Highest point ft	Gannett Peak
Other cities	Casper, Laramie,		13,804
	Rock Springs	Main rivers	Platte, Yellowstone,
			Powder, Green, Snake

Climate Semi-desert conditions throughout; true desert in the Big Horn and Great Divide basins.

Geography The eastern Great Plains rise to the foothills of the Rocky mountains; the Continental Divide crosses the state from the NW to the SE.

Time zone Pacific

People

			%
Population m	0.47	Under 18	29.6
% av. ann. growth 1980–92	-0.1	Over 65	10.7
Pop. per sq mile	4.8	Urban	65.0
Birth rate per 1,000 pop.	15.4	Male	50.1
Death rate per 1,000 pop.	6.9	White	94.2
Pop. below poverty line %	11.9	Hispanic	5.7
Doctors per 100,000 pop.	139	Black	0.8
Hospital beds per 100,000 pop.	638	School spending per head	$5,333

The economy

GSP $m	11,115	Av. income per head $	17,423
No. of new corporations '000	1.4	% of national average	88

Structure of GSP	%		%
Construction	7.6	Manufacturing	3.8
Transportation, public utilities	14.2	Wholesale/retail trade	9.7
Services	9.4	Finance, insurance, real estate	16.6
Government	13.1	Other	25.6

Principal industries Mineral extraction, tourism and recreation, agriculture

Main crops Wheat, beans, barley, oats, sugar beets, hay

Politics

Senate Malcolm Wallop (R; term expires 1995), Alan Simpson (R; term expires 1997)

House Craig Thomas (R)

State government

Governor Michael Sullivan (D; term expires 1995)

State Legislature Senate 20R, 10D; House 41R, 19D

Total expenditure (1992) $1,322m

List of presidents of the USA

April 1789–March 1797	George Washington (Federalist)
March 1797–March 1801	John Adams (Federalist)
March 1801–March 1809	Thomas Jefferson (Democratic-Republican)
March 1809–March 1817	James Madison (Democratic-Republican)
March 1817–March 1825	James Monroe (Democratic-Republican)
March 1825–March 1829	John Quincy Adams (National Republican)
March 1829–March 1837	Andrew Jackson (Democrat)
March 1837–March 1841	Martin Van Buren (Democrat)
March 1841–April 1841	William Henry Harrison (Whig)
April 1841–March 1845	John Tyler (Whig)
March 1845–March 1849	James K. Polk (Democrat)
March 1849–July 1850	Zachary Taylor (Whig)
July 1850–March 1853	Millard Fillmore (Whig)
March 1853–March 1857	Franklin Pierce (Democrat)
March 1857–March 1861	James Buchanan (Democrat)
March 1861–April 1865	Abraham Lincoln (Republican)
April 1865–March 1869	Andrew Johnson (Republican)
March 1869–March 1877	Ulysses S. Grant (Republican)
March 1877–March 1881	Rutherford B. Hayes (Republican)
March 1881–September 1881	James A. Garfield (Republican)
September 1881–March 1885	Chester A. Arthur (Republican)
March 1885–March 1889	Grover Cleveland (Democrat)
March 1889–March 1893	Benjamin Harrison (Republican)
March 1893–March 1897	Grover Cleveland (Democrat)
March 1897–September 1901	William McKinley (Republican)
September 1901–March 1909	Theodore Roosevelt (Republican)
March 1909–March 1913	William H. Taft (Republican)
March 1913–March 1921	Woodrow Wilson (Democrat)
March 1921–August 1923	Warren G. Harding (Republican)
August 1923–March 1929	Calvin Coolidge (Republican)
March 1929–March 1933	Herbert C. Hoover (Republican)
March 1933–April 1945	Franklin D. Roosevelt (Democrat)
April 1945–January 1953	Harry S. Truman (Democrat)
January 1953–January 1961	Dwight D. Eisenhower (Republican)
January 1961–November 1963	John F. Kennedy (Democrat)
November 1963–January 1969	Lyndon B. Johnson (Democrat)
January 1969–August 1974	Richard M. Nixon (Republican)
August 1974–January 1977	Gerald R. Ford (Republican)
January 1977–January 1981	Jimmy Carter (Democrat)
January 1981–January 1989	Ronald Reagan (Republican)
January 1989–January 1993	George Bush (Republican)
January 1993–	Bill Clinton (Democrat)

Notes

The research for *State facts* and *USA: the basic facts* was carried out in 1994 using the latest available sources (see page 208). Definitions of the statistics shown are given below. Figures may not add exactly to totals, or percentages to 100, due to rounding.

Balance of payments The record of a country's transactions with the rest of the world. The **current account** of the balance of payments consists of: visible trade (goods); "invisible" trade (services); private transfer payments (eg, remittances from those working abroad); official transfers (eg, payments to international organisations, famine relief). Visible imports and exports are normally compiled on rather different definitions to those used in the trade statistics (shown in principal imports and exports) and therefore the statistics do not match. The **capital account** consists of long- and short-term transactions relating to a country's assets and liabilities (eg, loans and borrowings). Adding the current to the capital account gives the **overall balance**. This is compensated by net monetary movements and changes in reserves. In practice methods of statistical recording are neither complete nor accurate and an errors and omissions item, sometimes quite large, will appear. In the country pages of this book this item is included in the overall balance. **Changes in reserves** are shown without the practice of reversing the sign often followed in balance of payments presentations. They exclude monetary movements and therefore do not equal the overall balance.

Cif/fob Measures of the value of merchandise trade. Imports include the cost of "carriage, insurance and freight" (cif) from the exporting country to the importing. The value of exports does not include these elements and is recorded 'free on board" (fob). Balance of payments statistics are generally

adjusted so that imports are shown fob; the cif elements are included in invisibles.

Congress and State Legislatures Names and numbers are correct as of May 31st 1994.

Crude birth rate The number of live births in a year per 1,000 population. The crude rate will automatically be relatively high if a large proportion of the population is of childbearing age.

Crude death rate The number of deaths in one year per 1,000 population. Also affected by the population's age structure.

EU European Union, also referred to as the European Community (EC). Members are: Belgium, Denmark, France, Germany, Greece, Ireland, Italy, Luxembourg, Netherlands, Portugal, Spain and the United Kingdom. New members from January 1995 (subject to national referendums) include Austria, Finland, Norway and Sweden.

Ecu European currency unit. Technically an accounting measure used within the EU and composed of a weighted basket of the currencies of all EU member countries.

Effective exchange rate This measures a currency's depreciation (figures below 100) or appreciation (figures over 100) from a base date against a trade weighted basket of the currencies of the country's main trading partners.

Fertility rate The average number of children born to a woman who completes her childbearing years.

GDP Gross domestic product. The sum of all output produced by economic activity within that country. GNP (gross national product) includes net income from abroad eg, rent, profits.

GSP Gross state product. The sum of all output produced by economic activity within that state.

Human Development Index This new index is an attempt by the United Nations Development Programme to assess relative levels of human development in various countries. It combines three measures: life expectancy, literacy and whether the average income, based on purchasing power parity (PPP) estimates (see below), is sufficient to meet basic needs. For each component a country's score is scaled according to where it falls between the minimum and maximum country scores; for income adequacy the maximum is taken as the official "poverty line" incomes in nine industrial countries. The scaled scores on the three measures are averaged to give the Human Development Index, shown here scaled from 0 to 100. Countries scoring less than 50 are classified as low human development, those from 50 to 80 as medium and those above 80 as high.

As with any statistical exercise of this sort the results are subject to caveats and the small number of indicators used places some limitations on its usefulness. The index should not be taken as a quality of life indicator since in particular it excludes any direct notion of freedom.

Inflation The annual rate at which prices are increasing. The most common measure and the one shown here (but not the only one) is the increase in the consumer price index.

Life expectancy The average length of time a baby born today can expect to live.

Literacy is defined by UNESCO as the ability to read and write a simple sentence, but definitions can vary from country to country.

Money supply A measure of the "money" available to buy goods and services. Various definitions of money supply exist. The measures shown here are based on definitions used by the IMF and may differ from measures used nationally. Narrow money (M1) consists of cash in circulation and demand deposits (bank deposits that can be withdrawn on demand). "Quasi-money" (time, savings and foreign currency deposits) is added to this to create broad money.

Population percentage figures These do not always add to 100 because according to the Census format persons of Hispanic origin may be of any race.

Poverty The poverty rate is the proportion of the population whose income falls below the government's official poverty level, which is adjusted each year to take account of inflation. It is intended to reflect the percentage of Americans living below a threshold of minimal need, estimated at $13,359 per year for a family of four in 1990.

Real terms Figures adjusted to allow for inflation.

SDR Special drawing right. The reserve currency, introduced by the IMF in 1970, was intended to replace gold and national currencies in settling international transactions. The IMF uses SDRs for book-keeping purposes and issues them to member countries. Their value is based on a basket of the five most widely traded currencies: the US dollar, Deutschemark, pound sterling, Japanese yen and French franc.

Total personal income This omits earnings of Federal employees and military personnel stationed abroad and of US residents employed abroad temporarily by private US firms.

Abbreviations

n/a	not applicable		**DC**	District of Columbia
...	not available		**GSP**	gross state product
–	zero		**Ind**	Independent
CMSA	Consolidated Metropolitan		**m**	million
	Statistical Area		**R**	Republican
D	Democrat			

States

AK	Alaska	**LA**	Louisiana	**OH**	Ohio
AL	Alabama	**MA**	Massachusetts	**OK**	Oklahoma
AR	Arkansas	**MD**	Maryland	**OR**	Oregon
AZ	Arizona	**ME**	Maine	**PA**	Pennsylvania
CA	California	**MI**	Michigan	**RI**	Rhode Island
CO	Colorado	**MN**	Minnesota	**SC**	South Carolina
CT	Connecticut	**MO**	Missouri	**SD**	South Dakota
DE	Delaware	**MS**	Mississippi	**TN**	Tennessee
FL	Florida	**MT**	Montana	**TX**	Texas
GA	Georgia	**NC**	North Carolina	**UT**	Utah
HA	Hawaii	**ND**	North Dakota	**VA**	Virginia
IA	Iowa	**NE**	Nebraska	**VT**	Vermont
ID	Idaho	**NH**	New Hampshire	**WA**	Washington
IL	Illinois	**NJ**	New Jersey		(state)
IN	Indiana	**NM**	New Mexico	**WI**	Wisconsin
KS	Kansas	**NV**	Nevada	**WV**	West Virginia
KY	Kentucky	**NY**	New York	**WY**	Wyoming

Sources

Associated Press.

The Banker.

Barone, Michael and Ujifusa, Grant, *The Almanac of American Politics*, National Journal.

Dun and Bradstreet Corporation, Economic Analysis department, *The Business Failure Record*, 1990.

Fortune.

National Conference of State Legislatures, Washington, DC.

Smithsonian Guide to Historic America, Stewart, Tabori & Chang, New York, 1990.

US Department of Commerce, Bureau of the Census, Washington, DC.

US Department of Commerce Economics and Statistics Administration Bureau of Economic Analysis, Washington, DC, *Survey of Current Business*, monthly.

US Department of Commerce, *Statistical Abstract of the US 1993: The National Data Book* (111th edition), Washington, DC, 1993.

US Department of Health and Human Services Centers for Disease Control National Center for Health Statistics, *Monthly Vital Statistics Report*, Vol. 40, No. 8, Supplement 2, January 1992, Washington, DC.

The 1994 Information Please Almanac (45th edition), Houghton Mifflin Company, Boston, 1992.

Washington Post.

World Almanac and Book of Facts, World Almanac, New York, 1994.

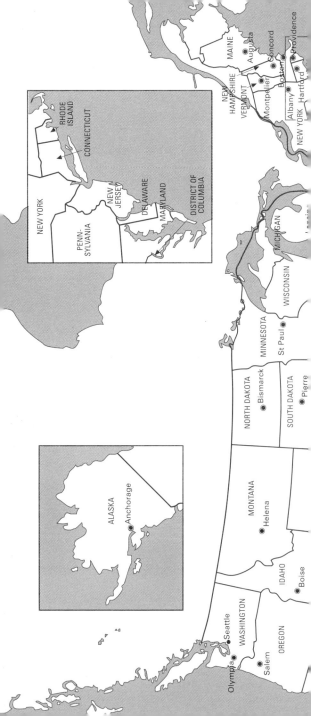